Dead Man's Journey

Phillip Cook

ISBN: 978-0-9922868-0-4

To my dear Mother, for that's where
the journey in the tent started.

FRANKIE
LOVE YOUR
HOSPITALITY
ENJOY THE READ
Phillip

ACKNOWLEDGMENTS

Thanks to all those who saw me through to the completion of this book. And thank you darling, you have been very, very patient.
Thanks to Brian for preaching the appropriate sermon at the appropriate time and for all those that asked me if I heard it.
Thanks to Iola Goulton for making my first experience with a professional editor a pleasant one that included much encouragement and good doses of humor.
Thanks to Sean Stanley for his great cover design work.
Thanks to Rob Filgate and Gareth and Anne (my dearest parents-in-law, and the greatest proofreaders) for their encouragement.
Thanks Smithy for your prayers and support.
And thank you Lord Jesus. May the eyes of many be opened.

Truly, truly, I say to you, whoever hears my word and believes him who sent me has eternal life. He does not come into judgment, but has passed from death to life. (John 5:24)

[11]For he will command his angels concerning you to guard you in all your ways; [12]they will lift you up in their hands, so that you will not strike your foot against a stone. (Psalm 91:11–12)

The poor man died and was carried by the angels to Abraham's side. (Luke 16:22)

Part One – Beginnings

CHAPTER ONE

Sunday, 5 November 2017, Bulimba, Brisbane, Queensland

SOMETHING UNSEEN AND MAJESTIC stood next to Patrick Fitzpatrick. He sensed it. In fact, the presence made him turn to his side to look. Goosebumps ran up his arms. His guardian angel?

Patrick stood on his front balcony, runners in hand, staring across the parklands. Their house sat in a quiet tree-lined street; tidy houses on one side, well-kept parklands interspersed with more tidy houses on the other side. A peaceful Sunday afternoon in Bulimba Village greeted him and washed away his thoughts of angels.

He sat down on the balcony's top step and laced up his runners. Feet now comfortably enclosed, he stood up and looked around. Through an open window he could see his wife sitting in her favorite sun-room chair. He turned and looked up at the blue skies overhead and saw dark clouds forming in the south. As if on cue, distant thunder rumbled. He walked down the steps and did some light leg stretches. A few moments later, he heard the front door open. He turned and smiled up at his wife.

Jill Fitzpatrick leaned on the balcony rail and pointed to the sky.

"It's okay, love. I'm not planning on getting zapped by lightning. I'll make it a short run." Patrick smooched up his lips and blew her a kiss. He headed towards the gate. Opening the gate he turned and yelled to his wife. "Love ya!"

Jill smiled and nodded. "Okay, just be careful."

Patrick closed the front gate. Jill waved him off.

Another low rumble of thunder sounded as Patrick turned into Oxford Street and headed down towards the river. Lightning flashed in the sky and the subsequent low rumbles told him the storm was some distance away. It was getting gloomy. A white van passed him. Its left hand turning indicator came on, blinking brightly in the gloom. He watched the van turn into a street. White vans always made Patrick think of surveillance vehicles and this one, with its dark side panel windows, fitted the mould perfectly.

Apart from the white van, things were quiet—no people, no cars. Patrick was near the river now. He turned onto the bike path that ran alongside the Brisbane River and led to Riverside Park. As always, he smiled as he saw his sons' initials in the concrete. He'd discovered the initials not long after the path opened—freshly laid concrete was always a target for such things. Jill wasn't impressed but Patrick thought a bit of mischievousness in the boys was good. Jill was petrified that the police were going to turn up one day. She believed they would track the boys down, as the boys left a calling card—their initials.

With his runners now pounding the bike path, his thoughts went to Aaron in Townsville and Jack in heaven. Patrick had regrets. His biggest regret was that he only gave his sons fleeting warnings about the battle of life. Jack had found life and was now at home with the Father, but Aaron was still on the hunt. Then again, it took Patrick a long time to realize the journey of life was about finding life.

As Riverside Park came into view, Patrick picked up the scent of freshly-mowed grass. He took a deep breath—he loved that earthy smell. The park was quiet with no people or cars in sight except for a white van parked near the entrance. It was the same van Patrick saw before. He noticed a person's head silhouetted against a side window.

Patrick Fitzpatrick was taught to be suspicious.

* * *

Some twenty kilometers south of Bulimba, the storm clouds were dark, almost black, as they hovered over Eight Mile Plains. The suburb housed a large technology park spread over thirty-three hectares. In one of the park's outer precincts sat a Department of

Urban Movement outpost, a small, inconspicuous building, set in well-landscaped grounds, just above a running stream.

Something black sprinted through the outpost's car park.

The thick storm clouds blocked the remaining daylight from shining through, activating light sensors in the car park. The small number of lights gave off a dim glow. Warm air spread over the car park, bringing a mint fragrance from the stream below. The air became still and calm. Birds were silent and returned to their resting places. Fallen leaves and discarded litter lay motionless. Small trees and shrubs cast their night shadows.

Through the branches of a small shrub, yellow eyes blinked. A black cat stared at something on the ground. The cat came out from the bushes and moved forward. It was curious.

A body lay on the ground. Blood trickled from a cut to the head.

The leaves and litter beside the body moved slightly. Suddenly, a strong gust scattered the debris. The cat, now alert, raised its head and looked at something above the body. The cat's hair stood up. Frightened, the cat hissed and slowly backtracked.

* * *

Patrick could see the cat. He realized he was floating above it and looked down at his body lying on the ground. He felt so light, and sensed no fear, no bombardment of thoughts, no limits. Freedom. The chains had gone. So this was death. Why did people fear this?

Still staring at his body, Patrick sensed something coming close to him, a powerful energy. He felt no fear and turned his head towards the energy source. Before him stood one large being, with another emerging from behind some invisible realm. The two beings slowly turned their heads, taking in the surroundings. They nodded to each other, maybe a signal that all was okay.

Patrick nodded his head in recognition. He knew they were angels.

The angels smiled. The leading angel spoke.

"Patrick, we are here to take you home to paradise. To guide and protect you, for the trip is through regions unknown and unsafe."

They came to each side of Patrick, tucked their arms in his and directed him towards the invisible realm. Patrick looked back at his physical body, still on the ground, as he entered what appeared to be a passageway. They passed a black wall of some kind, and Patrick heard screams.

An angel spoke, "That is what the lost have to fear, Patrick. Behind that darkness is a place of torment."

The angels moved their bodies closer to his. Their power enclosed him. Patrick felt God's peace upon him and knew that he was on his way to heaven. He thought of Jill, and Aaron. He thought of Jack and knew he would soon see him.

CHAPTER TWO

Sunday, 5 November 2017, Townsville

AARON FITZPATRICK STOOD ON a pathway, staring at the imposing outcrop of Mount Stuart as it presided over the city of Townsville. The city was situated in the tropical north of Australia, some thirteen hundred kilometers from Brisbane. From the top of Mount Stuart, the pristine waters of Cleveland Bay could be seen, along with boats returning from their trips to the Great Barrier Reef.

Aaron pondered the similarities between the mountain and the ruggedness of life. Some climb, some watch, some do nothing. He sought purpose to life, some meaning, a goal. The mountain kindled those thoughts.

The huffing and puffing of some joggers going past took his attention away from the mountain. Their sweat showed through the back of their singlets; Aaron could smell it. He watched as they turned on to the track that ran along the Lavarack Barracks' boundary fence. It was a long fence, as Lavarack Barracks was the largest military installation in northern Australia. The joggers were fit, and so was Aaron. He was a soldier.

When in his uniform, some of the old school saw his dad. They all knew his dad, an elite military man. Aaron was slightly taller than his dad but had a similar, solid build. The army stories Dad told Aaron and Jack had a lasting impression on both of them—more so Jack. His mother expressed her concerns. She believed this war stuff ran in the family genes and had told them that a few times.

Aaron's thoughts went to Jack. He closed his eyes and pictured

Jack before the accident. Aaron missed his brother. The accident was a wake-up call. He realized that the world was not such a pretty place after all. Would he ever forgive that drunk driver for slamming into Jack's car? Aaron's parents had but that was due to their belief system. It was all still confusing.

Aaron hadn't planned to join the army. That was Jack's dream. Aaron enlisted for his brother and Dad—he thought it would help the grieving process. He didn't take into consideration Mum's views on war and death, not purposely.

Aaron missed his brother. Death was so final.

* * *

After his reflective time with Mount Stuart, Aaron headed to the mess complex for the regular Sunday drinks. He took one more glimpse of the mountain. It wasn't escapism, more that he drew energy from nature. At the mess complex, he got himself a drink and walked out and joined his mates on the timber deck. Taking a sip of his lemon, lime and bitters cooled his dry throat. The grog was no longer a friend—it was the cause of his brother's death and he didn't like the strange things it did in his head. He preferred to be in control of his thoughts.

Aaron's phone rang.

He picked up his phone and looked over at his mates.

Nathan, about to take a sip of his beer, guffawed, "It's her ringing, mate."

Aaron would have been pleasantly surprised if it was Mackenzie. His mates referred to her as Aaron's sought-after but never caught girl. He had told them too much already and regretted it. He checked who the call was from, and felt guilty when he saw it was his mother.

"Hi, Mum."

"It's not his mum, he's having us on," Nathan said.

Aaron whispered to Nathan. "It is my mum." He gave Nathan a wink and nodded to the others as he left the mess complex and headed in the direction of his accommodation.

"I'm sure all's okay, Mum. He might have just fallen. See if Mackenzie's parents are home and then walk the jogging route Dad usually takes." Aaron kicked a stone off the path. What did Mum expect him to do when he was so far from home? "Make sure you take your phone in case Dad has had an accident or something, and take a torch. I know the track is well-lit, but take one anyway."

"I'm sorry for calling you, love. I know there's not much you can do, but I'm worried."

Annoyed with his attitude, he searched for something else to kick. "It's all going to be fine, Mum. Probably a twisted ankle and he's hobbling home now. If you don't have any luck locating him, go to the police station. They could help locate him."

Aaron opened the door to his unit and walked in, listening.

"Mum, everything will be fine. Make sure you call me as soon as you know something."

He placed the mobile on his bed, disturbed, went out to the balcony, and lifted his face to the breeze. Yes, he was a long way from home and did feel a little helpless, but there was nothing he could do about that. Dad's running routine worked like clockwork. He would be fine; he could look after himself. But soldier's intuition hinted something was wrong.

All he could do now was wait until he got the call telling him all was well. Dad would turn up, but the situation reminded him that Dad wasn't immortal. He felt the metaphorical shoe on his foot now—his parents had to deal with the possibility of death with Aaron serving in war-torn countries. He told his parents not to worry. Dad displayed the same anxiety as Mum, which always surprised Aaron—Dad had been there, done that.

He started calculating when he would get a call. It would probably take them an hour or so to walk Dad's running route, so Aaron decided to take a walk. He always thought of the tropical north landscape as lush green canyons with raging waterfalls, but here at the base, there were only pockets of greenery with some parts resembling the outback desert. But it was all still nature. He took a deep breath. His energy needed a top-up.

He returned. Hot and sweating after his walk, he opened the bar fridge and grabbed a bottle of water. His phone rang. He walked over and picked it up. Mum.

They hadn't located his dad and were heading down to the police station.

* * *

On Sunday evening, a loud clap of thunder shook the car Lucas Fell was dozing in. He woke with a fright and heard voices, dark evil voices. But they were retreating now, getting softer. Just to be sure, he turned and looked behind him, but there was no one there. He was alone. It was stuffy, so he wound the window down a little. The sound of noisy crickets entered the vehicle while the stale smell of marijuana smoke drifted out.

Lucas didn't know where he was. A drink bottle lay on the passenger seat, so he grabbed it, had a sip, and laid it back down on the seat. A moment later, he wondered about the cold feeling in his throat. He stared at the drink bottle. Did he just have a sip of water? *Wow, what kind of state am I in?* He sat for a while, then wound his window all the way down. He rested his arm on the window, and realized he was in the blue security car. Images of a big star on the front doors and roof popped into his head. Where was he? It was quiet, but slowly the sounds of birds were picked up by his senses. He looked out the window and saw the steps leading up to the house and worked out that he was at the property.

Lucas got out of the car and stretched. He took some deep breaths—rain was in the air. It helped to clear his head. He looked at his watch and realized that he needed to get back to the lab or office or whatever they called it. There was something he had to do there, but could not quite remember what. He got back in the car. It would come to him as he drove there.

As he turned the car to drive out, he noticed the white van and that the driver's window was open. With rain coming, the window needed closing. He pulled over and walked over to the van. A pack of cigarettes lay on the passenger seat and he wondered how his cigarettes got there. He opened the door and reached over and grabbed them. A quick glance in the back of the van told him all the hi-tech equipment was turned off. Lucas locked the van and went back to his car.

As he drove, he thought of two things: his mum and the green stuff. His mum hadn't concealed her habit very well, and Lucas had picked the habit up. It wasn't like he had a dad to copy. In her later years, Lucas asked her why she stopped. It was the voices in her head, she told him, and the paranoia. She said to be careful because the faulty wiring may have been passed on.

Lucas ignored her. He ignored the warning.

A sign appeared. BRISBANE TECHNOLOGY PARK 100 METERS.

Lucas preferred the van—it had more room. The blue security car was a tight fit for his solid build. He knew his appearance as the rugged, thick-necked weightlifter type had helped him get his current job, a security officer for a hi-tech organization that was part of the Department of Urban Movement. A menial job, but his mum said that was his own fault because he lacked drive and vision. She'd told him to watch out as he could become very, very lazy—that's what this stuff could do to you. He wished he could get his mum out of his head sometimes. With those negative vibes came the need for a hit, but he could wait a little while. He had no choice.

Lucas turned into the technology park. Clean, modern buildings sat on both sides of the road, most with lights on even on a Sunday night. People must still be working. A few drops of rain hit the windscreen, but not enough to turn the wipers on yet. He turned into another street, with fewer buildings, older buildings, different shapes and sizes, less lighting. He reached his destination and turned into the Department of Urban Movement outpost's car park.

A black cat sprinted in front of his car. The notion of bad luck popped into his head but he pushed it away. He steered the car towards the front of the building and was moving in that direction when something to the right of the building caught his attention. He stopped, grabbed the spotlight and scanned the area. Something lay in the shadow of a tree. This did not look good. He got out of the car and walked towards what looked like a body. It was. He leaned over it and searched for life signs. None. This person was dead.

Lucas needed a hit of that green stuff really bad. There was something familiar about all this.

* * *

Mackenzie had phoned late last night, saying they still hadn't located Dad. Aaron asked for some time off work, and booked a flight to Brisbane.

Aaron always preferred window seats. He did the things you normally do on a plane: buckle up, observe people, and flick through the inflight magazine. It would be nice to be flying with someone, but that would come in time. As always, his thoughts went to Mackenzie. She had volunteered to pick him up from the airport. He looked forward to seeing her.

Aaron rested his head against the window. The vibration of the plane gently massaged his cheek. He stared out the window, houses and properties getting smaller, and his thoughts went to that Man who looks down on the world.

He often thought of God when flying. Maybe it was a fear thing, trying to make a connection in case the plane decided to fall out of the sky. Dad found God later in life, not long after Jack's death. Aaron saw a change in his dad, a good change, although he didn't fully understand it. Once he flew with Dad, and Dad told him God views our lives from on high, from beginning to end. He told Aaron that people forget that God knows everything about us, that there is nothing hidden. Aaron remembered thinking about the day he and Jack put their initials in the concrete down near the river. He still felt guilty about that.

He had a book to read but he couldn't concentrate. Too much on his mind. He stared out the window, thinking of Dad again. They knew they loved each other: he was sure of that. They were not the hugging type—the firm handshake said it all. He loved Dad. His eyes were tearing up so he looked to the clouds to distract his thoughts. It worked and he soon dozed off.

A bump woke him. The clouds drifting had relaxed him but these same clouds brought the thing he hated about flying: turbulence. The seat belt indicator lit up. He tensed up and closed his eyes as the first wave of turbulence came. Why did Dad turn to God? The next wave came. He wondered what had happened to Dad. Another wave, he thought of praying but then wondered would God hear his prayers? The turbulence passed. He relaxed.

They were through the clouds now, and Aaron watched as the houses came closer. He straightened up in his seat and waited for the wheels to hit the runway. He looked forward to seeing Mackenzie. He smiled, but how he wished things could be different.

* * *

Mackenzie Gordon sat in her red Ford Fiesta, some distance from the domestic terminal. She was early, so had pulled over. She sat, thinking. Her fingers tapped the steering wheel in rhythm with the praise and worship music she had playing. She loved Aaron, but they were pulling in different directions. Her prayers that the stumbling block to his faith be removed had not yet been answered.

Her phone rang.

"Mackenzie?"

It was Aaron's mum, and she was sniffling.

"Not good news, my love . . . I've tried Aaron's phone but he must have it turned off. They've found a body way out at Eight Mile Plains."

"Eight Mile Plains?" Mackenzie said. "That couldn't be—"

"I think it is, love . . . I think it is."

"I'm sorry, Jill. Shall I get Aaron to call you?"

"Please do. They've asked that someone from the family come and confirm that it's Patrick. I'd like Aaron to come with me."

Mackenzie put down the phone and asked the Lord to not let it be Aaron's dad. She gripped the steering wheel, hard. Her chest tightened up. She tried hard not to cry, but the tears came anyway.

* * *

Aaron walked to the public pick-up area. The airport had undergone some refurbishments since the last time he was here, so he wasn't quite sure which way to go. He looked at his phone and shook his head, annoyed. He'd forgotten to charge it.

"Aaron."

He turned to see Mackenzie coming towards him. She looked wonderful, tanned with a black and blue sleeveless print dress, but he could tell that she'd been crying. He braced himself for what was to come. He gave her a hug, told her how beautiful she looked and waited for her to tell him. She tucked her arm in his and pointed in the direction they should go. They started walking—Aaron's suitcase producing a rhythmic sound, like a train, as its wheels dipped in and out of the contours of the paved sidewalk.

"Your mum phoned. You need to give her a call."

Aaron nodded. Mackenzie was giving his mother the courtesy of telling him.

"This is it . . . my red machine."

They sat in the car, silent. Aaron adjusted the seat for more leg room. Mackenzie gave him a smile.

"You're looking good, Aaron."

"Thanks, Kenz. One small problem though. My phone is dead. Could I borrow yours?"

Aaron watched Mackenzie dig into her handbag and find her phone. She handed it to him, then started the car.

"Well, I suppose we best get going."

Aaron nodded and put his hand on her leg. "You're looking real good, Kenz." She did look good. He wasn't going to let her teary red eyes take that away.

He took his hand away and watched the traffic as Mackenzie made her way out of Brisbane Airport, then called his mum. It was a brief call. His mum was a tough cookie and she knew he would be there soon. He placed the phone on the plastic console between the seats.

Aaron stared out the window. "This is all mighty strange, Kenz. Did Mum tell you?"

"Just a little. A body found in Eight Mile Plains?"

"Although I hope the body they're talking about is not Dad's, my gut feeling says otherwise. The police wouldn't want us to identify the body unless they had a strong inkling that it was Dad. So how did he end up in Eight Mile Plains? That's close to twenty kilometers from home. Dad wasn't a marathon runner."

Aaron paused and thought about emotional coldness. Should he be showing more emotion? His training had kicked in, to use sound judgment rather than emotions to make important decisions. He did feel different. He sensed toughness with his emotions, maybe a combination of army training and the death of his brother. The training gave him coping strategies, adaptability and resilience. His thoughts even sounded military, like a soldier going into battle.

"How's Paul?" he asked. Yes, he had changed. That was a strategic, cold question.

* * *

Aaron and Mackenzie's parents had been neighbors in one of the older streets of Bulimba Village for over twenty years. It wasn't really a village. In the early years Bulimba had covered a much larger area, but in time was truncated to a small area on the edge of the Brisbane River.

Mackenzie turned the car into their street. Aaron's heart sank. His mum stood, both hands resting on top of the old woven wire gate, obviously waiting for him. On seeing Mackenzie's car, she opened the gate and walked onto the footpath. The gate closed behind her.

Mackenzie parked in her family's driveway.

Before opening the door, he looked at Mackenzie and gave a sigh. "Thanks, Kenz. Appreciate what you've done. Best get to my mum now."

"Yep. Give her a big hug. We can catch up later."

He got out of the car, walked over and embraced Mum.

"Hello, soldier boy."

Aaron smiled. He opened the gate and walked his mum up the path, onto the front porch. They each sat in a wicker chair, a small glass-topped wicker table between them. An ornamental grapevine kept the porch shady and cool.

"Your dad brought me here to live because it's a place of heart. He told me that the Aboriginal name for Bulimba means 'heart', and if you look at the boundaries of Bulimba on a map, it's heart-shaped."

"I didn't know that, Mum." Aaron could see she was trying to distract herself. She followed a butterfly as it made its way through the grapevine, and then she turned to Aaron.

"He had a big heart. Aaron . . . it's him, love. They told me the clothes he had on. Not everyone goes jogging wearing a Beatles t-shirt. But we still need to formally identify the body. We can do this together, Aaron."

"We can." Aaron pictured Dad's t-shirt. It had the famous image of the Beatles crossing a zebra crossing. "You okay, Mum?"

"A bit numb, love . . . as you get older death becomes a regular companion. You know, friends die, relatives die, media personalities that you have grown up with die . . . but it's the unexpected ones that hit you the hardest, and this one is dear to my heart."

Aaron nodded. The world could see the love his parents had for each other. Death was such a confusing thing. The period after losing his brother in the car accident was one he would never forget. Sometimes he would seek out his brother only to remember he was gone. And he wondered why God did not prevent the accident. They told him God could have, but chose not to. It didn't make a lot of sense to Aaron but he knew they meant well. Apparently, Aaron's focus was on the physical side of things, and death was a spiritual thing. God was more concerned about the spiritual side of things. Dust to dust, ashes to ashes, they would say. It was beyond Aaron's understanding at the time, and still was. Would the aftermath of Dad's death bring the same thoughts?

"Something I'm learning in life, love, is that I have to pay closer attention to the prompting of the Spirit. He wasn't meant to wear that t-shirt. I told him it was dirty, but he didn't mind. Not sure why, but I think if he had something different on this would not have happened."

"You don't know that, Mum." Aaron was puzzled why she thought that.

"I think it's true, Aaron, but . . . what would he be doing in Eight Mile Plains?" Her gaze followed the flight path of another butterfly through the grapevine. "Did he get lost or something? He wasn't showing any signs of dementia or anything like that. I can only think that he was transported there by someone. But why?"

"We'll find out." He reached over and gave her a few pats on the hand.

"I spoke to someone from the police department a little while ago. They were making sure I was okay and told me that they will let me know as soon as anything crops up. The police person said something along the lines that they needed to establish if it was a crime scene or something else. They're coming to visit us tomorrow; they have a few questions they would like to ask."

Aaron thought about the incident being a crime. What else could it be? It must be foul play. Aaron believed Dad's body was dumped there. He wanted to know why and by whom. He got up from the seat, touched her on the shoulder, and told her that he was here to help her with things. They heard a low screeching noise—something needed greasing. They looked out on the road and saw Mackenzie pulling Aaron's suitcase over.

"Think it needs an oil, Mum?"

His mum smiled. "She's still cute, isn't she?"

* * *

Aaron and his mother sat on a bench at Riverside Park. A man and his wife walked past, their dog keeping them in tow. The couple nodded to Aaron's mum.

"You know them, Mum?"

"Yep, they've been coming to our church for a while. Think the husband is a politician of some sort. They looked a bit rushed today. Normally, they're a bit friendlier."

Aaron and his mum walked to Riverside Park after the interview with the investigating officers. During the interview, Aaron sat with his mum while the officers went over the last twenty-four hours of Patrick's life. Mum told them it was a quiet day. They went to church in the morning, and stayed a while after the service to help pack some groceries for needy families. Then they had lunch at their favorite café in Bulimba. She paused and repeated that it was a quiet twenty-four hours, nothing of significance: a quiet, peaceful day with no spilt drinks and no road rage incidents.

Aaron's mum laughed when they asked if there were any known conflicts with her husband. Aaron smiled too. He knew Dad as a kind man who minded his own business, but would be the first to come to the aid of anyone in distress.

The police officers asked about church and if there could be any conflicts there. Aaron's mum said that the world would be in a real mess if Christians were fighting with Christians. She did acknowledge that there was still some work to do with brotherly love and loving thy neighbor. No, she didn't believe there were any conflicts.

The breeze brought in a slight chill so they decided to head home from the park.

Aaron's mum had her arm tucked in Aaron's arm. "I'm sure there were no conflicts, Aaron. Everyone loved your dad."

"I'm sure you're right, Mum."

* * *

But there was a conflict—a private conflict that sat in the head of one person.

A boy told his father a story once. The boy told his dad that a man at church wasn't nice to him. What do you mean, son? Did he do something to you?

The boy was surprised by the attention his dad gave him when he told this lie. The boy was even more surprised how his dad put his arm around and told him it was okay to tell Dad what he did.

The boy just said it wasn't nice.

The father made an assumption about what happened. And he made another assumption that no one in church would believe his son, so he would take things into his own hands. He knew God understood these things.

The boy continued to tell stories. His father loved his stories; he always showed his son attention and affection when he told him these stories, but that was the only time. The stories stopped when something inside the boy told him it wasn't right to tell lies. His dad went back to his old ways when the stories stopped. No more attention, no more affection.

But a seed of revenge had already been planted in the father's heart.

CHAPTER THREE

AFTER THE VISIT TO the mortuary and a number of police interviews, focus turned to funeral planning—not something Aaron enjoyed. Celebrating a life, they called it. Tears flowed as they went through photos that could be used as part of the celebration.

It was Thursday. The funeral was scheduled for the coming Monday. Aaron finally was able to surface and take a breath. He borrowed his mum's Holden Cruze and drove to Eight Mile Plains. The traffic was starting to build up as businesses were beginning to close for the day, but he managed to arrive before peak hour traffic had fully taken hold.

He stood in the almost-vacant Department of Urban Movement outpost car park—either people finished early or not many people worked here. There was some police crime scene tape down in an area on the left. That must be where Dad's body was found. Aaron thought of the autopsy report as he walked down to the crime scene—it indicated death caused by severe brain damage when his dad's head hit the car park's pavement.

Aaron felt numb and confused. The police had interviewed a number of people around the Bulimba area that lived along Dad's normal jogging path. No one had seen anything. They did mention they were trying to locate the owner of a white van seen in the vicinity of the parklands.

Aaron's thoughts bounced around in his head. Did Dad fall? Did somebody dump the body here? What was he doing here? What attracted him here? Aaron looked around. There were no buildings in close proximity except for one that had been damaged by fire, about fifty meters from where Dad was found. A burnt ash smell still lingered in the air. The police had told Aaron about the fire. They didn't believe it was connected to his dad's death, as it was a couple of days after. Aaron wondered if it was a mere coincidence, just an unrelated event in close proximity and time.

A car pulled up not far from him. He turned to see an elderly Asian couple getting out of it. The man nodded to Aaron and walked with an arm over the lady's shoulder. Her body language showed grief—hunched, a figure of sadness. She had flowers in her hand. One flower dropped. They walked on towards two crosses planted in the ground near the entrance.

Aaron walked over and picked up the fallen flower. He walked towards them, tapped the man on the shoulder, and gave him the flower. The man nodded his thanks and laid the flower with the other ones. He turned and stared at Aaron.

"You are soldier?"

Aaron nodded. Why do people always say that? The haircut probably gave him away— short, light brown and neatly groomed— nothing unusual about it, styled so he could wear his military headdress. Probably his face too—a weathered look, a face of one who has spent considerable time outside. He also noted that English was not this man's language of choice.

"You must find people who did this. It is murder. They up to something, something secret."

Aaron could only nod. He placed a hand on the man's shoulder, both men fighting their own grief.

The woman turned and looked up. Her face begged for mercy. "Please help us, it not an accident."

Aaron wasn't sure what to say. "I'll do my best."

He left them to their grieving and headed back to his mum's car. So caught up with his dad's death, he hadn't realized that deaths had resulted from the fire. Could they be related? It didn't make sense. Were the deaths of the factory workers an accident?

He opened the driver's side door. Leaning on the open door, he looked back at the grieving couple and then beyond them to the bushland surrounding the building. A branch from a tree had snagged a piece of paper, and it fluttered in the breeze. He thought of the autopsy report. Something puzzled him. The report mentioned that the little finger on Dad's left hand was missing. Something he needed to check with his mum. Unless there was an accident recently that Aaron didn't know about, he was sure Dad had all his fingers.

Aaron climbed into the car and thought of the couple. They also had to plan a funeral. He drove out of the car park and headed towards Mum's.

It was getting cloudy. Heaven was up there somewhere. So many people have told him that is where his dad now resides. Religious things confused him. He wasn't quite sure why heaven was a better place. It seems everyone that dies goes to heaven. Mackenzie was the expert in this area, and one day he would get Mackenzie to explain it all to him.

* * *

Aaron watched Mum as she poured the cold water into a glass mixed with ice and lemon slices, and handed the drink to Aaron.

"Thanks, Mum."

He studied her as she returned to her kitchen tasks. He shook the ice in the glass and listened to the ice clinking inside the glass. Mum seemed to be holding up well. She stood at the sink rinsing some plates, occasionally lifting her head to look out into the backyard. He swallowed hard as he thought of the number of years his Mum and Dad spent together, and now his mum was alone.

"You okay, Mum?"

She turned towards Aaron and came and sat down with him. She placed her hands on top of his. "I'm okay, love. I'll always miss him. I know you find God things hard to understand, but my spirit is at peace. My journey continues and the Lord watches over me. I'll join your dad one day, but that's up to the Lord, and in the meantime I'll work through the grieving process. The Bible tells me that those that mourn will be blessed and they will be comforted. What about you, son? Are you okay?"

It dawned on Aaron. It was now just him and his mother. "I'll be okay, mum. The army has toughened me up and taught me some coping strategies."

"I'm sure they need to do that. Your dad had some bad memories in his head, and they would get to him at times, mostly at night-time in bed. But we would sit up and pray, and that seemed to calm things. You just be careful they don't toughen you up too much. You still need to be that sensitive boy we raised."

Aaron smiled. "I'll keep a check on that."

"I had a phone call earlier from one of the investigators. They asked me a strange question. They wanted to know when your dad lost the little finger on his left hand. I said that's news to me. Maybe it was part of the accident or whatever it was."

"Maybe you're right, Mum. It was in the autopsy report. Are you sure you don't want to read it?"

"No. I'll leave that stuff to you."

Aaron didn't want to elaborate on the missing finger—the report indicated no signs of an injury. It said the hand looked like it never had a little finger.

"Okay if I use the computer for a sec, Mum?"

"That's fine love, but you'll need to turn it on. It's in the spare room."

Aaron picked up his glass and headed towards the spare room. He sensed Dad's presence. Aaron swallowed hard. He had many regrets about his relationship with his dad. Over the last few years, he'd started seeing and thinking of Dad as a person and not a parent, but for most of that time Aaron had been away. Maybe that enabled the transition to take place in his mind. Now Dad was gone, and gone forever. Aaron swallowed hard again. If any misadventure was the cause of his dad's death, Aaron planned on finding out.

He found the computer and turned it on. He stared at the lemon in the glass, as he waited for the computer to load up. Once loaded, he googled the Internet for news items on the building fire.

A hi-tech company used the building. It was reported that an explosion had occurred in a secure room and seemed to be limited to that room. A security guard patrolling the premises raised the fire alarm. A photo of the guard—with well-maintained goatee and moustache—came with the news item. Apparently, he heard an explosion as he drove in to the parking lot. As there were no cars in the parking lot, he didn't realize that people were in the building. The two workers either caught public transport or rode bikes to work.

Aaron still pondered why Dad was in the vicinity. How did he loose a finger? Would this security guard know anything?

* * *

It was early on Sunday morning, and a clear sunny day. Mum had decided not to go to church today. She told Aaron that she wanted to spend some grieving time at home, alone with God. She was happy for Aaron to borrow the car and meet with one of the police officers.

Aaron sat on the bonnet of the Holden Cruze as he waited, watching a flock of parrots come up from the trees below the technology car park and fly over him. He followed their flight path and caught a glimpse of a plane in the sky. It reminded him that he needed to book his flight back to the base. His compassionate leave expired in a few days.

He was fortunate enough to be able to meet with the officer in charge of the investigation. The officer said he didn't normally work on the Sabbath but had no choice at the moment with his workload. But he was happy to catch up with Aaron. They agreed to meet at the incident site as the officer was glad to be able to get away from the paperwork that he was engulfed in.

A car pulled up.

Aaron turned to look at the car. It was not the investigating officer, but the people who'd visited yesterday. Aaron watched them get out of the car and start walking towards the crosses. The old man saw Aaron and hurried back to his car. He got something out of the car and brought it over to Aaron. It was a manila folder.

"You know man that died over there?" he said pointing to where Aaron's dad's body had laid.

Aaron nodded.

"Please take. It is writing my son had in his bedroom. I cannot read. Please you read." He looked behind Aaron. "Please hide. Police I do not trust."

Aaron turned to see a car coming towards them. He wondered how the man knew the unmarked car belonged to a police officer. Aaron nodded to the man, realizing the man's distrust of the police was probably a cultural thing. Aaron placed the folder on the floor and tucked it up under the seat. He closed the door and watched the man walk down to his wife. Aaron looked over to the unmarked police car.

It was parked in a shady spot, and the officer was heading towards Aaron. He was dressed more casually today, in jeans and a red and blue polo top.

"Hello, Aaron."

"Hello, Officer Olsen."

They shook hands, and the officer once again offered his condolences. They walked over to the scene of the incident. "This is where your father's body was found." He turned towards the building. "You can see a couple of CCTV cameras on the roof of the building."

Aaron nodded.

"We've reviewed the footage of the relevant camera and, I'm sorry to say, it hasn't helped us. Your dad's incident happened right on the edge of the camera range. It was like your father fell into the camera range, so we could not ascertain what caused the fall."

"I assume there were no witnesses?"

"None have come forward. Do you have any idea what your father was doing here? Our background checks indicate he wouldn't normally visit this business park. We also checked his phone and there weren't any calls regarding meetings or anything."

"I agree. It's not the type of place I would expect to see my dad, unless he had some business with whatever goes on in that building."

"That's a Department of Urban Movement research facility. We have checked with them, and they have no record of any dealings with your father."

Aaron looked over at the building and noticed a sign outside the main entrance. He might take a closer look at that later.

"I noticed you were talking to one of the parents who lost their sons?"

"I was. I met them the other day."

"You are aware there was a fire incident a couple of days after your father's accident? They believe the fire wasn't an accident. But they're unable to substantiate their claims—they have given us no evidence to why they think it was not an accident. We're going to wait for the Fire Investigation Unit's report and then take it from there. Can you see any connection between your father's death and the fire?"

Aaron shook his head. "Not really. Is it just a coincidence? I have no idea."

"The autopsy report indicates your father had a finger missing yet your mother indicates that wasn't so. We've double-checked with the coroner and that's definitely the case. Are you able to confirm this?"

"Well, a missing finger would be obvious if you have been married to someone for close to thirty years. And it's something I would have noticed growing up in the same household."

"Yes, I agree. Sorry, but I do need to ask these things. You mentioned when we met the other day that you're in the army. Where are you based?"

"Townsville."

A car started up, and the two men turned to see the grieving parents slowly drive off.

"Give me the best number to contact you on and I'll let you know if something crops up. At this stage though, the fire could just be a coincidence and maybe we are just looking at a tragic accident but my job is to confirm that. Here's my card if you need to contact me."

Aaron took the card. "I understand, and thank you for meeting with me, Officer Olsen."

Aaron stood next to his mum's car and watched him drive off. He appreciated what they did. He opened the door and reached under the seat and grabbed the folder. Opening it, he found a piece of paper and a printed picture. The picture looked like a shot from a black–and–white zombie movie. He put the picture to one side to look at later, and started reading the notes in the hope they would make things clearer.

We have seen evil things. Things not of this world. Yet we continue to progress this technology.

Who was writing this? What were they talking about?

Animals come back deformed. But we think we have fixed the technology so this no longer happens. Yet things appear that frighten us. We hear voices. We tell owner these things but they laugh at us. There is a man that comes with owner, he wears blue uniform with star on shirt pocket, he seems good man but we don't trust him. We have told him these things. He just tells us to fix things. We have, we no longer see the evil things. They no longer come through the walls.

Aaron looked at the picture again. It was a picture printed in grayscale. He wasn't sure what it showed—something coming through a wall: bony arms, bony legs, dirty torn clothing. What was it? There were some more notes at the bottom of the page.

Project signed off today. Technology being moved somewhere. We are glad this project now over. We now look for other work. We no longer want to work here.

Aaron closed the folder.

Thud! A small branch fell on the hood of the car. Aaron jumped, his heart racing. He stared at the branch. A dead branch: no leaves, just twigs. Like the skinny things in the photo. How could something come through a wall?

A crow squawking got his attention. He turned and looked over towards the front entrance of the building. The crow's beak nudged the flowers around the cross—a matte-black crow and flowers, all symbols of death. He wondered about the relationship between the cross and heaven. It seemed everyone was going to heaven, except, of course, for the murderers and the like. He thought of Dad in heaven and the day when they would see each other again. As long as he didn't murder someone between now and then.

Aaron got out of the car and walked over to the front entrance of the building, to the crosses and flowers which sat under the entry sign. There were pictures of the boys there. They looked so young.

He wrote down the contact details from the building's entrance sign, and had a good look at the building and its surrounds—a secure building with a high perimeter fence. There was a track along the outside of the fence and through some bush. It looked as though it was formed by human traffic, to help people get somewhere. Curiosity got the best of him and he followed the track into the bush.

The track made its way through an army of small gum trees and melaleuca bushes, with lots of weeds as undergrowth. Shade pockets gave off a damp smell with insects zigzagging all over the place as Aaron invaded their domain. Further into the track Aaron picked up a different smell, a cheesy smell. There was an area in the weeds that looked flattened. He walked over and found the decaying body of a cat, with only blotches of fur remaining. He stared at the decaying body, something once living and breathing. For some strange reason, he wondered where it had gone. Did a spirit depart from this animal? *Where are these thoughts coming from? The grieving process?* He returned to the track and further on found another decaying body. This one was bigger, maybe a dog.

Aaron kept walking. Coming out of the bush, he ended up in another commercial block with a few buildings and a shop where you could buy food. So, hungry humans had formed the track. Heading back, he noticed another skeleton. Moving a branch to get a closer look, he pricked his little finger. With his finger in his mouth, he looked down at a large dog, which was well into the decaying process. Why so many dead animals? Somebody didn't like pets. There must be many saddened pet owners close by.

He thought about the notes. Was there a connection? Maybe these animals had been 'tested'. Should he go back in there to examine the bodies for deformities as mentioned in the notes? He decided against that. He looked at his little finger: the blood flow had stopped and dried up. Then he remembered his dad's hand. He looked over at the building. Was there a connection between whatever was going on in there and his dad's death?

Aaron walked back to the car, trying to decide whether or not to call Officer Olsen. Would it be of any benefit? He decided to investigate the matter further, then provide the police with solid information that would bring this to a speedy close. Anyway, that was the theory.

The perimeter fence had strategically-placed signs advising monitoring of the property twenty-four hours a day. The signs provided a contact number. Aaron looked up at a security camera. It was pointed straight at him.

* * *

The cameras on the building were motion-activated, and the man's movements were being recorded. Lucas watched, alerted by a text message triggered by the sensors.

He played the video back and watched as the man had bent over and looked at things on the ground. He made a silent bet with himself that the bodies of the animals they'd discarded had not been buried. He looked around for something to throw. Nothing. *Calm down, Lucas, calm down.* He knew he should have checked. People are incompetent. Who can you trust?

This man looked like a detective. So he was investigating, and Lucas decided he wasn't going to find anything. Lucas took a long draw on his joint and powered down his tablet computer. He stood up, stretched back his arms. The little voice in his head told him everything was going to be fine.

* * *

A large white cross stood on top of the main auditorium building. The cross could be seen from a distance, advertising the love of God and attracting the lost. The funeral service was being held in the smaller auditorium which still seated a large number of people. Patrick Fitzpatrick came to church here.

The national flag lay draped over the coffin with an Australian Army slouch hat resting on the flag. A cushion displayed Patrick's medals, symbols of courage and national pride.

Lucas Fell leaned on the Minister for the Department of Urban Movement's car as he watched the pallbearers coming down the stairs. He shook his head. He had no national pride—the country stank. He did this once, carried a coffin. At his mother's funeral, he remembered, they called it a celebration. Why? What were they celebrating? They have mentioned the word celebration here too, a celebration of life. Well, this person may have had more to celebrate than his mum.

Lucas was glad he didn't have to enter the church building. The last time he entered one of those buildings, at his mum's funeral, it freaked him out. Something happened to her in her last days. This man kept coming to see her. She went religious on Lucas, and then she died. Lucas smoked some cannabis about thirty minutes before his mother's service and he had some terrifying visions during the service.

It was a funny world. Some days back, Lucas had reported the outpost incident to the authorities, and now here he was, attending the funeral of the person he'd found.

Something about this dead man bothered Lucas. Something didn't sit right and he couldn't quite sort it out. Was he losing the plot? The voices in his head bothered him. He just needed to stay away from the green stuff for a while. Maybe the demons or whatever they were would go and bother someone else. Maybe they fed on the green stuff. He smiled and decided he would starve them. Then they would definitely go away.

Lucas saw the Puffer Fish come out of the building. That's what he called the minister at events like this—he puffed up with all the media attention, which was probably the only reason he was here. Lucas smiled as he thought about the recent unwanted media coverage the minister got—he'd recently lost his license due to a drink-driving offence. He had supposedly repented of that behavior, but the media gave him a good serve.

Lucas was the chauffeur today. The minister attended the funeral because the incident occurred in close proximity to one of his department's research centers, the one known as the outpost. The minister had taken a shine to Lucas after Lucas gave him a guided tour of the hi-tech lab at the outpost. So Lucas alternated between being a chauffeur and being a security guard.

After loading the coffin in the hearse, the pallbearers stepped back. One of the pallbearers was decked out in full military uniform. A girl walked over to him and gave him a hug. This girl did something to Lucas's heart—he wanted to be near her, to know her. Lucas grabbed his iPhone and took a photo, and another, and another.

He climbed into the car and waited for the Puffer Fish. He checked out his photos, and then looked out the window for her again. He found her. How come he was so infatuated with this woman? Well, the body was a good start. But then maybe Cupid was shooting arrows around. Wasn't Cupid an angel, and didn't angels hang out at church? That's it: he's been hit by one of those arrows. That could explain the uncontrollable desire that had come upon him.

One of the photos brought him back to reality. The man in uniform looked familiar.

Lucas got out of the car so the minister would see him. He saw the minister talking to a lady. Soldier boy walked over and shook hands with the minister. The lady and soldier boy hugged. Lucas looked around. Where was she? He found her, but there stood another man, a different man, with his arms around her.

* * *

Aaron had not seen many of his dad's friends for a while. Now all were coming up to him, one by one, telling him what a great man his dad was, and if there was anything they could do to let them know.

He had just met a politician who gave his mum a hug. Apparently, they knew each other—both attended this church. A break from the well-wishers came, so Aaron found a seat on a concrete wall not far from his mum. He sat there, taking in the surroundings. People were heading to their cars to join the procession to the cemetery.

He noticed a government car with a bulky person leaning on it. Alarm bells went off in his head. He looked like that security guard he saw on the internet clip. Aaron decided to walk over and check out his hunch.

"Aaron."

He turned to see Mackenzie not far away. Paul was in tow.

Aaron shook hands with Paul. They chatted and agreed on a get-together before Aaron headed back to base. Aaron tried not to be rude but he really wanted to get to this chauffeur to confirm his suspicions, so he kept the conversation short. He sensed Mackenzie's annoyance.

They left and Aaron looked down toward the government car. He saw the minister getting in his car and then felt his mother's arm tuck into his. "Come on, love. We need to get the procession underway."

* * *

Aaron sat at Gate 44, waiting for the boarding call for the flight to Townsville. He hoped the flight wasn't crowded. Aaron watched as Mackenzie came back with a bottle of water.

"Whatcha looking at?"

Aaron smiled. "You're such a pretty thing." She would see it as jest but his heart saw it as something else.

"Thank you, Aaron."

The call came. They hugged and he boarded the plane.

He took his seat and put his backpack under the seat in front of him. His hopes were met: it wasn't a crowded flight and the seat next to him was vacant. If there was someone sitting next to him, he felt obligated to talk and on this flight he didn't want to do that—he wanted to think. Unfinished business. Dad, Mum, Mackenzie—he would come back soon. The last few days have been a blur with so many visitors. Back at base he would get his thoughts in order and decide what to do next.

Maybe he should contact Officer Olsen and tell him to check out the chauffeur, but he remembered that the officer already mentioned they had interviewed the 'security guard'. What new information would come to light—a scratchy picture, dead cats and dogs, jumbled words. He grabbed his backpack from under the seat and got out the notes and read them again.

Where had the technology been relocated to? Is he holding back important evidence by not contacting Officer Olsen?

CHAPTER FOUR

IT WAS A CLEAR and sunny Saturday morning. Grant Windsor stood in the dining room looking out on to the street. He was dressed in casual brown trousers with a navy blue polo shirt. A white Toyota Aurion pulled up, right on time. The driver got out and stretched. It wasn't Lucas today but the other driver. That was okay.

He walked to the front door and opened it. "I'm off, love. Will be back later today. Enjoy your shopping."

Windsor waited for the response. He wasn't sure where his wife was.

"Okay, see ya." It came from the main bedroom.

Windsor closed the front door and headed down toward the waiting vehicle. The driver stood there with the door open.

"Good Morning, Tony."

"Morning, sir."

"Well, let's get this trip underway," Windsor said as he climbed into the back seat. "Can't keep the Professor waiting."

Tony walked around and got into the driver's seat. "Sorry, sir. I didn't catch the last thing you said there."

"That's okay, Tony. I was just saying that we can't keep the Professor waiting. You've got the directions I hope."

"Certainly have. Entered in the GPS navigator. We should be there in under an hour."

"Let's have a good trip Tony. And a safe one. It's Saturday, and all the crazies get let out of their cages on Saturday mornings. Bit harsh, I know. But all these lawbreaking idiots just don't seem to care about the laws of the road. Respect has gone out the window." Windsor smiled and connected with Tony's eyes in the rear-view mirror. "I know. I'm just a grumpy old man."

Tony started the car and drove in the direction of the motorway.

Windsor had a quiet chuckle to himself. The good Lord has a sense of humor. Those drivers out there drove Windsor crazy and he ended up in a job where he had to think about them and how to improve their plight. He helped form a new department and was now the Minister for Urban Movement, as it was called.

On the motorway, Windsor watched as cars weaved in and out and sped past them. "Cars everywhere, Tony. You know we have an important job to do. There are over four million cars on Queensland roads and we need to keep them from hitting each other and keep them moving. I tell everyone that our department is an innovative one that combines the fields of transport planning and engineering with urban design—integrating transport systems with moving people. Sounds impressive, hey?"

"It does."

"That's why I'm meeting with the Professor. We have some innovative testing under way and I wanted a demo before we get too far into it. And hopefully, I may get some control over those idiots out there sooner than later."

"Sounds good to me."

"You're a good man, Tony. I hope that Lucas boy isn't leading you astray. I sometimes think he has a hint of madness about him. Don't know why. Maybe it's in the eyes."

"It's all cool, sir."

Windsor wondered if the word 'cool' was still cool. The word seems to have been around for years. He wasn't sure if he would use the word cool to describe Lucas. He stared out the window and noticed dark clouds moving in.

"Looks like the fine weather is leaving us," Windsor said.

"I think you may be right."

The rest of the trip was reasonably quiet as Windsor reviewed some of his business correspondence.

Windsor looked up from his papers. Drops of water had started hitting the car windows. The windscreen wipers came on. Windsor watched the rain drops racing down his window. He noticed an old rusted car sitting in a well-grassed paddock. He remembered seeing it on the last trip, so he knew the house wasn't far from here. The car slowed as the GPS told them they needed to make a left-hand turn soon. They turned. Some coins started rattling in the unused ashtray.

After bouncing along the dirt road for a few hundred meters, Windsor could just make out the old Federation style home through the mist. Wheels crunched as they turned on to the gravel driveway. As they got closer, Windsor saw a figure sitting in the shadows of the deep shaded veranda. The car now parked, Windsor watched the man stand up and place a wide-brimmed hat on his head. He walked down the steps, waving, and came towards them.

Good to see the Professor again. God brought the right people into your life at the right time. He wanted to do something about these lawbreakers.

Windsor's door was open before he had placed all his business correspondence in his bag. Impressive. Windsor stepped out of the car.

He gave the Professor a warm handshake. He turned to Tony. "Tony, I would like you to meet the Professor. His real name is Bruce Starke, but we refer to him as the Prof, the Professor, or just plain Starkey." The Professor and Tony shook hands. Windsor continued. "He's the brainchild behind the technology, the innovative technology, I am so looking forward to seeing. He wants the world to know about it, and we are going to help him achieve that."

They left Tony to his own devices and headed up towards the house. Windsor towered over his friend. Starkey was a small, slightly-built man. Starkey once told him that his build was the result of nervous energy from years of thinking too much and eating too little.

Windsor was puffed from just walking up a few steps. He was out of condition and needed to do something about it. But he had told himself that on numerous occasions.

"Okay to sit out here for a moment, Starkey."

"Glad you suggested it."

Windsor stared at the openness of it all. The quietness: no traffic, no people. He took a deep breath.

"They working you too hard, Grant?"

"No, not at all, Starkey. It's just life. Wears you down. I seem to be getting grumpier and less tolerant the older I get. That's what everyone tells me anyway. What about you? This stuff I got you working on stressing you out?"

"Loving it, the stress and all. I'm nearly sixty and bouncing along. You're helping me bring something together that I've waited thirty years for. It's like all those years, with all those companies all over the world, all those ideas and bits and pieces, all those crazy scientists and physicists, are finally culminating into something. Yes, you're giving me the opportunity to bring it all together."

Windsor nodded. He had no doubt about Starkey's ability and talents. He also knew Starkey was being driven by the desire to prove himself to others. A prominent entrepreneur tripped some negative thought patterns in Starkey's head. Apparently, Starkey heard this entrepreneur talk about him in a demeaning manner—that was a spark that set off a forest fire.

He noticed that Tony had made himself comfortable under a tree. He wondered what the magazine was he was reading. Most probably something to do with body building.

"Well, I'm keen to see what this build up of thirty years has brought about. I just hope you're not going to have some supernatural being come thundering out of the sky."

"Not quite, Grant. Thor will not be attending. Let me go over it with you. The technology works as the testing has shown. It involves placing an energy field around an entity or entities. We can call the energy field a package or attachment. This package is pushed into an invisible realm and transported to an identified location."

"Just like my e-mails." Windsor added with a smile.

"Well, sort of. The invisible realm acts as a transporting mode—like placing a canoe on a river."

Windsor pictured a canoe with the occupants dressed in business attire. "Do you have any reservations?"

"Not really, Grant. You and I are spiritual type people, so I will tell you that I still lack confident knowledge about the invisible realm. I'm not entirely sure what happens when they are in the invisible realm."

"Maybe nothing happens. Maybe it's just like driving along a road or canoeing in a river, as you say. Maybe there isn't even an awareness of the realm."

"Well, we will find out. I just want it to be used. Your strategy, although flaky in some aspects, will utilize the technology and that's all I want. Maybe we will be famous one day. And Grant, I do thank you for the opportunity. Now, come inside."

* * *

They entered the house, their feet echoing on the timber floor. Windsor walked into a large lounge room where he saw a comfortable-looking couch, and a large iridescent mosaic tile coffee table, which reminded him of stained glass windows. Something sat on the floor covered in a sheet—maybe a precious piece of furniture protected from the dust.

Starkey told him to be seated. Windsor looked around the room and saw a large brown shed through the window. He turned back to see Starkey place an aluminum briefcase on the coffee table and then walk over and remove the sheet. Starkey came and sat next to Windsor. They sat together staring at a lifelike mannequin.

"That thing looks spooky," Windsor said, staring at the mannequin. The longer he stared, the more uncomfortable he felt. "I think I understand why you see more headless mannequins in the shops now. The longer I look at the mannequin's face, the more disturbed I seem to be getting."

Starkey made some adjustments to something in the briefcase. "What you're saying about the mannequin, Grant, is known as the uncanny valley effect."

"Uncanny valley?"

"Yes, they say the closer the mannequin or robot resembles human form it creates a feeling of uncanniness . . . familiar but foreign . . . attracted to, yet repulsed." He smiled at Windsor. "Are you ready for a demo?"

Windsor gave a slow nod.

A humming noise started. Then silence. An energy wave engulfed the room. The mannequin vanished.

Windsor pushed his back hard against the couch and then leaned forward. "Where did it go?"

Starkey stood up. "Come outside with me."

They headed down to the large brown shed Windsor had seen before. The mood outside felt strange—there seemed to be different vibes in the air. Windsor could see Tony still sitting under the tree. *So nothing's happened out here.* Starkey opened the shed door.

Windsor was hesitant. What lay behind that door?

Starkey must have sensed Windsor's apprehension. "There's nothing to fear, Grant. You won't end up in the invisible realm or anything."

Windsor walked in to what looked like an office: benches, desks, chairs and monitors. An aluminum briefcase, similar to the one in the lounge room, sat on a bench. There was another door with a digital keypad.

Starkey entered a number and pushed the door open and gave the signal for Windsor to follow him.

There on the floor sat the mannequin. Windsor could feel adrenaline pumping through him at the sight. He was back in the uncanny valley.

They walked over to the mannequin. Half its head was missing.

"Still needs some fine adjustments, but you get the gist?"

"So it does work . . . not that I ever doubted you Starkey. I'm impressed, and I get the gist."

They started walking back to the house.

"Yes, I'm impressed Starkey. After all those meetings I've finally seen it in action. And you are a clever man, and I may say, soon to be famous." He patted Starkey on the back. "Lucas is also impressed. He has been keeping me up-to-date with the testing." Windsor wanted to tell Starkey about the mistake he made, but he couldn't. He just wanted to give someone a scare. Windsor preferred not to think about the consequences of that scare.

Windsor realized that Starkey was talking and quickly refocused.

"It's just a matter of bringing up the entity you want to move on a screen or entering their GPS location. They get enclosed in an energy field, and then sent off to the specified destination."

"There's my email analogy again, but this time it's like sending an attachment to someone."

"That's a good way of looking at it."

They walked up the veranda steps and sat down on a timber bench. Windsor again took in the quietness, taking a deep breath to grasp the freshness of it all. In nature, he saw balance and order. But in man's world, things lingered, where they needed to be in order. He believed what he believed because it gave order to the chaos.

"Was the fire necessary?" asked Windsor.

Starkey looked at Windsor. "I hope you're not accusing me of having something to do with that fire and the death of those workers? No . . . no, it was a genuine accident. Those men were talented men, they enabled the technology. We best hope there are no more bugs with the technology as our experts are now gone. I'm saddened by what happened."

"I'm sorry . . . it wasn't an accusation, Starkey. Are we able to fix the problem that just showed up with the mannequin?"

"Yes, I have that one under control. It's a proximity thing. We need to specify the distance range involved in the transport. I forgot to put that in the code."

"Is that what happened with the recent incident?

"Yep, I think so. They realized as soon as they did the transfer. A wrong setting. It won't happen again. And, of course, he was meant to be transported back to point of entry."

"We're making life sound so cheap."

"We are . . . I'm not sure why Lucas chose this man. That was not our intended strategy—we were meant to be focusing on those that would not be missed if something like this did happen. As for now we have moved into dangerous territory. We could be held responsible for his death. So, before we go any further, we may need to consider if it's all worth it."

Windsor's chest tightened. It was only a suggestion. That's all it was. Why didn't Lucas put up a fight, suggest someone else? There was nothing personal there for Lucas. It was just another person.

"The person was a Christian, Starkey. That's one positive thing. He's gone to a better place." That was lame but he couldn't let guilt get in the way now. They had come too far. Sitting in that funeral, and knowing what he knew, was one of the hardest things he had done.

"So you say, Grant. But it's irrelevant. What is it they call it?

Accessory after the fact; I think that is more relevant. Is it worth us continuing? Are the risks getting too high?"

"I believe it's worth it, Starkey. We need to help society. I don't think we can see the changes in society your technology is going to bring. I think it is going to go beyond your wildest dreams. The death of one or two, compared to well over a thousand deaths on our roads each year, not to mention the follow-on deaths and suicides . . . it's a small sacrifice. I know the loved ones will feel differently, but we need to ride out this storm and introduce your technology to the world."

"You sound like a politician, Grant. And you have won me over. Let's soldier on."

"Soldier on, we will." Windsor chose not to let Starkey know that he'd known the man who died.

Windsor tried to relax. He found the timber and cast-iron bench hard on the backside. It creaked when he moved. He looked out over the property and noticed a large dead gum tree. Everything dies eventually. In the choice of life or death, what would he choose? His fellow believers would say death, because that would get them home, to heaven. We're dead men on a journey, they would say. Only meant to be here for a short time. We're not to love the world or the things of the world. Windsor wasn't sure if he thought the same, but he kept those thoughts to himself.

Windsor's ears picked up a sound, a distant sound. He looked up, and beyond the dead tree he saw a silver glitter in the sky.

Windsor pointed to the sky. "As on cue . . . I was on a plane the other week and my thoughts, or should I say, my thanks went to the aviation pioneers and how we have benefited so much from what they did. I'm sure some died so that we could benefit."

"I'm surprised you didn't bring your religion into it, Windsor. Isn't that what your faith is about, a man dying for the benefit of mankind?"

"It is, Starkey. And it's a good point . . . so you do know some things, hey?"

"Let me show you a trick." Starkey pointed his phone at the plane and then showed Windsor the result: a little thumbnail displayed showing the flight number, speed, altitude, last port of call and destination, and how far away it was from them.

"Technology . . . it's amazing what they can do these days. And it makes me worry about that man's death. Will they be able to trace it back to us?"

"Lucas viewed the security video. The victim actually fell into the view of the camera, so the authorities would have no idea what caused him to fall."

"Why didn't Lucas just move the body?"

"It would have been caught on video."

"Makes sense. So what's next?"

"We'll need to do a few more human trials. But we will be much more selective this time."

Windsor agreed.

CHAPTER FIVE

IT WAS THE FIRST day of summer, a hot morning, and the rail tracks were already shimmering in the sun.

Judy's head rested on the window. She enjoyed feeling the rhythmic vibrations from the train's wheels as they rolled over the rail joints. She smiled as she felt the sun's rays filter through and touch her face. She saw many people dozing as she looked around. Eyelids heavy, she soon joined them.

A loud screech woke her. She was confused. It was dark. More screeches, and she realized she was in a tunnel with the dark dirty walls amplifying the sound of the wheels as they made slight adjustments to stay on the tracks.

Another train passed. Heads flicked past in the lighted train carriage windows. It reminded her of a PowerPoint slide show. People just don't look happy she thought, looks of nothingness, looks of gloom—what dread awaits them? She laughed silently when she answered her own question: the dread of work!

Her mind started to rev up. The other train had passed now. Staring out the window, past her own reflection, always wondering what creatures lurked in such dark places. Rats—big rats—and homeless people. She caught a glimpse of some graffiti and added graffiti writers to her list of those that lurked. Light penetrated darkness; she knew the station was getting closer.

She watched some passengers stand and head towards the door before the train stopped. She preferred to stay seated until the panic to get out died down. Once stationary, she got out of her seat and stepped out of the train. She moved toward the escalators with her handbag over her shoulder, and mentally tuned into the phone resting in her hand. She hoped the call would come.

Off the escalators and towards the exit, she walked down the steps towards the pedestrian crossing. *Please, God, get him to call.* And then she wondered how God received such requests. Did he a have big screen that he monitored? How silly. She didn't even believe in God.

She slowed as she reached the pedestrian crossing. The vibrations started in her palm: it gave her a mild shock. Excitedly, she brought the phone up for viewing and kept walking. She opened the screen, her heart picked up a couple of beats—it was him. She saw her phone sailing through the air before pain and confusion overtook her. She experienced a brief period of light then entered darkness. She was in a place of torment.

* * *

The early morning sun reflected off the roof of the white van. The city haze hadn't yet settled in, but the cars and smokers came descending on Brisbane City. The white van sat parked on a street above Central Station. Lucas stood outside, leaning on the van, smoking. The blue haze of his cigarette climbed up the side of the van and then drifted up to join the other pollutants. Lucas stubbed his cigarette on the pavement and kicked the butt into the gutter. He opened the back of the van and climbed in.

In the back of the van, Lucas could just make out the continuous wailing and 'he-haw' sounds. Ah, the sounds an emergency brings to the city. He looked around at the gadgets in the back of the van—just a few gadgets, nothing like the Houston Mission Control Centre. The image on the computer monitor was focused on the pedestrian crossing. Lots of things seemed to be going on down there. His heart skipped a beat because he saw that girl again, the one from the funeral. What a coincidence. He zoomed in on her, such a pretty thing. Maybe this was meant to be. He noted the time.

Lucas took in the scene unfolding below. A car had hit someone, thankfully it wasn't his girl. The driver got out of his car and needed some assistance. Maybe he was in shock. Lucas could see a body in front of the car. There was no movement.

His mobile phone vibrated. "Not yet," the voice said. "There's too much police activity down at the crossing at the moment—looks like there has been an accident or something." Lucas nodded in agreement and watched as more police vehicles pulled up at the crossing.

Lucas climbed into the driver's seat and started the van. He drove off, past a man sitting on a bench wearing a red and blue cap. Lucas remembered the bench and the man: he did a successful test on that man recently.

The man stared at Lucas as he drove past.

* * *

It all happened so quickly. She just walked straight in front of his car. Her legs were swept from under her, throwing her on to the bonnet of the car. Her head crashed against the windscreen. He hit the brakes hard, sending her forward. She hit the road like a rag doll. Her mobile phone bounced ahead of her.

The man got out of his car, surveyed the scene, and would have collapsed except for the quick hands of a man close by. The driver stared at the girl sprawled in front of his car. She lay still, very still. He shook his head and covered his face with his hands. They told him to sit down, and he did.

He thought of his dad and his reaction to this.

* * *

Aaron was back in Brisbane city and was out for a run when he came across the incident.

The driver was out of the car and swaying, so Aaron grabbed the man to steady him. It was obvious the man was in a state of shock. A few people came and assisted Aaron. They sat the man down where his view of the body was obscured. Aaron thought the driver looked familiar—maybe they had crossed paths sometime in the past.

The ambulance arrived in less than ten minutes. The paramedics worked on the young woman for a while, and then placed a white sheet over the body. Aaron told the police he didn't witness the accident, but arrived just after the event. They still took his details. One of the paramedics came over and checked on the driver of the car. Aaron stood back and looked around. There were gawkers everywhere. Why didn't these people leave and go to work or wherever they were to be going?

A stranger stood beside Aaron. "Terrible thing this, and will you look at those gawkers. And look at those taking pictures."

Right on! Why were those idiots taking pictures? The person's dead. Rage was building up inside of Aaron, best he continue his run.

"Excuse my insensitivity," the stranger said, "but where do you think that person has gone: heaven or hell?"

Aaron looked at him. He didn't know how to react. "You're right mate. That's a bit insensitive. Maybe you're as bad as those gawkers." He walked off, angry and keen to continue his run. Just before he started running he turned and looked back at the scene and the stranger, there was something odd about him. The stranger was gone, a funny sort of gone, like he just vanished. Aaron decided that the man had just ducked around the corner. He felt better thinking that. Besides, what else could he think?

* * *

Mackenzie and Paul heard the sirens and then saw the Emergency vehicle lights flashing as they came out of Central Station. Paul nudged Mackenzie to cross the road in the opposite direction, as their normal route was closed off. They crossed, and Mackenzie looked back, wondering what had happened. She saw a sheet being placed over a body and a man sitting down on the footpath with a few people around him. A man with a runner's singlet and shorts stood out among all the business attire. He looked a lot like Aaron, but she didn't think he was in town. The lights changed, and Paul told her to cross. She turned and obeyed.

Mackenzie had a funny feeling, a premonition. Normally, the clutter of the day drowned out the presence of the Spirit but she sensed him now—it got her attention. She turned again to look at the scene. She felt the blackness of the road drawing her. Something else was going to happen here, something that was going to rock the harmony of the place.

* * *

Aaron thought as he ran along the Story Bridge walkway, thought about the question the man asked about heaven and hell. It bothered Aaron. Why did it matter? When you're dead, you're dead.

Thoughts of his dad popped into his head. Dad's death was still quite raw.

Back in the base, they'd a big discussion about the subject of death and the conclusion that seemed to be reached involved good people going to heaven and bad people going to hell, as simple as that. Nik the Muslim summarized it nicely for them, saying that no one shall enter hell who has an atom of faith in his heart. Most of his mates had nodded their heads in agreement with his view. A few wanted to know more about the virgins in paradise that were often mentioned with suicide bombers.

Aaron looked down at his runners pounding the walkway. Past his runners he could see the water through the cracks in the bridge's walkway. The Brisbane River flowed down there, a long way down. A CityCat glided past.

Suicide bombers. Suicide. There had been a number of suicides from this bridge. Such things saddened Aaron. The despair or desperation a person reached to commit such an act confused him— wrong thought patterns, illness—he just wasn't sure. He asked Mackenzie about it. She preferred not to talk about suicides, but rather she felt for the people that were left behind and believed the people that did such things were not in their right minds. She believed they were influenced by evil.

They had moved on to talking about heaven and hell, and Mackenzie said that non-believers must get a real shock when they end up in hell. But then Aaron would get confused about the good person thing. Mackenzie told him bluntly, a few times, that unless he was saved he will be going to hell. But then Aaron would say he was a good person and she would say, "You are, Aaron, but you're not saved." Aaron wondered about the suicide bombers and their virgins in paradise. They couldn't be going to paradise—they kill people.

He came off the bridge, and ran along the riverside. He missed the breeze that cooled him on the bridge. He started getting hot. Mackenzie . . . thoughts of her darted in and out his head.

Ping pong in the head, he called it. One voice told him that he joined the army to run away from his feelings for Mackenzie. The other voice told him not to be stupid, and to get on with his life. But Mackenzie took up prime real estate in his head. At every opportunity, a thought of Mackenzie jumped to the front of the thought queue. He needed to build a Mackenzie firewall but had not quite worked out how to do that.

His thoughts went back to the accident. Life could be so sad. The driver of the car would have to deal with accidently killing someone. The parents of the girl were going to get some shattering news—maybe they already had. Then that man raising the subject of heaven and hell . . . there was something strange about him.

As he ran, he passed a house with a huge FOR SALE sign planted in the lawn. It reminded him of the first time he met Mackenzie . . .

* * *

Aaron had been ten years old when he first set eyes on Mackenzie from his front balcony. He peeked from behind a bush and watched as a pretty girl and her family walked past the FOR SALE sign on the house across the road, and walked up the stairs to the front door. A man greeted them. Mum told him that man was a real estate agent. He knew about agents. He was going to be a secret agent when he grew up. The man had a dark suit on and probably carried a gun. Aaron hoped no shooting took place.

The next time he saw Mackenzie was at school. Their teacher, Mrs. Trewin, welcomed Mackenzie to the class. He remembered praying to God that Mrs. Trewin would sit her close to him. God heard his prayer and she ended up in the seat right next to him. He was too scared to say anything to Mackenzie, so he just smiled every time she looked at him—which wasn't often, because she really paid a lot of attention to the teacher.

He decided to follow her home after school because he wanted to know where she lived. The bell rang, and few of the girls in the class came over to Mackenzie. One of the girls practically pushed him out of the way to get to Mackenzie, but that was okay because he needed to fade into the background because he was going to be a secret agent and follow her home.

He walked behind her after school. She didn't see him as he blended in with all the kids, bikes and bags. A lady met Mackenzie at the school gate. Aaron thought it must be her mum. He followed them down the street, but he felt grumpy because they headed in the opposite direction to where he lived—so they didn't buy the house on his street. Rats. As they turned into Thorpe Street he remembered that he rode his bike to school, so he ran back to get the bike.

He peddled madly back to continue his following act but could not locate them. To make things worse, the bike chain broke, so he had to push the bike home. He headed home with his shoulders hunched, kicking anything he found on the footpath. He happened to look up as a car passed, and got a shock—it was the car he was looking for, and Mackenzie sat in the front seat. She looked at Aaron, appeared excited, and waved. Aaron straightened up and headed home with the biggest grin, but a bigger surprise was around the corner. Their car was parked across from Aaron's house and that man with the black suit was back. He stuck something on the sign outside the house and shook hands with Mackenzie's mum. Aaron's grin got even bigger when he saw the thing on the sign read SOLD. He was in love.

* * *

Back from his run and back to his city accommodation. His short stay had been adventurous so far.

Aaron hoped his mum wasn't going to be annoyed. They sent him back to Brisbane for some training and then he decided to take leave for a few weeks after that. He had to stay in the city for a few nights due to his training requirements.

A shower cooled him down from his run. He walked out on the balcony and called his mum. Pictures of his mum walking out in the passageway and heading towards the phone came in to his mind. Her shoulders were not hunched, but tall and straight. That was the image he wanted. One where she is strong and on the mend. It had only been a few weeks but he wanted these things. He didn't want to think of his mum struggling with the loss of her husband.

Aaron told his mum that he would drop round, pick up his fishing gear and have a cuppa with her. He would bring her up-to-date with what he was up to. He told his mum he'd catch the ferry there, and asked if it was all right to borrow the car. That was fine.

Aaron planned to work things out with a fishing rod in his hand.

CHAPTER SIX

THE WHITE VAN CRAWLED along. Movement was snail's pace, at times even slower, the congestion due to the incident. Lucas had to get the Professor to walk a few blocks before he could pick him up.

After a good hour or so he finally picked up the Professor, then maneuvered the van onto the Pacific Motorway and relaxed. Lucas told the Professor that he saw one of their 'test dummies' sitting on a bench. They hardly spoke the rest of the trip. They nearly hit a wallaby as they turned into the property, which generated a brief sparkle of excitement in the van.

Lucas pressed the button and watched the garage door open. He drove the van in and told the Professor he would join him soon, as he needed to shut down a few things first. After tidying up things he went over to the shed. He saw a mannequin on the floor and assumed that they must have done some testing. It was just as well they didn't do a transfer, as this would have spooked the people. They slipped up—it should have been removed. He picked it up and carried it out with him and threw it on a pile of rubbish. The face on the mannequin stared back at Lucas, so he covered it with some of the other rubbish.

He lit up a smoke because he knew he wouldn't get another chance for a while. The image on the cigarette package was gruesome. It reminded him of the face of the mannequin. He hoped they'd fixed things up, because he wouldn't want to see these things happening to humans. There had been signs of problems—the first human test they did, the man stayed intact. He died from the fall, not a deformity. He thought of the man with the red and blue cap—he was intact and seemed to be functioning okay.

Another car was coming down the road. It was his boss, the Minister for Urban Movement. He quickly put out his cigarette as the minister didn't particularly like smokers. Tony the chauffeur got out of the car, raised his arm towards Lucas, and pretended to get him in a headlock. The chauffeur opened the car door for the minister. The minister nodded to the chauffeur and headed for the steps. He waved Lucas over.

"How are you, Lucas?"

"Not bad, sir."

"You're nearly looking as good as my chauffeur. Maybe you two should get into wrestling and form a tag team or something." He laughed.

Lucas had heard it all before. In fact, the minister's constant referral to his chauffeurs and wrestling gave birth to Tony getting the nickname of Tag. Lucas missed out on a nickname. He wondered if he might end up being called Tag2.

"I heard we had to delay things this morning. Bit of an accident, I believe," the minister said.

"That's what I heard." He hoped the minister would expand a bit more, because Lucas hadn't heard much.

"Sad, a person died, just because she didn't follow the rules. What are we meant to do with these idiots? They think they're immortal."

Lucas just nodded.

"Come join us, Lucas. You're a part of the team. And one other thing Lucas . . . you're not immortal either, so you better give up those cigarettes. You people just don't realize, you can smell a smoker a mile off."

Lucas followed. He imagined grabbing the minister in a head lock and blowing smoke in his face. They both reached the top of the stairs when the door opened.

"Ah," the minister said. "The mad professor. Are we safe to enter your domain?"

"Of course, there are no mannequins inside, only my spiritual guides."

The minister turned to Lucas. "He believes this stuff."

They walked in. "But don't you, Minister?" the Professor asked.

"What? Believe that stuff? No . . . no. I'm a Christian, mate. God forbids us to consult such things."

Their talk concerned Lucas. He looked around the house. He sensed an evil presence.

Lucas heard something.

"I must stop calling you the mad professor because you're not mad, but a good friend. Lucas probably doesn't even know your real name. Do you, Lucas?

Lucas, still looking for the source of noise, turned back towards the minister. "Yes, I know his name. It's the nutty professor." His humor always came out when stressed. He wasn't afraid of much, but invisible things and voices in his head spooked him.

They laughed. They sat around the coffee table. The minister placed his phone on the coffee table.

"No it's not the nutty professor. It's Bruce Starke, if you all don't mind.

"I knew that," Lucas said.

The Professor walked out of the room and came back with some beer cans. He threw one to Lucas and another to the minister.

"You know, Lucas," the Professor said, sitting on a chair facing them, "someone once asked me where thoughts come from. That question sent me off on a journey. I started reading lots and lots of books, new age books as they're referred to. I met many people also looking for the source of their thoughts. I came to believe in reincarnation and started visiting people who could tell the future and some who fixed up the holes in my aura."

"Holes in the aura?" Lucas mentally changed the man's name to Mad Nutty Professor.

"That's why he's so skinny, Lucas. Things leak out of him." The minister laughed, "He needed to be patched up. And Lucas . . . you know that impressive thing on your face, the goatee and moustache? If you removed the moustache and trimmed the goatee, just leaving a small patch, do you know what the remaining patch is called?"

"You got me there."

"A soul patch." The minister paused, thoughtfully. "I think that blends in with what we're talking about."

The Professor continued, ignoring the minister's attempts at humor. "I know it sounds far-fetched, but when you venture into the spiritual world these things become clear. I'm sure you're familiar with things like tarot cards and séances. I started communicating with angels of light who I have come to know as spiritual guides. I don't see them but sense their presence through people, things, and coincidences."

The minister shook his head. "It's all hogwash, Lucas, and downright dangerous stuff to get involved in. Those angels of light aren't necessarily angels of light. I keep telling him that, but he says it's a hobby. As long as it doesn't affect his work, it's okay with me. I think these beliefs move on, you know, like a passing fad."

"Don't think so, Minister. I believe they helped me develop the technology. Anyway, enough about me. We might have to find out a little about Lucas sometime."

"None of that stuff interests me." Lucas wanted them to get off the subject. It made him feel uneasy.

"Let me summarize it for you, Lucas. The Professor believes spiritual guides trigger thoughts, whereas I believe we have an angel on our right shoulder and a demon on our left popping thoughts into our heads. We just have to listen to the right voice."

"You're both mad, and I'm going outside to have a cigarette." The minister was just as mad as the crazy man he was dealing with.

* * *

Lucas lit up a cigarette but he would have preferred a joint. Tag was resting on the front of the car reading a magazine. Tag looked up, so he gave him a wave. He often wondered why Tag never attended these meetings. Sometimes wished he could swap spots with him, but knew if he did that he wouldn't have any idea of what was going on.

He walked to the end of the veranda and stared out towards the shed. Dark storm clouds were forming to the right of the shed. More rain coming. People would soon be in the shed. He imagined their fear and panic after a transfer. They had set up sophisticated surveillance equipment inside and outside the shed. He had watched videos of all the transfers so far, and they seemed to be working quite well, although he did feel for the poor homeless people they used as guinea pigs. He also had strange feelings about the first transfer he did—he wasn't quite sure what happened there.

They continued to test on humans. They needed to get it right, for they had great plans for this technology. They hadn't had any more deaths. Lucas was thankful for that, and he was also thankful that the investigations into the first death had not involved them. He was now well-trained in the technology and getting plenty of practice. He preferred using the mobile units, each the size of a briefcase, rather than using the van. The van was normally used to hook up all sorts of monitoring and testing equipment.

He did his first 'mobile' zap last week—he followed the man into the railway tunnel, and just as the man lay down on an old battered mattress, Lucas brought the man into view on the device's screen. The transfer location was already set, and Lucas pressed the green button. He knew the man would return shortly. The configuration of the equipment in the shed sent them back within a short period of time. He had watched the man as he returned. The man stood there scratching his head, as he had ended up next to the mattress. They needed to be more precise with the settings—he wouldn't have liked the man to end up on the railway tracks.

For the past few weeks, Lucas had travelled into town to locate appropriate street people and zap them with the technology. He would then venture back to the property and check the videos to make sure the transfer was successful.

The vanishings had been getting publicity but no one believed the street people. Normal people equate homeless with mindless, which is why the Professor had suggested they use the homeless. Lucas was getting concerned about himself as he felt his heart getting colder. Sometimes he would watch some of the videos and feel enjoyment at the confusion and suffering of these people. It was like it was feeding something inside him.

He shook off the thoughts and went back into the house. Once again he sensed something, and the squeaky door just added to the deep dark atmosphere.

* * *

The smell of beer permeated the room. The drinkers didn't smell it. Their senses got swamped, and their tongues loosened up.

Lucas sat down and grabbed a can. He noticed the minister's eyes had a glazed appearance and his face was flushed. The Professor just had a permanent smile.

"Why did you still want to meet, Minister?" Starkey asked.

"No more Minister stuff, either, Starkey. Same with you, Lucas. It's Grant to both of you. Now that we sorted out the pleasantries, I thought we would still have the meeting because this accident today just speeds up my resolve to sort this mess out. The poor driver and the girl's family are shattered. But we need to do a bulk transfer because this will bring the attention we're after. They need to know about this technology sooner rather than later."

Lucas took a sip out of his can. He hoped this meeting didn't turn into another drinking session. But at least if everyone was drunk, the tongues got wagging and he could find things out. He took another sip and looked at the pair. Bruce Starke had the same lack of fashion sense as Grant Windsor, but his taste for bow ties wasn't as flamboyant.

"Out of curiosity, how long have you two known each other?" Lucas asked.

Windsor raised his eyebrows and looked at Starkey. Windsor spoke. "Many years. We attended the same secondary school and university. Starkey had the brains while I was the streetwise one. You know, better people skills and charisma." Windsor gave Starkey a wink. "That's why I'm a politician, and I mean no criticism of Starkey when I say that."

"I have no problems with having a brain, Windsor."

It seemed to take Windsor a while to work that one out. He let out a burp. A few more years down the track, and Windsor would look like an older version of Harry Potter's Uncle Vernon. Lucas laughed at that thought.

"Lucas, have I told you when Starkey came to me with the technology?"

Lucas didn't get a chance to remind Windsor that the story came up at the last meeting before he continued.

"After many had knocked his idea back and even had a few laugh in his face, he came to me and I listened. Big ideas started to take shape in my head. My department's an innovative department, I'm an innovative man, and Starkey had an innovative idea. You know, Lucas, I always believed that there must be a better way to punish minor offences. The rich find fines to be a minor nuisance; they pay the fines but don't change their behavior. The poor can't pay their fines, end up in jail and are the worse for wear from it."

Starkey asked if anyone wanted another beer.

Lucas watched as Windsor looked at his can, responded in the affirmative and then took a big sip. Lucas declined. His eyelids were getting heavy.

Windsor carried on. "For traffic offences there was talk of impounding vehicles for a short duration, the theory being inconvenience would change behavior. I saw merit in this, but thought a better way of inconveniencing people would be to impound the person. I believed such a strategy could be used for a number of offences, not just traffic offences. And we now had the means to impound people."

Lucas was looking to the ceiling. There was a scratching sound.

Starkey looked at him. "It's okay, Lucas. There's no insulation, so you can hear the birds walking on the roof.

Lucas nodded and raised his eyebrows. "Are we still going to impound them in the shed?"

"For now." Windsor's phone rang. He picked it up and looked at the number. "My son . . . excuse me for a moment." He got up and walked out on to the veranda through the squeaky flyscreen door.

A short time later the door squeaked and Windsor walked back in the room. Lucas thought he looked pale. "Something's happening." He was shaking his head. "My son was the driver who hit that girl. That dead girl. He killed that girl. Something's at work here. My son's devastated."

Lucas agreed there was something strange going on. He remembered the two workers at the department's outpost making claims about evil things. Lucas wondered if they were venturing into something unknown and causing events.

He thought he heard a chuckle.

CHAPTER SEVEN

AARON WAS ON HIS way to do some fishing. He finally burst through the city traffic. His mum's car radio kept him up-to-date with the day's events—the accident this morning was mentioned briefly in the news and then discussed on talkback shows. Apparently the victim had walked straight on to the road, ignoring the pedestrian signals, totally preoccupied with her phone.

And of course the stories came in. A lady told of seeing a person fall down a manhole while texting, another walking into a street sign, and another with a broken nose after someone texting walked straight into them.

A sign advertising the greatest-tasting coffee in Brisbane caught Aaron's attention. Good advertising? He wasn't sure. Maybe it was just that he needed a caffeine hit. One sniff of the air as he entered the café told him they made good coffee here. The café had a number of small tables with cane chairs and a jar with a floating frangipani centered on each table. A few tables were occupied. The breeze from a large free-standing fan in the corner had the palms in pots dancing.

Aaron ordered. They handed him a little stand the shape of a pelican with number seven attached to it. He grabbed a newspaper and sat outside so he could see the river. He thought of his dad. They loved fishing together.

He started from the back of the paper as he always did. The Australian batsmen were making lots of runs in the cricket Test, but there wasn't much else happening in the world of sport. He flipped the paper over to the dreaded front page, where the major headline stated 'Australians addicted to speed', as some 21,000 motorists were fined for speeding in the past week and police were at their wits' end trying to curb this blatant breaking of the law. Fines and police patrols weren't working.

His thoughts went to the man that he helped that morning. How did you recover from something like that? The man had kept saying that his dad was going to kill him for this. What did he mean by that? Maybe his dad was in a position of power. Maybe it was his car.

Just as a heading caught his attention, his coffee and breakfast arrived. He thanked the server; she said he was most welcome. He smiled and watched as she walked off. She was nice.

The table was a good size for both a plate and a newspaper. He returned to the article that caught his attention. It was about the homeless in the city. They were talking about vanishings that have been happening over the past few weeks. People just disappeared and then reappeared a short time later. They were all saying the same thing: they heard a humming noise then found themselves in some kind of tunnel before ending up in a white room for a short period, then reappearing back where they were before the disappearance. Authorities had not been convinced of the vanishing stories, or putting it down to a number of things including mental illness, alcohol and drugs, paint sniffing, copycat behavior.

Aaron stopped reading and stared at the river. But what if it was true? How frustrating for those telling their stories. He heard a putt-putt noise and saw a man with a black and yellow life jacket and dark sunglasses cruise past on his Jet Ski. Aaron sensed something going on in his head. What was it? Thoughts jumping around, trying to connect to each other, trying to sort out all he had been bombarded with over the past few weeks, trying to untangle the mess. Vanishings. Is this what happened to Dad? He disappeared, but didn't reappear back at the same spot. How were the people transported? Loud revs—the man on his Jet Ski shot off, gone.

He told himself to chill. The eggs were to his liking and the coffee too. He was tempted to order another one, but the river's calling was stronger. Pessimism sells papers. It made him wonder why he bothered reading them. He folded the paper, pushed his chair back, stood and placed the newspaper back where he retrieved it from. He thanked the staff for a nice breakfast and headed out, brushing a palm tree on the way.

* * *

The Brisbane River is a majestic river meandering through the city of Brisbane. The river had a glow about it this morning. The fish were waiting for him, ready to latch on to his bait. A few pelicans rested on top of the pier poles—he wondered why the poles didn't bend with their weight. Aaron retrieved his fishing gear from the boot of the car. He watched a canoeist drift past.

He baited up and threw his fishing line in, concentric circles rippling out from where the line hit the water. As he watched the circles, he wondered if 'street people' was the correct term to use. Many didn't live in the streets, but in shelters or special housing. What if there was an element of truth in their disappearing? In time, people would start mocking the street people. They would say it was aliens: alien spaceships coming at night-time, zapping the street people up to their spaceships and conducting experiments—the perfect guinea pigs. No one was going to believe the street people. But this needed to be taken seriously, because he was starting to suspect a connection between the vanishings and his dad.

Seagull squawks caught Aaron's attention. He looked around and saw a small colony of gulls gathered on a small sandy beach on the other side of the river. A few had taken off flying in Aaron's direction, coming to check out what he threw in the water. They would be disappointed—it wasn't food. He pictured a man humped over a large garbage bin looking for food, isolated and alone. Yep, maybe there was an element of truth with the street people story.

A nibble on the line signaled he had a bite. He jerked the rod back hoping to hook the fish. The line went tight. He had hooked something and started reeling it in and saw flashes of silver as the fish got closer to the surface. The fish was too small, so he threw it back. He put some more bait on the hook and cast the line back in—ripples again, squawks again. Aaron turned his head towards the Gateway Bridge. Marveled at the cleverness of man—what holds these things together? So much concrete hanging so high in the sky. He often wondered what would happen if an element that was part of the formula holding these things together was removed—bridges would collapse, skyscrapers would fall. He supposed we should be grateful for the forces that do hold these things together. He was once told that God sustains all things . . . he wondered if that was true.

Aaron fished and kept thinking. Triggers . . . he recalled an event that happened a few years back on a crossroad just before the Gateway Bridge. Some idiot cut in front of Aaron, he tooted and got the 'finger'. Rage took control of Aaron and there was a dispute. He was victorious in his eyes but lost in Mackenzie's eyes. They broke up not long after that. She said they were on different roads. It was a bad time of Aaron's life. He had already lost his brother, his best mate. Now he'd lost Mackenzie, his soul mate. He joined the army not long after that.

No more bites. Aaron wound in his line. The bait was still on the hook, so he removed it and threw it in the water. He watched as some toadfish came to inspect what had just appeared in their environment. Toxic things they are, a bit like his life was back then. The small brown spots over the back of the toadfish reminded him of Mackenzie. She had a small band of freckles across her cheeks. She was always in his thoughts. He would always watch out for her.

His fishing urge was satisfied for the time being. He would do some more fishing next week. He threw his fishing gear in the boot of the car, jumped in the car and wound the windows down to get some air circulating. He felt a bit tired so he reclined the seat and laid back. A short snooze was on the cards.

He was out, dreaming. Thirty minutes later, he woke up. He wasn't sure whether a truck or the large boat cruising past on the river woke him. It sounded like a horn. Stretching, he thought of his dream—it was a strange one. A caterpillar and death. The caterpillar did not want to die. But he was told he had to. Something great and wonderful awaited, but he had to die first.

Part Two – Bulimba to the City

CHAPTER EIGHT

LUCAS KNEW THE AREA pretty well. The minister didn't live far from here and there'd been a few pick-ups and drop-offs at his house. Now they were at the house of the lady who lost her husband in the 'accident'. The minister wanted to drop in and pay her a visit.

Windsor told Lucas that they were in the clear. No one had been able to establish a link between their technology and the death. Lucas was surprised that Windsor knew the couple so well. He wondered about the event—he wished he could remember the evening of the accident better. Cutting back on the green stuff had helped his thinking clear up a bit. He had a vague memory of Windsor suggesting he try the park for their first live test. It was a secluded area with no security cameras operating. It had all made sense at the time, although Lucas's senses were duly wacked.

Lucas sat there waiting for the minister to conclude his visit. With the window down, a breeze found its way into the car making the cardboard air freshener flap—there was no scent as it was well past its use-by date. He heard some peaceful music, and turned to see a car pull up beside him, windows down. He thought he was dreaming. It was that girl again. The breeze carried her scent into his car. Or maybe he just imagined that. He closed his eyes to take it all in. He heard the revs in her car increase as she turned into the driveway. The girl lived, or maybe stayed, over the road from this house.

Her number plate was one of those personalized ones: KENZIE93. What sort of name was that? Well, anyway, maybe he now knew the year she was born.

He continued to be amazed at how this girl kept coming into his life. He was energized and decided he needed a stretch and a quick stroll. The car window screeched as he wound it up. He sat there for a moment thinking about her. The name Mackenzie popped into his head.

* * *

Mackenzie Gordon needed a break. She was shocked when she found out that the accident she witnessed had involved a girl from work. The ensuing spiritual battle that took place at work had worn her out.

She took Thursday and Friday off.

The traffic lightened once everyone got to work. Mackenzie had taken advantage of this to go visit her mum. And, secretly, she was also hoping to see Aaron. He called her on the weekend and said he was in town, busy with a training course, but he would be taking some time off—starting around about today, she believed.

Mackenzie had just parked her car, and Mum came running down the porch stairs. Could Mackenzie go and get some milk. Of course she could. Mum hadn't yet worked out the benefits of mobile technology—she could have called before Mackenzie arrived. But that was okay, Mackenzie wouldn't have answered anyway, not while she was driving. Mackenzie was a model citizen, or trying to be. A good old-fashioned girl. That's what her workmates called her—a good, old-fashioned, boring girl.

Mackenzie reversed out of the driveway. She noticed a white car parked outside Aaron's place and was surprised she didn't notice it when she drove in. Her mind must have been elsewhere. It had a government look about it except the windows were dark. It made sense—the dark windows must give the occupants privacy. She could just make out the outline of somebody sitting in the driver's seat.

She hoped Jill was doing okay.

* * *

With the milk sitting beside her, she turned on the indicator and waited for an oncoming car to pass. She noticed the white car still parked there, but the dark shadow in the front seat was no longer there.

She started to turn into her parents' driveway but paused to let a man pass. He gave her a thank you wave. She thought he just needed a leather jacket on to make a good biker, and then told herself off for stereotyping. Why did a goatee and a moustache make a man a biker? She watched him walk off, and noticed that he turned back to look at her. It made her feel uneasy, but she brushed her thoughts aside and parked the car.

Mackenzie got out of the car. The driveway had been upgraded—there were no large cracks anymore. Must have been done in the last couple of weeks, since the last time she was here. Or maybe she didn't notice it then. She smiled, thinking about how the cracks used to bug her dad so much. He kept saying they were going to get bigger and bigger and the kids will fall through to one of those underground gorges. His stories about the underground realm used to scare Mackenzie and her sister. She smiled, and looked forward to seeing Dad later that evening.

Mackenzie started heading up along the path up to the front door. Just as she started walking up the steps she heard a dog barking. She looked over towards Mr. Smith's front yard and saw Jethro on the front balcony, tail wagging.

"Hello, Jethro."

The Border Collie acknowledged her with another bark. She heard the front door open.

"Hello love," her mum said. Kathy Gordon had on her favorite kitchen apron, plain and black, with her glasses hanging around her neck on a black cord. Mum turned and looked in the direction of Jethro. "I don't think that dog will ever forget you . . . come in."

The apron told Mackenzie that Mum had been cooking. She followed her down the passage, taking a quick glance at the family portrait on the side table. "It was just those walks I used to take him on. He really used to look forward to getting out and sniffing out his territory and anything else that he came across."

"And Mr. Smith appreciated you doing it, too."

"Least I could do. How's he going?"

"He's doing fine. I think it's been five years since his wife passed on. He's active in the local church and still keen on his golf. But he does miss his darling. He takes the dog for long walks now, so there's fewer holes under our fence."

Mackenzie heard a car and turned to see a car drive past the Fitzpatrick's house. She turned to Mum. "Have you seen any sign of Aaron?"

"Saw him briefly yesterday. He dropped in and said a quick hello. He's attending a training course or something, and every break he gets he's off fishing . . . probably doing the same today."

"Did he ask about me?" Mackenzie was annoyed with herself. She should have kept that question to herself. Now Mum was going to worry about her and Aaron getting hitched and God being left out of the equation. Not that Mum didn't like Aaron. It was just the unequally yoked thing. But Mum needn't fear. She knew Mackenzie loved Paul. They had discussed it many times and Mackenzie was in agreement about the unequally yoked thing—she wanted her partner to be pulling in the same direction and not a worldly direction. Everybody was praying for Aaron. He was practically part of the family. But he was still lost.

"Of course he asked about you . . . why wouldn't he? You're his best mate."

They reached the kitchen. Mackenzie stared at the size of the cheesecake. "You're wicked, Mum. But good timing . . . I haven't been for my morning run. So I can eat and run it off later."

Mum smiled. "You're looking well. That man of yours must be looking after you." They'd been going out for over six months, and friends and family had been teasing them about weddings bells in the future.

"He is," replied Mackenzie.

Mackenzie watched Mum put the kettle on, then walked out to the lounge room which looked on to the street. She stood there staring out on to the street.

Mackenzie sensed her mum's presence.

"Deep in thought, love?"

"Always, Mum."

They both stood looking out at the Fitzpatrick's front yard. Mackenzie saw the biker man walking past again. She didn't say anything to Mum, but tried to convince herself that he was on his way back from the shops. The man crossed the road and headed towards the white car.

"What's with the government car, Mum? Is Jill okay?"

"Jill's doing fine, love. That's just one of her friends from church. He's a government minister."

They headed back to the kitchen. Mackenzie sat down on one of the kitchen stools.

"You mentioned on the phone that you're tired from work. Are they working you too hard?" Mum asked as she poured water into the cups.

"No, work's fine, Mum. It's just the atmosphere. One of the girls died in an accident, so it's a bit grim. She wasn't a Christian. There are so many people who don't believe. Most of us at work went to the funeral. You know, Mum, I still get a bit confused about things."

"You will 'til the day you die, love." Mum pushed Mackenzie's cup towards her.

"That's depressing, but I know what you mean."

Her mum sat down on a stool next to Mackenzie. "Some people believe there are different paths to God. And, as you know, there are some who don't believe at all. We've been blessed with both you and your sister, for when God's spirit stirred in your hearts, you both responded."

Mackenzie nodded.

"I suppose, love, the environment has a lot to do with it. It gives you an advantage in your choice. If you're exposed to God's love, you lean towards him. If you're exposed to the way of the world, you lean towards the world."

Mackenzie always believed her mum was a wise person, so she listened.

"I do think being baptized as a child, as the Catholics and some Christian denominations do, may present a problem in that you may grow up thinking you're a 'Catholic' or 'Christian' but you have no relationship at all with God. You know he's there, but at a distance. I think many Catholics, and Christians too, think good people go to heaven and truly evil people don't. But what's a good person?"

"That's the tricky question . . . 'for all have sinned and fall short of the glory of God'."

Kathy smiled.

Jethro barked a few times.

"Sounds like Jethro would like some company. Let's go sit outside," Mum said.

Mackenzie listened to Jethro and thought about the invisible things dogs see. At least, she hoped it was something invisible. As Mum searched the cupboards for a serving tray, Mackenzie walked out to the lounge room and looked out the window. Jethro must have been barking at the man walking out of Jill's house. He definitely looked like a politician. He got in the car.

The driver's seat window came down. Biker man looked over at Mackenzie. There was something in that look, like there was unfinished business. Did she know this man?

* * *

The backyard had timber fences on all three sides, with a laneway behind the fence at the end of the yard. A number of native plants, all attractive to the local bird life, screened the end timber fence. Daylight filtered through gaps in the fence palings. Mackenzie didn't like the end of the yard. When she was young, she didn't like being in the backyard by herself. She would often think there was someone watching, that they could see her but she couldn't see them.

Mackenzie and Mum went into the backyard and sat down at the small table hidden in a shaded pocket of the yard. The cheesecake sat on a serving tray with their cups of tea. Mackenzie wrapped her hands around her cup and took a sip. She could hear Jethro running up and down his side of the fence, puffing, pausing and peering through the small gaps. Mum nodded towards the fence on the other side of the yard. A family of Blue Wrens were hopping along the top of the fence—they'd been doing that for years. Mackenzie could remember them from her childhood.

"Jill now has a dog, a gift from her church friends," Mum said. "It's a Golden Retriever. She told me they're the most sociable and least aggressive dogs. She loves it and takes it for regular walks."

"Aaron will be excited with the new family member." Mackenzie smiled as she continued to watch the wrens. "It's funny, Mum, how Aaron's so much into nature, yet he can't see God. He gets so excited if he sees a dolphin pass by while fishing or an eagle flying above. He would always tell me about these things."

"It is, love. A veil covers their eyes, the heavens declare the glory of God, the skies proclaim the work of his hands. We'll keep praying that one day the veil will be lifted." Kathy paused. They both watched as the wrens decided it was bath time and took turns diving into the birdbath. She turned to look at Mackenzie.

"How did the funeral go?"

Mackenzie thought about the girl from work. Mackenzie hadn't been close to Judy and had only ever had a few conversations with her. She sensed the girl was always on edge and seemed to want to impress everyone she met. Her language was colorful—she was always cursing the Lord and using other profanities, and not just to express intense emotions. It felt like Judy was looking for something and Mackenzie knew that His hand was outstretched, but like so many, Judy had pushed it away.

"So different to Aaron's dad's funeral . . . I found this funeral a bit flat."

"Was she a believer?" Mum asked as she placed a piece of cheesecake in front of Mackenzie.

"Don't think so. She knew I went to church, but like most of the people I work with, she had no interest in what they refer to as 'religious' things. I had a conversation with her recently and she told me she was seeing a clairvoyant. I asked her why and she said she wanted to know what the future held for her. She said the clairvoyant told her some amazing things, so she had no doubt the clairvoyant was genuine."

Her mum shook her head. "Frightening stuff, hey? Probably a number of demons, masquerading as angels of light, working with the clairvoyant—faking the voice or image of a dead person. I wonder if they told her she was going to die soon?"

Mackenzie continued. "It's so hard . . . you want to help these people. They either believe in heaven or nothing and that includes no belief in hell. Then they think we're crazy because we believe in hell." Mackenzie grabbed a fork and dug it into the cheesecake. "I sat in the funeral service thinking about it. I watched people that I work with who I know haven't got the slightest interest or belief in God or church, yet they stand up there and read God's word."

A hmmm came out of Mum. "Funerals are funny things. The

funeral's more for the comfort of the family than the deceased."

"It must be hard for pastors to conduct a funeral for an unbeliever."

A fly had decided to inspect the food. Mum shooed it away. "How do we know if a person's an unbeliever, love? You just don't know the kind of plea for mercy that girl may have prayed out in the nanosecond before her death."

"That's true."

"I was reading an article recently. It impressed me so much, I cut it out of the paper."

Mackenzie watched as Mum pulled something out of her mobile phone wallet. She unfolded a sheet of paper and put on her glasses.

"The article said what I often thought about funerals but haven't been able to put into words. It's from a retiring Anglican Archbishop. It speaks about the cost of individualism, and the shift to self-love, and the consequences this had for the quality of our community, family life and how we treat death. He mentions a famous song called *I Did It My Way*. Have you ever heard that song?"

"Not sure I have, Mum. But definitely a self-centered title."

"It is. It sums up modern society pretty well. Anyway, he goes on to say that funerals are now used for eulogists to attempt to resurrect the dead by the power of fine words." She looked up at Mackenzie and then down to the article again.

"It goes on to say that the last words at funerals come from friends and family, and their aim seems to be to build up the reputation of the dead person, so everyone will believe how good a person he or she was. It all seems designed to avoid the truth that the person is gone, that death is horrible, that bodies turn to dust, that the person hasn't a chance of avoiding hell based on the quality of their lives."

"Wow. He is being brutally honest."

"He is, Mackenzie. But we need to be too, because friends and loved ones are going to hell. We see it as a celebration for believers who have finished their work and have gone home to the Father."

The fly returned. Mackenzie did the shooing this time.

Mum continued. "Others, the unbelievers, see it as a celebration as well, but more of a closure event, something for those left behind.

But then I often wonder, for those left behind, where has the person they're saying goodbye to gone.

"What sort of funeral do atheists have? Those that specifically don't want God involved?"

"Similar in structure, but with no mention of God and no Bible readings. They still celebrate the life of the person and recall fond memories, but that's about it. I often wonder what would happen if the deceased unbeliever was able to come back during the service and report on where he has ended up. I can just imagine the smell of his burnt clothes and hair as he stood there, and the people streaming out of church screaming, 'It's true, it's true. Hell exists'."

Mackenzie laughed. "Oh, Mum, your imagination runs off the rails sometimes."

"Sorry, love. I get frustrated too. I have had relatives die around me over the years and it hurts to know that I may not see them again, but I still hold on to some hope that I will. I think, deep down, most people believe they're going to heaven."

"That's okay. I have learned a lot and I think you're right. Most people believe they're going to end up in heaven because God is love, but they forget he is also a just God. "

"That's good, my love. Not too many grasp the just side of God, so you're doing well. Now, to lighten up, when are we going to see Aaron?"

Jethro barked, and ran down to the end of the yard. He stayed at the corner barking. Mackenzie was sure she could see the gaps between the palings darken, as if someone was walking past.

CHAPTER NINE

SEEING MACKENZIE'S RED CAR parked on the road, Aaron sprinted inside, gave Mum a hug, and told her he was shooting over to Mackenzie's and would be back soon. She told him off as he sprinted out the door, leaving behind a trail of muddy footprints.

He rang the doorbell and waited, and the echo of the doorbell was soon replaced by the sound of footsteps. Mrs. Gordon opened the door, with Mackenzie standing behind her. Mackenzie squeezed past and gave him a great big hug.

"Hello, army boy," she said. "Wow, look at those muscles. I thought you would at least wear your uniform when you came to visit."

Aaron looked down at his shorts, singlet and mud-covered footwear. "This is my uniform." Jethro must have thought that was funny, because he gave a bark.

He noticed Mrs. Gordon staring at his feet. "The tide was out and I had to retrieve a fish, hence the state of my feet. I tried to clean them. I'll forgive you for not inviting me into the house. I was just keen to see your lovely daughter." Aaron gave her a wink. She returned it with a smile.

Mackenzie tucked her arm in Aaron's. "That's fine. We'll sit out here."

Mackenzie led Aaron to the teak bench on the front porch and sat down with Mackenzie still holding on to his arm. The bench was surrounded by a number of potted plants and a fountain, which Mrs. Gordon turned on. She told them that she loved the sound of running water— it was soothing for their souls.

Mackenzie laughed. "Mum's got to bring God into everything."

They watched her walk off.

Mackenzie turned her attention back to Aaron. "It's so nice to see you, Aaron. How long are you here for?"

"A few weeks. I'm off overseas in January." Aaron watched Mackenzie as she looked down at the wooden floor. She was such a pretty thing. He loved her hairstyle—short, blonde, and tucked behind her ears to reveal small silver earrings.

"Your dad would be so proud of you, Aaron. Is your mum okay about you being posted overseas?"

"She's okay. She's a bit of a worrier, especially with the recent news of some Aussie deaths in Afghanistan."

"I can relate to that." She looked over towards Aaron's house. "You know, my Mum always tells me the story of watching you on the big skateboard ramp your dad built. She watched you standing on top of the ramp, overcoming your fears. She said she realized then what a determined boy you were going to be. Fear was not going to defeat you."

"Well, I try not to let fear get a hold of me, Kenz."

"I can imagine that isn't always easy to do."

"Yeah, it's not at times, but I don't want to be fearful. It could get in the way of things. But how are you going? How's Paul?"

"Paul's doing well. He's interstate with work at the moment, back tomorrow and said he's looking forward to catching up with you then."

"Tomorrow?"

"Church . . . you hadn't forgotten?"

"I had, but it's no problem. I just have no idea what day it is when I'm on holidays, and church on a Friday is different. In fact, I'm staying not too far from your church. I decided to book into a motel complex nearby for a few days."

"Why aren't you staying with your mum?"

"No room. She has some friends staying—easier to kick me out than them. Besides, I wanted to catch up with some army friends who live out that way."

Mackenzie looked at her watch and appeared to be pondering something. Aaron just stared at her and wished he could turn back time. The video clip of Cher singing to a large group of sailors aboard a battleship jumped into his head. He was slipping more and more into holiday mode.

She looked up. "I have to go soon. I'm helping out at a sausage sizzle for the homeless in town. And seeing I don't see you much, I think you should come with me."

He wasn't going to argue. Cher's song was fighting for room in his head, but then the word homeless caught his attention, reminding him of the news item and the vanishings.

They went into town together on the ferry. Aaron liked to think of it as a romantic ride on the majestic Brisbane River with his beautiful Mackenzie. But it was just a practical thing to do, as Mackenzie was coming back to Bulimba to stay with her parents for the night and it saved the parking hassles in the city.

They sat at the front of the CityCat. Mackenzie kept looking around. She seemed quite edgy.

"Are you okay, Kenz?"

"I'm fine, Aaron. Besides, I have you to look after me."

Aaron nodded and smiled. *Yes, Mackenzie . . . always.*

* * *

The CityCat glided quietly through the still waters. The Story Bridge came into view. They looked up to the summit of the bridge, some seventy-four meters to the water, similar to a twenty-two story building. Mackenzie and Aaron stared up at the bridge as they passed under. Mackenzie shrugged up her shoulders. She felt so tiny under the massive steel structure.

Mackenzie heard a soft sigh. She turned to Aaron. He was looking in the water. "Whatcha thinking about?'

"Suicides . . . people actually jump off this bridge . . . take their lives. Apparently jumping from a height is a done deal. Not like an overdose, where there's a possibility of no death, a way out, a call for help. I just don't understand why people do such things. But then again, maybe I do, because it's a pretty sad world we live in."

Mackenzie returned her eyes to the bridge. "It's sad, Aaron. You'd often hear relatives or friends say that these people were in a dark place. It's like they couldn't be reached. It's sad and breaks my heart when I think of these things." She turned to look at Aaron. "You're going to see a group of people today that have battled through some pretty dark places, and some are still battling."

"It's good what you do, Kenz. You know . . . helping these people."

Mackenzie knew that, but she didn't do it for people to see. She'd be happy out at the back doing the dishes, helping others. She grabbed Aaron's arm and gave it a squeeze. "It's a battle Aaron. You're off to fight a battle, one that we can all see, but there is an invisible war going on. I know you don't like me getting religious, but I'm seeing more and more that the prince of this world is not a nice person."

"You got me there, Mackenzie. Who is the prince of this world?"

"The devil, Aaron. The devil."

"But what has that to do with suicides?"

"It's a battle for the souls of the people. I'll be blunt. That's what I believe, Aaron, and I say this to you because you're going to a dangerous place. If you die without knowing the truth, your soul is lost."

"Phew . . . I asked for that."

Mackenzie watched Aaron as he turned to look back at the bridge. Trying to lighten what she just dumped on him, she said, "But, more importantly, wouldn't you like to see me again in the afterlife?"

He gave her a small smile.

"And I know for certain that your Dad has gone to heaven."

"How do you know that, Mackenzie?"

"I know, Aaron, and I hope that one day you will too."

The CityCat slowed and then docked. They got off and headed towards the City centre. Mackenzie tucked her arm in Aaron's. She felt his tension, and rubbed his arm in comfort.

"Sorry for hitting you with all that religious stuff, Aaron." *Rats! Why do I do that?* She didn't like dumping religious things on Aaron. But what was she meant to do? He might die soon, and then where would she end up?

* * *

Aaron used tongs to put the sausages in the bread, adding onions if they wanted them. Mackenzie handed out the slices of bread.

Things got quiet. Mackenzie told Aaron to check out a group of untidy-looking men standing around a man with a red and blue cap. The men all burst out laughing, some patting the side of their legs, some bending over. Something was funny. One of the men broke away from the pack and headed over to Mackenzie.

The man grabbed a slice of bread, said something to Mackenzie and they both laughed.

"Just go over to Aaron there and he'll give you a sausage." The man walked over, and Mackenzie followed. "Aaron, this is Chris . . . go on Chris, tell him."

"You see the bloke with the red and blue cap over there?"

Aaron looked in that direction. "Yep."

"Well, he reckons he used to be a doctor and he's telling us about one of his patients. He reckons this patient came into his office and said to him 'Doctor, doctor, I keep thinking I'm invisible'."

Aaron wondered where this was going.

"The doctor looked around the room, pretended there was no one there and said, 'Did someone say something?'"

A chuckle came out of Aaron.

"He's a good man, but I don't think he's a doctor. He's just trying to relax us because there are some strange things happening in the city at the moment. People are vanishing."

Chris nodded and started to walk off.

Aaron's mind started spinning. "Hey, Chris, what do you mean by 'vanishing'?"

Chris stopped and turned to face Aaron. "It's like people get transported somewhere and then back again—hasn't happened to me yet. No one believes them but I do. I reckon someone is testing something."

"Has it happened to anyone that's here today?"

Chris had a look around. "Nope, don't think so, at least those that I'm aware of. Some don't tell because no one believes them. But then you get some saying they've vanished just to get the attention. And they may add an alien green man element to it." Chris smiled and winked. "No one believes street people; we're all mad as hatters."

Mackenzie grabbed Chris on the arm before he left. "Chris, I want you to be extra careful out there, okay?"

"I will, love. You be careful too." Chris turned towards Aaron, gave him a wink and walked off.

Aaron watched Mackenzie staring at Chris as he walked off. She had a big heart.

Mackenzie turned to Aaron. "I had a premonition. I've had a few lately. Maybe I'm tuning into something. I sensed something is going to happen to Chris."

CHAPTER TEN

THE REVEREND WAS OUT on the footpath staring up at the church. It was an old building, one of the oldest churches in the city. A high-rise development dwarfed the church on one side, while open public space greeted it on the other side. Entrance to the park was guarded by two bronzed lion sculptures—some street people claimed to have seen these lions come to life at night-time, prowling around and roaring.

The only prowling roaring lion that the Reverend Peter Thomas knew was his enemy, the devil. But the Reverend was aware of the enemy and he was sober-minded and alert, as his Father had instructed.

The Reverend had reservations about coming to a church in the city considering he was a country boy through and through. Home was the Pilbara district, a massive remote area in the north-west of Western Australia, rich in natural resources. He'd had reservations about coming from such a spacious open place to a cramped city. But he came here to help those attracted by the density of a city, those seeking refuge in the city, seeking to blend in and become invisible, to take on new identities and vanish from their loved ones.

The Reverend reflected on the verse that he studied in his quiet time this morning. It reminded him of his servanthood.

To him who loves us and has freed us from our sins by his blood, and has made us to be a kingdom and priests to serve his God and Father—to him be glory and power for ever and ever!

I'm here to serve you Father, he said to himself.

The Reverend commenced his regular morning circuit of the church grounds. He was vigilant about this, not wanting any used needles and beer cans polluting the church grounds, especially at the weekends when the young ones liked to run around on the lawns.

He noticed some egg on his left shoe from a little incident this morning. He wiped it on the grass and continued his circuit. He had found a few empty beer bottles today. As he was picking up another bottle, a movement caught his eye. He turned to see a man crumbled up against the back wall of the church, partially concealed by a red flowering bottlebrush plant.

He moved closer to the person and pushed a branch away so he could see the man better. He tapped him on the leg. "Are you okay, mate?"

The man was startled and stared back at the Reverend. "Who are you?" He pushed his arm out in front of him. "Are you real?" The man closed his eyes and opened them again. He let out a low groan. "No, it's still there."

The Reverend said a quiet prayer. "Who's still here?"

"An angel . . . but he's moving away at the moment."

The Reverend thought for a moment. Some of the street people he had come across had lost touch with reality, and this looked like another example. "Can I help you up?"

The man moved his head around, taking in his surroundings. "Where am I?"

"You're in the grounds of the City Community Church on Ann Street."

"Who are you?"

"I'm one of the ministers of the Church." He put his hand out for the man to grab which the man took hold of. The Reverend pulled him up and helped the man regain his balance. "People around here know me as Reverend Peter."

The man was taller than the Reverend, only by a few inches. His clothing had bits of grass and twigs from where he'd been lying; they both started brushing these things away.

"I'm not crazy. I was pretty scared last night . . . I remember now. I sometimes sleep rough, but something awfully strange happened last night."

"Would you like to come inside and refresh yourself—I make a nice cup of tea. Or coffee, if you prefer. Probably have some leftover cakes or cookies from the last meeting held here."

The man nodded.

The Reverend led him inside the church. They walked past all the pews.

"It's been a long time since I've been inside a church except for funerals and weddings."

"That's okay."

They continued into an area with a large kitchen bench.

"This is where we serve supper and have fellowship after our services. What would you like?"

"Black tea is fine. Thank you."

"Sit down on the couch over there. I'll join you in a sec." He pointed to a blue two-seater couch. The man sat down.

The Reverend looked over at the man while he made the drinks. The man was staring at the many things scattered around on the coffee table near the couch. The Reverend organized everything onto a serving tray, which he carried over to the table. The man picked up a brochure with the headline, 'Where is God?' in large letters across the page. He saw the man shake his head, maybe in agreement with the question. The Reverend placed the cups and cookies on the table and sat down beside him.

"Are you feeling a bit better?"

The man lifted the cup to his mouth and slowly blew some cooling air into the cup. "A bit." He placed the cup back on the table. "This place has a nice feel about it."

"That's nice to hear." The Reverend decided to re-introduce himself. He wasn't sure if the man recalled his previous introduction. "My name is Peter. Most people around here call me the Rev." He put out his hand.

"And I'm Chris. Thank you for doing this."

"My pleasure. Can I ask, do you normally sleep rough?"

"I sometimes sleep in shelters but most times I sleep rough. I feel safer out on the streets, and in a funny sort of way found freedom on the streets, but all that depends on where I'm sleeping."

Odd. "How come you find it safer on the streets?"

"I know you probably think that's strange—most people do. The shelters are not overly peaceful, lots of coughing and spluttering, and germs freak me out. And you know, there are predators out there. Some people follow us when we leave shelters, particularly if we're by ourselves, and they can do some nasty things. I've been followed before but was lucky enough to escape. Sleeping rough, I've been urinated on, bashed, spat on. But I found a good secure place. No one else knows about it, and I've been able to keep it secret for a while now but after last night, I don't know."

"Are you able to tell me what happened?"

Chris rubbed both his knees. "Last night was strange. I sensed the presence of someone, something, not close, but I felt I was being watched. Then I heard a loud humming noise and found myself lying on a floor in a large room. Then I heard the noise again and I was back where I started. I consider myself of a sound mind and wasn't sure about was going on, but then it got worse."

"You weren't dreaming?"

"Let me tell you the rest. I thought, yes, it was only a dream. But then I started seeing things. It started with a crackling sound in my head, you know like when you try and tune the car radio." He paused and picked up his cup.

"Here comes the crazy part . . . a being floated down in front of me." Chris stood up and walked around the coffee table.

The Rev watched Chris walking around. This wasn't the first time he'd heard of people seeing things that no one else can see. He would hear him out and then see if he could help him.

"What sort of being?"

"An angel."

"How did you know it was an angel? Did it have wings or something?"

"No wings. But I just knew. And he told me."

"He told you?"

"I grabbed hold of a branch that was close by because I was frightened. I closed my eyes and opened them again. And there was nothing there—I was relieved. But I did the same again, closed my eyes hard, like this—" He closed his eyes, pushing his nose up to his eyes. "And then I opened them, and I nearly fell over because the being's face was inches from mine. And then the being asked, 'Can you see me?'"

He watched as Chris sat down again on the couch and wrapped his hands around the cup. "What did you say?"

"'Yes', was all I could say. I thought I was going crazy. I closed and opened my eyes again. The being was gone. I was about to open and close my eyes again but decided to say a little prayer—not that I knew what I was doing. I just told God to get rid of whatever it was. I opened my eyes again. And then the being was there and spoke again."

"What did it say?"

"It said something like, 'Don't be alarmed, I'm your guardian angel. For some reason you can see me.' And then something else floated down beside him and it wasn't nice. Then I heard a noise like a slashing sound and saw a head or something like that bounce past me. That's when I got up and ran. I was in a bit of a state, so I wasn't sure where I ended up."

The Rev wasn't sure where to go from here. "Have you seen anything since you have been here?"

"I saw the one who said he was my guardian angel. Outside, where you found me. But he moved away. I think he sensed I was scared. I seem to be able to switch between seeing the things when I open and close my eyes—it's like changing television stations."

"Did you want to try and see what happens in here if you do the open-and-close routine?" The Rev didn't expect anything to happen, but watched as Chris closed his eyes hard.

Chris took a while to open his eyes. The Rev could understand why he would be hesitant. Chris opened his eyes.

"Wow," Chris said, shaking his head.

* * *

When Chris opened his eyes, there were two angelic beings. He recognized his guardian angel, but the other was a being of such strength and beauty that Chris felt that he needed to be on his knees.

His guardian angel must have read his mind. "Don't bow down to us. Stay seated. Do not fear us; we are God's messengers. You have been given the power to see us, so be still and let God's peace rule in your heart. Tell Reverend Thomas that God was with him when he dropped the egg this morning."

Chris turned to the Rev. "There are two next to you. One of them just told me to tell you they saw you drop the egg this morning." He watched as the Rev opened his mouth and then bowed his head.

The Rev looked up again, his eyes watery. "Chris, there's no way you could have known about that. So I would say what you're seeing is real. You won't understand what I'm about to tell you, but we need to test the spirits. I want you to ask the angels to acknowledge that Jesus Christ has come in the flesh and is from God, and that Jesus is Lord and the Messiah."

Chris turned and looked up. He tried to remember what the Rev said, but there was no need. The angels were nodding their heads slowly, gracefully. "We are fellow servants with Reverend Peter. We hold to the testimony of Jesus, we confess that he came in the flesh, that he is from God and he died and rose again. He is our Lord and King."

"They have confirmed what you asked. What does that all mean?"

"Chris, many don't understand the invisible world. You may have heard of people trying to contact spirits to see what the future holds and things like that. God forbids people to do that, and for good reason, because evil can masquerade as angels of light. So you can put them to the test because evil won't acknowledge that Jesus Christ has come in the flesh."

Chris was starting to struggle with all that was being pumped into his brain.

"You have been given a gift and I'm sure God doesn't want to overload you. Let me pray for you." The Rev placed his hand on Chris's right shoulder. "Heavenly Father, your Word tells us that the angel of the Lord encamps around those who fear him. Father, you have revealed this to us in such a powerful way today. Father, I lift up Chris to you. Lord, it is a fearful thing for him to see what is invisible to all others. Please put your peace into his heart. Help Chris to see that nothing happens in this world that you don't know about it, that this is all part of your plan, and you are in charge. Amen."

Chris was struggling with something. "But I don't think I believe in Jesus, so where does that put me?"

"Have you ever thought about it?"

"My wife would nag me about going to church. But church wasn't my thing. The wife and kids loved it though."

"I have to assume that you're no longer with your wife or family?"

He didn't answer the question. His head felt heavy. All the events were taking a toll. He needed to rest. The Reverend suggested a bunk at the back of the recreation hall that he could use. He thought about it and was too tired to go anywhere else so he took up the offer.

As soon as his head hit the pillow, he was out like a light.

Then the screams came. The car took the bend way too fast and lost control. He reached over and placed his arm to protect his wife from the impact that was coming. With his other arm, he reached out for his kids in the back. The look of fear on both their faces he could not forget. He lost them all.

He sat up quickly and looked around. He closed and opened his eyes. His guardian angel was beside him. Chris noticed that the fear had gone.

"Thinking of your wife, sir?"

Chris stared at the angel and nodded.

"She is with the Father and the children also. You will become like them. You will become a believer, and you will see them again, but for now God has work for you to do."

CHAPTER ELEVEN

Friday evening, 8 December 2017, Mount Gravatt, Brisbane, Queensland

THIS CHURCH WAS BIG. There were hundreds of people here and the music was loud. Aaron sat, looking up at the preacher, who was dressed in jeans and a white casual shirt; neat and not over the top.

Are you afraid of death? The question popped into Aaron's head. He had no idea where it came from. In his mind's eye he saw the girl's body on the road, and the distraught man. He saw his dad's body lying in that car park. But the words of the preacher brought his focus back.

"And besides all this, between us and you a great chasm has been fixed, in order that those who would pass from here to you may not be able, and none may cross from there to us."

It was the story of a rich man and a poor man. Aaron had vague memories of the story—Aaron and his brother, Jack, had attended a few Sunday school sessions. The story stuck in his mind because it introduced him to that fellow with the pitchfork and where he lived. Jack told Aaron that if Aaron died before him, he was to come back and tell him if it was real or not. Aaron smiled at that. Maybe he should have made reciprocal arrangements with Jack. He lowered his head. *I miss ya, Jack.* Aaron never thought about hell . . . maybe it took on significance as one got older and closer to death . . . maybe it was time to revisit his belief system. Not yet. There were too many other things to focus on . . . Dad, Afghanistan.

His legs were falling asleep, so he moved them around to get more comfortable. He looked around. Most people were paying attention, the occasional lights from people looking up verses in their Bible e-books or iPhones. They believed this stuff, yet he struggled. And indeed, a great chasm came between Mackenzie and him—it was called religion.

"And he said, 'Then I beg you, father, to send him to my father's house—for I have five brothers—so that he may warn them, lest they also come into this place of torment.'

But Abraham said, 'They have Moses and the Prophets; let them hear them.'

And he said, 'No, father Abraham, but if someone goes to them from the dead, they will repent.'

He said to him, 'If they do not hear Moses and the Prophets, neither will they be convinced if someone should rise from the dead.'"

Maybe it didn't matter about the reciprocal arrangement with Jack because, apparently, if he did come back, no one would believe him anyway. Aaron turned to look at Mackenzie. She was taking notes while Paul listened intently. Aaron hadn't had a chance to speak to Paul yet. He was a nice bloke—Mackenzie had done well with him. The jealousy had passed. It wasn't an easy journey—a few drunken episodes—but Aaron had finally pushed away the feelings.

Preacher man was concluding, heads were bowed, eyes closed, the man was seeking out those that were lost, something about eternal life. Aaron had a peek: quite a few people were raising their hands. Did raising their hands mean that they were no longer lost? They prayed for the lost and they were all asked to join in. Aaron snuck out at this point. His legs were screaming for a stretch.

So he had a choice: heaven or hell. He tripped on the way out.

* * *

Grant Windsor didn't have his head bowed.

He was thinking about the amazing relevance of sermons. It was like pockets of the sermon were a reflection of his life at a particular time. Windsor believed that there were different chasms, and he knew that soon many more would also have this same belief. That's what they were doing with their new technology, shunting entities along some kind of chasm.

Windsor was raised in a Christian home. He believed God was calling him to do something about society. He always had this belief, and now had progressed to a position of power where he actually could do something.

He saw a young man trip on his way out of church. *What a goose.* But then his thoughts went to his own son and how he wished God would remove the dark cloud that had closed in on Timothy.

In some ways he blamed the church for those dark clouds, especially those men that looked after the young.

* * *

When Aaron tripped on the way out of church, he felt the whole world was watching. It sometimes felt like mild paranoia ran in the family. He made his way out of the auditorium, smelled coffee and followed his nose until he found the source. An attractive girl was serving the coffee. Aaron ordered.

"There you are." A voice came from behind. Aaron turned to see Mackenzie with Paul in tow.

"Hi, Teresa," Mackenzie said to the coffee lady.

"You remember Teresa don't you, Aaron? Year 9, not one of your best years was it? Remember, the party at Teresa's place and one blown-up letter box? The things you used to do to get our attention."

Teresa and Mackenzie laughed.

Aaron remembered. He'd been home-bound for a few weekends after that incident. He turned to Paul. "Does she still make up stories?"

Paul smiled and gave Aaron a hug. "You're looking good, Aaron. This army life seems to suit you. I hear you're on your way overseas soon."

Aaron felt uncomfortable with this hugging caper and he was sure people picked up those vibes. He nodded and sipped his coffee. There were no bad vibes for Paul. The idea of Paul and Mackenzie as a couple was quite settled in Aaron's mind—although it had taken a while for the adjustment to take place. Paul was good for Mackenzie and Aaron really only wanted the best for her.

He caught a glimpse of Mackenzie out of the corner of his eye.

She was sipping a diet Coke and about to hand Paul a full-strength Coke. Those lovely blue-grey eyes turned towards Aaron.

"Did you enjoy the church service, Aaron?"

"I think so, changed a lot. Music's good and loud." He was sure Mackenzie wanted to press a bit deeper but she just nodded.

"The pastor who delivered the message is an ex-military man. He's a nice man. Maybe you should catch up with him sometime. Have a chat."

That was the press. "Why?" He hoped that didn't sound rude because it wasn't meant to.

Mackenzie paused and reflected. "You know, going off to war, that sort of stuff. How do you feel about going off to Afghanistan?"

"Ah, Kenz, we're all well trained. And besides we have chaplains that we can talk to if we were that way inclined."

"But you are, Aaron, aren't you"

She was pressing a bit deeper now. "Sorry?"

"That way inclined."

Aaron stared at his coffee for a moment, raised his head and smiled at Mackenzie. He really didn't know where he stood.

Mackenzie continued. "I'm sorry, Aaron . . . I'm being too pushy. I just worry about you and I'm probably nervous about you going to war. Sorry."

"That's okay, Kenz. I know the Lord will be watching over me. He has got me this far." Now he was being politically correct. The words sounded like they came from an empty drum.

Aaron was invited to an after-church get-together at a local café. He was told his mum was going so he should too.

On the way down the entrance stairs, Aaron noticed a white government car with dark tinted windows, parked not far from the church entrance. From the side, he could see two silhouetted figures sitting in the front seat.

Aaron noticed Mackenzie staring at the car. There was something about the way she stared. Did she know the people in the car?

* * *

They waited to be seated. It was a light and bright large café, with two walls of glass doors opening onto extra-large alfresco patios at the front and at the back of the cafe. A row of comfortable sofas sat on colorful patterned carpet, with a large number of potted palms giving the place a breezy feel. Mackenzie advised that the noise from the road was bad at the front, so they asked for seats at the back. Paul offered to buy the coffees and started wandering towards the counter.

"Paul, remember, it's table service here,' Mackenzie said.

Paul turned and sat down again.

Aaron looked over at his mother. It was good for her to be out and about. She looked young and vibrant with her group of church friends. He noticed a large sophisticated man talking to his mum. Aaron remembered him from the funeral. His mum nodded to the man and he joined the group. A few tables behind his mum sat two men, one with his back to Aaron. They were also large, but their bulk was muscle.

As the waiter took their order another waiter walked past carrying a tray load of food. The smell drifted down to Aaron and convinced him that he was hungry. He ordered a steak sandwich and chips. He started watching the café staff in anticipation of their order arriving—the order came not long after. Paul and Aaron chatted about Bible references on military rifles. Apparently they were inscribed on the telescopic sights attached to some rifles. Aaron wasn't sure if they did it anymore. The arrival of the food interrupted their discussion.

As Aaron bit into his steak sandwich, he looked over at his mum. He hoped 'big guy' didn't have his sights on her. A son wants only the best for his mother. The other large men had gone. He looked around and saw them outside, and one was smoking. Big healthy guys smoking didn't look good. The one smoking turned and stared at Aaron, as if he knew he was being watched. It was that security guy.

"Aaron."

He turned to Mackenzie.

"Do you know that man?" Mackenzie asked.

"No, Kenz. Do you?"

"He was hanging around my mum's place earlier today. But I think he's a chauffeur or something for that man sitting with your mum."

This was getting too close for comfort.

* * *

Lucas was glad Tag was with him tonight. He'd given in to the voices in his head and had some green stuff earlier. It was the girl's fault. He'd got all muddled in the head after seeing her this afternoon, so he sat down and smoked a joint or three. He couldn't remember how many.

The minister had wanted to go to church straight from work. As Lucas hadn't been in a fit state to drive, he asked Tag to do the driving. Lucas had wanted to catch up with Tag anyway and go out later. They tended to get into mischief together, which didn't bother Lucas too much; it was all in fun. They enjoyed the occasional fight with the low-lifes that go out in packs looking for fights. Lucas and Tag enjoyed the adrenaline rush from fighting as long as the packs weren't too big.

At the church there was a battle going on in Lucas's head—a voice fighting its way through the fog. The church was familiar, it was the same church they were at the other day with the funeral. He wondered if the minister came here regularly. He saw some funny things jumping off the church building when they got there, skinny bony things with torn flowing robes.

And then he saw the girl again.

The fight in Lucas's head was a fierce one. The voice in his head was putting up a good fight, like he wasn't going anywhere. A door was trying to close in his head but the voice thing kept pushing it open, as if he had his foot in the door. Lucas shook his head, hoping the thing would drop out of his head, fall through his ears and tumble to the ground.

Things had got worse at the café. "No, go," the voice told him. "That bloke's up to no good with his girl. That bloke needs to be kept away from Mackenzie. Maybe you and Tag should let him know these things."

* * *

Logan Road was quiet on Friday nights.

Aaron headed back in his rented car to his accommodation. He had another quick look in his rear-view mirror. The car was still there. The white limo had been behind him since they left the café, the two big dudes in the front. He couldn't see into the back, but he hoped the other big boy sat in the back seat. Aaron flicked on the right indicator and paused in the turning lane. The limo drove past. The shadow silhouetted against the tinted back passenger window was big. *Good, he's not still with Mum.* Aaron thought briefly that they might have been following him—he wasn't sure why—but then Logan Road was a main road back to the inner city suburbs where the big man almost certainly lived.

He parked the car in the space allocated for unit seven.

He opened the door to his motel unit, threw his keys on the bedside table and sat on the bed. It was quiet except for the humming of the air-conditioning unit. He looked at the bedside table and wondered if there was a Bible in one of the drawers. He opened the top drawer . . . nothing. The next drawer . . . there it was. The Gideon Bible. Another memory from Sunday school and a Beatles song his dad would sing: something along the lines of a person named Rocky checking into a room and finding a Gideon Bible.

Aaron looked in the notes in the Bible to find the story of Gideon. The story involved a large number of clay jars with torches hidden inside, then the jars were smashed to reveal light in the darkness, sending a panic through the enemy camp.

He placed the Bible on the bedside table, lay on the bed and thought about Rocky with a raccoon wrapped around his head, about smashed jars, candles, Mackenzie, and Dad.

It was a warm night and he had pumped too much coffee into his bloodstream. He felt like a drink, so he opened the fridge door and grabbed a bottle of spring water. His mobile phone played its text message tune. Aaron viewed the message—he needed to be back at base on Thursday for deployment. Six more days. Anxiety crept in—there must be something going on to be recalled early. Christmas overseas, and Mum's first Christmas without Dad. He had a big sip of the water and placed the plastic bottle on the bedside table next to the Bible. The Bible stared at him. He opened it, flicked through the pages and it came to rest at Psalm 91. Towards the bottom of the page he read:

For he will command his angels concerning you to guard you in all your ways; they will lift you up in their hands, so that you will not strike your feet against a stone.

It would be good to have that inscribed on the rifle he would be carrying in Afghanistan. He decided to write it down anyway and started searching for a pen and some paper.

A loud banging on the door startled him.

He was about to open the door but that little voice inside his head told him to be careful. The curtains were drawn on the window facing outside. He walked over, drew the front curtain open a little and saw those two burly fellows from the cafe. One turned to see Aaron peeking, tapped his mate on the shoulder and pointed towards Aaron. They banged louder.

Aaron yelled out to them to give him a moment to put some clothes on. He wasn't sure what these men wanted, but the last thing he was going to do was let them in the room. Aaron wasn't afraid. His training had kicked in. He opened the door, came out on the balcony and quickly closed it behind him as the Mr. Goatee tried to push him back in the room. His mate stood behind him.

Glazed eyes stared at Aaron. *Spaced out.*

"Take it easy," Aaron told him.

With that came a hard punch to the stomach that bent Aaron over, but Aaron was able to take out Mr. Goatee's legs and deliver a solid elbow to his throat. That brought a grunt as Mr. Goatee fell to the ground. Aaron saw a boot coming towards his face, but moved quickly and grabbed the foot, twisting the man's leg as he forced it up.

"Hey, what's going on?" someone yelled. Aaron turned briefly to see who yelled, and with that came darkness.

Aaron's head started clearing. It was the motel manager, sitting with Aaron on the step outside the unit. He had given Aaron a frozen bag of peas for his face. Aaron rested the bag against his jaw. It was a bit sore.

"Are you okay?"

Aaron took the cold bag off his face. "I'm okay, just a bit puzzled about what that was all about. Probably mistaken identity."

"Did you want me to call the police?"

"No . . . not worth the hassle."

"Okay. I didn't get the number plate. But it was a blue car with a big star on its door."

"Sounds like a security car. You know, the star representing a sheriff-law-order type thing . . . definitely mistaken identity. Thanks for helping me." He put the bag of peas against his face again.

"That's okay. You don't look the troublesome type."

"Thanks, I'm not. I'm a soldier, off to Afghanistan in a few days, so if I see those fellows before then I will shoot them." Aaron tried to smile. "I'm sure they won't be paying us another visit. They would expect us to call the police."

The manager helped him up. "Just make sure you don't shoot them here. The publicity wouldn't be good, but then again, it could attract customers."

Aaron smiled. It hurt. He thanked the manager again and went back into the room. It was past midnight. He placed his head on the pillow. Wondered what that was all about while his body recovered from the adrenaline rush. His body compensated by putting him to sleep. He dreamed of a man with a goatee and a moustache, and of two large beings standing next to him as he stood before Mr. Goatee.

Mackenzie and Paul had gone away with some friends for the weekend. Mackenzie was quite apologetic about it, which surprised Aaron. But as it turned out, Aaron's body needed healing, so he did nothing the whole weekend, just rested.

CHAPTER TWELVE

THE PATROLLING SECURITY GUARD, who had raised the alarm regarding the fire near where Aaron's dad died, had a goatee and moustache. He kept popping up in Aaron's life at the moment, including that rather nasty visit the other night. It was obvious that this man didn't consider how memorable his flamboyant facial hair would be. Aaron doubted that the man would even remember his most recent visit. He'd clearly been stoned.

It was the start of a working week and Aaron decided he would take a punt and try and make contact with Mr. Goatee. He found the number of the security firm that he had copied down from the sign on the fence and telephoned it.

"Sheriff Security, can I help?"

"Oh, hi. I'm looking for a security guard that may be able to assist me with an issue at the Department of Urban Movement research building. I have had dealings with the security officer before, if it helps. He had a goatee and moustache."

"Oh yes, that would be Lucas. I could get him to contact you if you like."

"Is he on shift today?"

"I'm sorry, but I can't disclose that sort of information. Can you give me your number?"

"My phone is dead. I dropped it recently, so at the moment I can only give you my home number and that's out of town. I'm just a visitor. Look, I just want to show him a hole in the perimeter fence. Could you give me an indication of a possible time to meet him at the site?"

"Hold for a moment please." There was a delay of a few minutes. "Hello, you there?"

"Yep."

"Lucas can meet you at the building at seven."

Aaron automatically converted that to military time: 1900. "Thank you."

* * *

Monday evenings could be quiet, the work week not yet cranked up. By seven, there were only a few cars left in the car park, and a few lights on in the building—most of the workers had gone for the day.

The signage light illuminated the cross and flowers. Aaron sat on a bench outside the main entrance staring at them. They belonged to the parents of those lost ones. He hadn't forgotten the parents. Losing loved ones wasn't something to be taken lightly, and he was hopeful the security man would help him solve the crime. He heard a door open and some quiet chatting. The building lights went off but the signage light remained on. He looked up and nodded to some workers as they walked out the main doors.

One of the workers stopped and looked at Aaron. "Are you okay? Are you meeting someone?"

"I'm fine, thanks. Yes, I'm meeting someone. It's someone from the building security firm. They should be here soon. We won't be going in the building. Thanks for your concern."

"No worries." The worker walked off.

Aaron watched the cars leave. Not long after, a car turned into the car park. The driver parked the car near the building entrance and sat in the car staring at Aaron. It didn't look like this man was going to get out of the car. Aaron waved, got up, and headed toward the vehicle.

Aaron placed his hand on the roof of the car. "Lucas, is it?"

"Yes."

He didn't think that this man had an ounce of fear in him. "Remember me from the other night?" There was no immediate response. Aaron could almost hear the gears turning over in Lucas's head.

"I do, but it was a mistaken identity. Not sure how I can remedy that."

Aaron pressed his fingers hard into the car's roof. "Mistaken identity? Not sure if I believe that, Lucas. You see, my father died just over there not too long ago and I believe that you know what caused his death."

"Now why would you think that?"

"Deformed animals." Aaron thought he smelled a whiff of the cheesy scent of the decaying animals.

Lucas snickered. "Listen, mate. I have no idea what you're talking about, except that some pet hater has been dumping cats and dogs over there in the bush. If that's what you're talking about, then I'm not that pet hater and you've got the wrong man."

"Are you responsible for the death of the workers? They left some proof, you know."

That got him. It was a small pause, but enough to convince Aaron that he was on the right track.

"What proof? What are you talking about, man?"

"The technology you were working on, the experiments. They were causing deformities." Aaron considered dragging this man out of the car. "My dad's autopsy report indicated a deformity."

Lucas just stared up at Aaron. "You're a brave man coming here and making these accusations. Can I suggest you stop right there, because you're entering dangerous territory. I know your lady friend, Mackenzie. I assume that's her name, that's what her personalized plate said, unless of course that wasn't her hot little red car. And if what you say about the technology is true, I would be a worried man."

That caught Aaron off guard. How did he know about Mackenzie? He took his hand from the roof of the car and clenched his fist. There was a strong urge to grab this bloke by the scruff of the neck.

The man continued. "Your dad's death was an accident. No one's going to believe what you just told me. The plan for the technology is for positive purposes. We've made some slip-ups, but overall this is going to be good for society. Any deaths related to the technology have happened by accident."

Aaron's fingernails dug into his hand. Lucas had basically admitted his involvement. Plan for the technology? Positive purposes? What was this man talking about? "But my dad's dead, and if you're involved, you're not going to get away with it."

"I'm sorry, that's all I can say. If you decide to take this any further then your Mackenzie is in danger."

If Aaron's fingers went any deeper they would draw blood. "You know I can't let you get away with such threats."

"Yes, you can. You have to."

Anger rose within Aaron. The man was full of himself. How dare he make such threats? "Why don't you get out of the car?"

The man's arrogance seemed to be growing. "I don't need to."

Aaron reached his right arm through the window and grabbed the top of Lucas's polo shirt. "Listen . . . you touch Mackenzie, you're a dead man."

"I won't touch her unless you make me." The man looked down at Aaron's hand on his shirt. "Could you please let go of my shirt . . . I wouldn't want to hurt such a beautiful girl. I have noticed of late that I'm becoming a bit unstable. Keep that in mind. And don't involve the police."

Aaron gripped the shirt a bit tighter. He saw Lucas grab something. A high-voltage current hit Aaron, bringing instant pain. Aaron jolted back, stunned, disoriented. He tried grabbing the roof of the car but couldn't focus. His thought process was scrambled, like the enemy has blasted his radar system with noise. Dazed, he staggered back and fell to his knees. He tried to focus on the head in the car. He saw Lucas's lips moving. A smirk?

Lucas held up the stun gun. "Does Mackenzie carry one of these?"

He reached out to grab the man, but his movement had not yet returned to normal. He tried to focus on the car as it drove off. The brake lights reminded him of Christmas.

Aaron staggered over to the bench at the entrance and sat down. His muscles seemed to be coming back to order. Those tiny neurological impulses travelling through his body had recovered from the shock and were back into their normal routine. He rubbed the back of his neck. His head was clearing.

He pictured Lucas's grotesque smirk. In fact, when Aaron was under the spell of that stun gun, all of Lucas's head looked gross. Maybe his real face changed. Aaron had heard stories of faces changing when evil was present. And now he knew the other night wasn't an accident. It was intimidation. Mr. Lucas Goatee was trying to scare Aaron, and it was obvious that drugs were clouding his thinking and judgment. His warning, although delivered in a confident manner, came out sounding panicked. Aaron was concerned about Lucas: his mind appeared unsound. And Aaron was more than concerned about Mackenzie.

He sat there alone in the car park, looking up to the heavens. There were only a few stars out. More would sparkle when the light faded. *Are you there, God?* He didn't normally talk to God. He missed Dad. He missed the direction Dad gave him. Mackenzie told Aaron that God is the father of the fatherless. Oh, how at times he wished he could understand. He wanted so much to revenge his dad's death, but doing so would now put Mackenzie's life in danger. What would God do?

He walked towards the car. His muscles were still sore. What were they up to with the technology? What was the technology anyway?

There wasn't much choice. He was off to Afghanistan in a few days. There was only one thing he could do for now, and that was let it be. At least Mackenzie would be safe, but he had to make sure that was the case. He had to get Lucas to understand who he was dealing with. No one was going to harm Mackenzie.

* * *

Lucas shook as the adrenaline wore off. He was surprised at how tough and convincing he was—it was like something took over. Now he was exhausted and just wanted to get home.

He heard a thump. He had no idea what it was. He heard it again. Thump, thump.

He kept looking in the rear-view mirror, but there were only a few cars out. He was sure that man would take a while to get back to normal again. Besides, he'd have no idea which way Lucas went after driving out of the business park. But being on a main arterial road was maybe not a good idea. He'd get off this road soon and find an alternative way to his flat at Morningside.

Thump, thump. Lucas wasn't even sure of the type of car the man drove. He looked again in his rear-view mirror. Thump, thump. There was still only a few cars. One had been right up his tail, but had now had pulled out and came alongside Lucas's car. Lucas's heart pounded and he had goose bumps. He turned to look at the driver. It wasn't the man he just incapacitated. The men stared at each other, then the driver pointed to the back of Lucas's car.

Lucas pulled over. The other car continued on its journey, his deed done. Lucas got out and walked around the car. One of the rear tires was flat. He banged the top of the car. He was tired . . . but he had to fix this.

He was glad it was the passenger side. His car shook from the draft of passing cars. One of the wheel nuts proved hard to get off, but he managed to get it loose. Thank goodness for his gym work. Some yobbos gave him cheek as they drove past. Lucas just ignored them. Besides, he didn't understand a thing they said.

Tire replaced, Lucas dropped into the driver's seat. He was glad that was done. Lucas continued his journey homeward. Still just the occasional car behind him. He thought about his mum, about paranoia. He looked at the rear-view mirror again. There was a car behind him. He thought about paranoia again. Now he just wanted a joint.

He didn't use the side streets, and he soon forgot about checking to see if he was being followed. When Lucas parked and locked his car, he didn't notice a vehicle pull up and park not far from him. He didn't notice a man in the car watching him when he appeared on the third floor landing. And he didn't notice the car drive off after he entered his flat and closed the door.

* * *

Lucas gave notice to the security firm on Tuesday. A week's notice was all that was required. He was being stretched; the minister was using more of Lucas's time than he had. The minister suggested to Lucas that maybe he should quit his security officer job and just focus on the work the minister had in mind for him.

The receptionist at the office told Lucas that she would miss him. She also told him that someone had phoned asking about the type of shifts they worked, the hours of the shifts and the days. He said he was thinking of applying for a job. The receptionist had suggested the caller should drop in his resume, because one of their best had just resigned. The caller said he'd think about it.

It was the end of the Tuesday shift. Lucas parked his car, walked over to the entrance to the apartment block and started his climb to the third floor. He pressed the stairwell light button for the first level and started heading up the stairs. He did the same on the second level and continued his ascent. Lucas heard the stairwell door close on the third level. He pushed the light button but no light came on. It was amazing how dark that last flight of stairs was. He could just make out a shadowy figure coming towards him. He paused, smelled perfume, and then the light from a miniature torch revealed his presence. It was his neighbor, and she gave him some cheek about trying to scare her.

The third floor landing was as dark as the stairwell. He wondered when they were going to fix these lights. Maybe he needed to download a Flashlight app for his iPhone. A squeaky noise came from the shared laundry facility at the end of the landing. Probably a mouse. He had seen a few of them recently.

He placed the key in his door. Something cold touched his face. It was the barrel of a handgun.

"You're dealing with a soldier, Lucas, not a boy scout. I'd have to say I didn't enjoy my experience with you yesterday but I won't return the favor. But let me tell you, you go near Mackenzie, and you're dead."

* * *

Aaron didn't like being sneaky, but he didn't want to alarm Mum. After getting her comfortable out in the backyard he made an excuse to come back inside where she couldn't see him. A vase sat on top of the fridge. Aaron grabbed it, turned it upside down, caught the key that fell out, then walked over to a solid timber cabinet in the family room and unlocked it. His dad's shooting trophies sat above the cabinet. Aaron gave them a quick glance before he grabbed the handgun out of his backpack and placed it back in its case. He locked the cabinet.

"What are you up to, Aaron Fitzpatrick?"

It was Mackenzie. Aaron tensed as if he had been sprung stealing, but quickly got himself under control.

"Admiring my dad's shooting trophies." It was not a lie but a half-truth. "And what are you up to, sneaking into the house?"

"Spoke to your mum on the phone. She told me the door was open and come out the back, but then I saw this hunk of a man."

Aaron smiled and looked at Mackenzie. Denim shorts should be banned. He walked over and gave Mackenzie a hug, wishing his tour of duty was not on. He wanted to protect Mackenzie. That Lucas character wasn't to be trusted, particularly if he was to find out that Aaron was going to be out of the country for a while. He noticed Mackenzie staring at the trophies.

"Shooting, guns, war. Why are we involved, Aaron? Why are we involved in these conflicts overseas?"

Aaron smiled and looked at Mackenzie. "They tell us it's not about destroying things, but to build, to develop the provinces and win over the locals. We train them and help them build bridges, hospitals, shopping centers—things we take for granted. And then we need to protect them. I feel I'm doing something worthwhile, Mackenzie. I'm contributing to a good cause. But the sad thing is, it's taking these countries a long time to learn from their mistakes. We seem to have to keep going back to help them. "

Mackenzie gave him a hug. "Just be careful. Always remember, many people will be praying for your safety over there. Not the wishy-washy standard 'you are in our prayers stuff'. There will be committed people praying for you." She looked up at Aaron and smiled. "We best go join your mum."

He gave her a peck on the cheek.

They discussed Christmas coming up, the first one without Dad. Aaron wanted to take special leave to be with his mum. She disagreed—she felt that if the army needed to send troops over there at this time, then the need was urgent. He was told that he needed to go, and besides, Christmas was only one day and she was going to spend it at church and with her Christian friends. Mum won.

Mackenzie and his Mum dropped Aaron off at the airport later that day. He had a smooth, quiet flight back to Townsville.

Aaron flew out from Townsville on Sunday morning to start his tour in Afghanistan. It felt like he was leaving one war zone and entering another. He started thinking about where he was going and that he would not see Mum or Mackenzie for months. *No.*

Aaron started the process of blocking out the things of 'back home'.

CHAPTER THIRTEEN

WINDSOR WAS AT HOME in his office when he heard the car pull up. He walked over to the window, drew the curtain and saw the Police Commissioner getting out of his Lexus. *Why would he be visiting?* Windsor went to the front door to greet him.

"David, what brings you to this part of town?" He looked at the Commissioner's face and then knew why. "He's done it, hasn't he? Timothy's dead."

A gasp caught Windsor's attention. Windsor turned and walked over to his wife. He put his arms around her and turned to the Commissioner. "How did he do it?"

"Drug overdose."

Windsor grimaced and bowed his head. "The demons finally got him . . . what do we need to do?"

"If you're up to it, you can assist with visual identification, then we have to report it to the Coroner."

"Why?" asked Windsor's wife.

"It's just a formal thing. All unexpected deaths need to be reported so the cause of death can be determined."

Windsor took his wife over to a couch and sat her down. He turned and looked at the Commissioner. "I appreciate what you have done . . . coming here, delivering the message in person. We knew it would come one day, but that doesn't make it any easier. Timothy was in a dark place and we just couldn't pull him out. If only that stupid woman didn't walk in front of his car."

The Commissioner nodded.

Windsor stared at the Commissioner, his hat tucked under his arm. "I'll come with you now."

His wife chose not to go.

Windsor saw this heartbreak as further confirmation to his plans. It just made him more determined to wake these lawbreaking people up. Such stupid people. Now he had lost his son thanks to one of those thoughtless people. Yes, he was now much more determined to make things succeed and he would.

* * *

Windsor's wife took the death of her only son hard. She often asked him why God took her Timothy. She asked if he was in heaven. She turned Timothy's room into a shrine.

Windsor, on the other hand, wanted revenge on those that contributed to his son's death, those that were a law unto themselves, those that make up their own laws. It was inside him, he felt it, rage, a burning rage. The new technology had taken on a much greater purpose now. But that's how God works—it all becomes clearer as things unfold.

And something else started to unfold.

Another plan came to Windsor regarding his son. Windsor believed it was another godsend. He'd seen it in the paper a few days back. He went out to the recycling bin and found the article he was looking for, found a name and researched it some more on the internet. A cryonics facility had commenced operations outside the city. He spoke to them and acted upon it—desperate action from a desperate man. He also used his influence to prevent an autopsy being performed on his son, using religious objection as the reason—the cryonics people told him that an autopsy could impede the preservation process. They did some things before the funeral and moved the body after the funeral, before the casket was buried—not many stay behind to watch a casket be buried. They use tractors, not shovels, and people need to be out of the way. The funeral director was sworn to secrecy.

* * *

Windsor needed to tell somebody, so he told Starkey.

His son was now stored at a facility in a device the company referred to as a cryostat—they likened the storage device to a big thermos bottle, with the body floating in liquid nitrogen. Windsor told Starkey how they used antifreeze mixtures and procedures to eliminate freezing. The bodies harden like glass rather than crystallizing.

Starkey supported what Windsor had done. He reminded Windsor of the advances they had made with their transportation system, and that the idea behind cryonics was the expectation of future medical technology that may be able to restore life to those that have been put in cryonic suspension. Technology was continuing to advance.

Windsor was glad it all made sense to Starkey, as he'd made the initial decision out of desperation, although he'd now researched it more.

They had discussed cryonics and the brain.

"It is really quite simple, Windsor,"

Windsor knew Starkey liked to pass on his knowledge, oblivious to what others might already know.

"The brain stores the memory and personality. It is like a computer hard drive. You turn it off, but the data is still there. You turn it on, revive the data, and presto: business as usual."

"Wouldn't something have to kick in to access the data? I wonder where the soul sits in relation to this."

"You have a point there, Windsor. Maybe the soul is the operating system that communicates with the brain structure accessing memory and personality." Starkey pondered that idea.

But where did the operating system come from? It got too hard for them. They would discuss it further another time.

* * *

Lucas looked out over the paddock at the fog, slowly disappearing. There must be a creek over there or something. It all looked peaceful. The fog would probably be gone by lunchtime. Where did it go? Deep questions, Lucas. His mind was getting clearer. That's what he wanted to believe. He'd been off the green stuff for a few weeks now.

He gripped the steering wheel harder. Although it had been many weeks, that event with that army guy had shaken him up a bit. He rubbed his cheek; he could still feel the coldness of the gun's barrel. The speedometer showed he was just over the speed limit. He needed to be careful, as the last thing he wanted was to have this government vehicle booked for speeding. Lucas had to drive today. Tag was off, supposedly sick. Lucas reckoned it was the trip distance, about an hour or so out of the city in the middle of nowhere. He looked in the rear-view mirror and saw the minister reading something on his latest toy. The minister looked up and his eyes locked with Lucas's.

The minister smiled and held up a tablet device. "It's taken me a long time Lucas but I'm well into these tablet devices now. In fact, I prefer them to the newspapers." The minister tapped on the tablet. "Looks like a few of our soldiers got injured in a bomb blast. It says an IED, an improvised explosive device, detonated near them during a mission. A dangerous job, hey Lucas?"

"Yep, sounds like it." The minister sometimes treated Lucas as if he was a dope. He laughed to himself—maybe he was a dope for smoking dope. Remembering what an IED was indicated that his brain was still working okay. He'd had his doubts recently—he didn't quite understand what was going on in his head. At least he wasn't hearing the voices as often.

Hills started rolling by.

"Welcome to Beaudesert, Lucas. Just drive through. There is a turnoff just outside the town."

Lucas turned the car into a small business centre and parked. The minister had the door open before Lucas could turn the ignition off. The minister got out of the car and told Lucas he wouldn't be long. Lucas watched as the minister walked up to what looked like some kind of storage facility. He scanned something, and the door opened.

Lucas sat staring at the door the minister went through. What is this place? *Why don't you go and find out.* The voice was back—not for long, he hoped. Lucas shook his head. These voices were starting to worry him. His mother had warned him of this.

He was starting to believe that people could read his mind and that God was talking to him. At times, all this head stuff frightened him. He preferred the minister not to know about his personal life, so he had a chat with the Professor about it.

The Professor told him that he believed drugs, including alcohol, were an opening to the spiritual world. He mentioned to Lucas how that sometimes people refer to alcohol as 'the demon drink'. The Professor wasn't sure about the demon possession thing but he believed that demons could influence people's lives, particularly if they let their guard down. Drugs let the guard down. Lift up the boom gates and these pesky little things come running in. The Professor stayed right away from drugs but believed in good spirits. They were the ones he preferred to be in contact with, not the pesky ones.

Lucas thought about his mum. She told him there was a problem with alcohol in the family—actually, it was pretty obvious. Mum told him he might have faulty wiring, a predisposition to addiction, and that he needed to be careful. Well, he was. He didn't drink alcohol but smoked dope instead. Mum didn't know much about dope initially, and neither did Lucas. They had been oblivious to the idea that dope smoking could also aggravate the faulty wiring and trigger an existing psychotic condition.

After that conversation with the Professor, Lucas decided that he needed to get on some medication. The voices in his head were getting too active, too frightening, trying to dominate. Maybe it wasn't God. Yep, he needed to see the doctor. He hadn't had time to make an appointment, but he would.

He saw the minister heading towards him. He jumped in the car.

"Let's go, Lucas. My visiting hours are up."

Lucas raised his eye brows, not sure what the minister meant by 'visiting hours'. He started the car and drove off.

The traffic was light. Trees were replaced by houses. Driving back, the minister asked Lucas if he could put the radio on. He felt like hearing what was happening in the world instead of reading about it.

Background crackle made Lucas look up to the sky, but there was no hint of a storm, no dark clouds. Lucas gave a silent shake of his head as he listened to the musical introduction to the news. That jingle must be as old as the radio station itself. Lucas hated the news. He had dark memories of having to sit through the news while his parents fought. But he could grin and bear it, let his mind float elsewhere while the minister found out more about the happenings of the world. Just before his mind floated off, he heard the news reporting on the IED incident.

"Hear that, Lucas? Aaron Fitzpatrick. His father was the one who died. It looks like he's going to be okay, and he's on his way home."

Lucas's mind came storming back. So that was his name. And what? He was on his way home? He'd been away? Voices spoke to him: *It's all a lie. That man's not injured. He's faking it so he could get back to Mackenzie. Can't let that happen, Lucas, better do something soon.*

* * *

Lucas had driven the minister to church a few times but hadn't seen Mackenzie. The minister rarely went on Friday nights, so Lucas reckoned this was the service Mackenzie must attend. Anyway, his preference was to stay away from church. He felt he stood out in that environment. He tracked Mackenzie down elsewhere.

He found she lived on the other side of the city to her mum. In his opinion, it was a bad choice, because the traffic was worse and life seemed much more cluttered. Trains ran to Mackenzie's suburb, but not to her mum's. It was only a short train trip from Mackenzie's apartment to the city, and things being more cluttered, more busy, helped Lucas.

Lucas had followed Mackenzie a few times. He didn't enjoy trains—he felt trapped when the doors closed. He positioned himself in the last carriage so he could see which station she got off at. Once he had the station, he put the jigsaw pieces together. He 'borrowed' some letters from her mum's letter box, found out her surname, did some Google work, and he had her address. He just needed to establish her routine. That took a few weeks.

She was such a law-abiding citizen. She would stand at pedestrian crossings and wait for the 'walk' signal. Most people would just cross, but she just stood there, waiting. Her mate was just as bad. Lucas hadn't worked out who she lived with, but knew it wasn't the man that hung around with her. The man stayed late sometimes but never stayed the night. Strange. There was no way Lucas would leave that girl.

This mate of Mackenzie's didn't bother Lucas, not like the army bloke did. There was some kind of connection between Mackenzie and the army fellow. Lucas couldn't quite put his finger on it, but the voices in his head were threatened by soldier boy.

He hadn't followed Mackenzie today, but the notes in his lap told him she would be walking past soon. He had parked on a tree-lined street that looked down on Mackenzie's street, so she wouldn't be walking directly past him. Yep, here she was, right on time. She looked up towards Lucas's car, but only a fleeting glance. She'd be back in twenty minutes, on her way to the gym. He was going to do it then.

He was hot. He wound his window down a bit and rubbed his face. After one of the train trips and a near panic attack, he had some good green stuff. It was a reward, like after a workout at the gym or a run when you stuff your face because you deserve it. His reward for staying off the dope was to use a bong, which he normally avoided because he smoked too much and it soaked up his money. He got stoned quickly using the bong and the voices returned. They were having a party and Lucas had joined in. The party guests still remained.

He sat staring straight ahead, arguing with a voice in his head. The voice wanted him to zap Mackenzie and then she was all his. But Lucas was thinking of the deformities. She's such a pretty thing—what would happen if something went wrong? Would he still love her, still want her, if she was deformed? He lit a smoke and wound the window down further.

Lucas stared out the front windscreen, his eyes heavy. He checked the time. She was like clockwork—she would be walking past soon. Right on, she came into view. Lucas threw his cigarette out the window and wound the window up. He had the computer on his lap with the transfer app loaded. She paused and started rummaging through her bag. Had she forgotten something? At that instant Lucas decided he wanted her, deformities and all. He looked at the screen, and found what he needed to tap.

* * *

Mackenzie found her phone. It was a text message from Paul. She looked up the street and saw an elderly lady walking towards a car. On the other side of the street, a man with a yellow t-shirt was trying to drag a golden Labrador away from something it was sniffing. The dog had moved on and soon was happily sniffing a message left by another dog.

Mackenzie looked back at the car. Something was not right.

Mackenzie returned to her phone, put it back in her bag and started walking off again.

* * *

A loud knock on the driver side window startled Lucas. He turned to see huge eyes staring at him, magnified by glasses, and a mouth moving like it was chewing grass.

Lucas was confused. He wound the window down.

"What ya up to mister? You trying to start a fire or something?"

Lucas heard scratching and saw her leg moving, a twisting motion—obviously emphasizing that she was putting out his cigarette butt.

The lady continued. "You better get out of here or I'm calling the police."

Lucas stared at those eyes. They blinked, waiting for a response. He thought of his mother. Be nice, he said to himself. He turned and looked back down the street. Mackenzie was gone. *Be nice.*

"I'm sorry, lady. Best you stand back."

He drove off. He looked back in the rear-view mirror. A hunched-over figure watched him drive off. She threw her arms up in the air, like she was shooing him away, and then turned back towards her castle.

No Mackenzie. No deformed Mackenzie. That was good. He thought of his mother. No, he would never use the technology on Mackenzie.

* * *

Was it right to be disappointed that the message was from Paul and not Aaron?

She had hoped it had been Aaron; she wanted to hear that all was okay. Since he'd been gone, he'd communicated with Mackenzie on what he called a 'welfare phone'. Only a few calls, and he would always use video chat software. It was like Aaron was monitoring her well-being. She was fine, and no, there were no strange men chasing after her. She was starting to think war was making him paranoid. But she hadn't heard from him for a while, and then Aaron's mum told Mackenzie about the incident.

A car drove past. It was the car that was parked up the street. The driver was rubbing the left side of his face. He had such big hands, they covered half his face. It looked like he was stressed out about something.

She'd been told Aaron was okay, a minor injury but he would be transferred home now. The injury made him unfit for overseas duty.

Mackenzie got a message notification as she made her way up the stairs to the gym, then another. The first one was from Aaron and said, 'The eagle has landed', which sort of made sense. The next one was from Paul and said, 'I love you', which made a lot of sense.

It was okay to be disappointed. She loved them both, just differently.

Part Three – The Vanishings

CHAPTER FOURTEEN

June 2018

IT WAS A DAY of firsts: the first day of winter, and the first day of the working week. Neither event generated a great deal of enthusiasm, as displayed by the passengers' faces on the morning train coming in to the city on the Ipswich line.

Mackenzie heard somebody cough. She looked around the train carriage looking for the culprit. Was it the lady with the brown and green scarf? It wasn't an overly cold day. Mackenzie pictured germs and other invisible things floating around in the carriage. Was she developing some kind of phobia? Hopefully not, although she was washing her hands a lot more these days. Mum always said to let the body's immune system harden up, then Dad would chip in that you can't really build up good muscles without doing exercise. It had taken her a while to work out the relevance of that one.

They pulled into Central Station, platform six, right on time: 07.29. More people were being added to the thousands already disembarked by the rail network. Mackenzie waited for the 'swish' of the doors to open and then braced herself for the noise of the station. And it came, the whooshing sounds of trains coming and going, the occasional horn and whistle sounds, announcements being made, a chorus of chatter as people hit the train platform and started making their way out of the station.

Paul helped an elderly lady out of the carriage. Mackenzie smiled and smiled again as she looked at Paul's red shirt. It was his favorite color and it suited him. Paul took Mackenzie's hand as they headed towards the exit. Mackenzie noticed the blind man ahead of her on the escalator with his guide dog. She often saw him and had a quiet admiration for him. He had a humble demeanor, smiling all the time. They headed towards the pedestrian crossing at the intersection of Creek Street and Ann Street.

They stopped at the traffic lights. Many people subconsciously tuned in to the slow beeping, making them pause. Mackenzie looked at the blind man and his dog, wondering how the dog decided when to go —at least dogs were obedient. Some people waited patiently for the beeping to speed up, for the red man to change to green. Others crossed when they felt it was safe—they made up their own laws. The road was clear, but the walk symbol was red, so the jaywalking started, the confident people first and then those influenced by others.

Mackenzie heard someone yelling behind her. She turned to see a tall man with a look of panic on his face, rushing towards the intersection with two police officers in pursuit. The man turned to look behind him and crashed into her. They both fell towards the road. Paul went to grab Mackenzie and stumbled as well.

The blind man's dog started barking. A humming noise engulfed the area. Somebody screamed.

Mackenzie looked around. People were turning their heads trying to locate the source of the sound, their hands raised over their ears. The air became distorted. Mackenzie saw something coming towards her. It was like a wave but she could see through it. People on the footpath on the other side of the road had been knocked over from the wave's force. It passed over the jaywalkers and they vanished. Vanished? It was getting closer. She moved her hands to her ears. She turned to Paul just as the wave hit him. Gone.

Now she was floating. Rising up. She looked down. A lady started screaming and yelled out. "Where have they gone . . . where have the people gone?"

Then there was silence.

* * *

Mackenzie picked herself up off the floor. *Floor?* What had happened to the road? Where was she? There were others. Where was Paul? Her heart was thumping and her head was throbbing. She looked around at the others—everyone trying to work out what had happened. She helped pick up a lady from the floor who was struggling. Mackenzie was thankful that the floor had been softened with some kind of thick flooring material. She looked around again. Where was Paul?

Some people had their mobile phones out, trying to make calls. She heard some crackling. It was coming from a speaker mounted near the ceiling.

"Hello, people. Please don't be alarmed. You are all perfectly safe and have been transported to a holding house. We ask that you make yourselves comfortable. We will join you all soon. Please note that mobile phones will not work here."

Mackenzie watched one man moving about, the one who crashed into her. He was like a caged tiger—she hoped he would settle down. The others looked dumbfounded.

"Did he say 'holding house'?" someone asked.

Mackenzie confirmed this as she looked around. She did a count. There were seven of them: four men, three women. Most were dressed for work—they didn't expect to end up on a dusty floor in a 'holding house'. A few were still dusting themselves down. There was a table of refreshments and a stack of white plastic chairs. She heard a quiet whirring noise and looked up to see a video camera scanning the room. *What is going on?*

The caged tiger was the most casually dressed. Mackenzie watched him as he walked over to the only window and tried a few things. Then he went into a small room, and came back out shaking his head.

"A toilet and only a small window," he advised no one in particular.

The man then decided to try and open the main door. He gave it a kick and then looked at Mackenzie and raised his hands.

"It's like Fort Knox," he said. "It'll be difficult to get out of here."

Time ticked by and nothing happened. One of the businessmen suggested they best stay calm and maybe take advantage of the refreshments offered on a table to the rear of the room.

Mackenzie looked at her watch. The train had arrived at 7.29. It was now eight-thirty. She wondered when their kidnappers were going to join them.

CHAPTER FIFTEEN

WAR IS DANGEROUS, AND dangerously loud.

Aaron was now back in Brisbane city and office-bound. The Bushmaster troop carrier's unique design and armor plating had saved them. They were evacuated by helicopter to the Tarin Kowt military hospital—a hospital that Australian Army engineers helped rebuild, and staffed by nurses and midwives trained with Australian aid. Aaron always emphasized these things when he spoke to people—he believed there was purpose behind it all, and what he had seen confirmed that.

Aaron had recovered from his injuries from the IED blast but was left with slight hearing damage, which limited his military options and prevented him completing his tour of duty. He struggled with not being able to go back to Afghanistan. He desperately wanted to remain in active service, to remain a soldier, to honor his dad and his brother Jack, and to serve his country.

Mackenzie and Lucas were always at the forefront of his mind. He had caught up with Mackenzie a few times and he was feeling more confident as days went past that maybe his threat to Lucas had a lasting effect. He'd asked Mackenzie about the minister guy and his drivers. Mackenzie hadn't seen them at church, although she did stress that she went to a 'younger' service than his mum's. That Friday night service Aaron had attended, the one where they'd seen Jill and the minister, was a special event.

Paul and Mackenzie were still going strong. That was another reason why he would have loved to have gone back to Afghanistan. Out of sight, out of mind. Maybe he should have moved interstate—he quite liked Townsville.

He followed up news articles to see if vanishings were still happening, but there was nothing. He came across a general article on suicides. One of the stories included a government minister losing his son to suicide. Although no names were mentioned, Aaron believed it was the man he had helped that day at the intersection, after the incident with the girl. Maybe that incident was the cause of his death.

His army training and experience had taught him a lot about post-traumatic stress disorder, and he knew it contributed to a large number of suicides. On his return from Afghanistan, he had to make a few visits to a psychiatric practice to make sure he was okay. Aaron constantly checked his thoughts. He was lucky. Although his war experience wasn't overly pleasant, he hadn't experienced excessively frightening or distressing events as some had.

He was challenged. The doctors told him that he had just been through a traumatic event in Afghanistan. It was a battle, but Aaron convinced them he was okay. The event had minimal impact on Aaron, even though the same event could have caused severe distress in another individual. Aaron decided it was the wiring in his head; he had inherited solid coping skills from his parents. He was thankful for the good wiring job.

He caught up with the detective that was investigating Dad's death. He was apologetic: not much progress had been made. The investigator's report on the fire gave no leads. It looked like it could have been an accident. They were unable to trace the white van, but they would keep Aaron posted if anything else cropped up. Aaron felt bad when he got off the phone. Maybe he should have passed on the information he had.

Aaron thought of Lucas. He told the image of Lucas that he was coming to get him.

* * *

The *M on Mary* had 43 levels of apartments. Aaron's was a mid-level apartment. It was a good-sized one-bedroom apartment, purchased with Dad's life insurance payout when Aaron returned from Afghanistan. The marketing spin for the apartment included words like style, elegance, opulently finished. To Aaron it was a simple investment that allowed him to live close to work and enjoy the city life.

Aaron had a late start this morning. He sat in his small study dressed in uniform camouflage trousers and brown t-shirt, reviewing some documents that he needed for a meeting this afternoon.

Although it was a cool morning, he had his balcony doors open. There seemed to be an abnormal number of sirens and sounds of emergency vehicles this morning. He got up from his chair and headed towards the living room balcony, grabbing a shirt that draped the back of a chair on the way. It was a bit chilly so he put his camouflaged shirt on.

Where was the sun? He looked up and saw a large thick cloud moving across to conceal it. He then looked in the direction of the sounds. It was the same direction as his route to work, near Central railway station. It looked like a huge ruckus going on. A train accident? He was leaving for work soon and would check out what had happened then.

Out in the streets, as usual people stared at his General Duty Dress uniform. They stared at you more in Brisbane than Townsville—curiosity, as there were few army personnel based in the city. He was getting closer to the ruckus. Some crowd barriers had already been put in place and it looked like more were needed. It was that intersection again, where he'd seen the accident. Was the intersection cursed?

It looked like a scene from a Hollywood action movie. Traffic was stopped behind several police cars, their red and blue lights bouncing of the glass of the surrounding buildings, search and rescue vehicles, news wagons with their satellite dishes extended, and people everywhere.

Aaron watched crowd barriers being moved to let an emergency vehicle through. Emergency staff disembarked from the vehicle and started to assist with getting the crowds under control. What was going on? Another vehicle came through with 'Gracie Rentals' painted on the side, carrying a load of rent-a-barriers. It looked like a big event.

Aaron noticed a lady and a police officer on their own, away from the crowd. The lady turned and pointed towards the intersection, and he recognized her. It was Kathy, Mackenzie's mum. Something was wrong. He walked towards them.

"Excuse me, officer."

The officer turned.

"I know this lady—"

"Is that you, Aaron?" Kathy looked up. "Oh, Aaron, please help us."

"What's happened, Kathy?"

The officer replied, "We're not sure, a few people have gone missing and we're trying—

"They've vanished, Aaron, Mackenzie and Paul. Both vanished."

The officer continued, "Maybe six or seven, maybe more have gone missing . . . could I leave this lady with you? I need to get back and help with managing the incident."

"Sure."

Aaron took Kathy's arm and led her over to an area where they could sit down, a low concrete wall supporting a garden bed. Aaron looked around the street. It was eerie with no traffic. Some people were rushing to the barriers closest to the incident but being discouraged and directed away by police and emergency service workers.

"I'm sorry, Kathy. I've just got here so I've no idea what's happened."

"I can tell you . . . based on what I've heard from others, Mackenzie and Paul cross this street every work day. But this morning they vanished . . . just vanished."

Aaron frowned. "What do you mean, 'just vanished'?"

"That's it, Aaron, they just vanished, like they fell through a hole or something. But there are no holes."

Aaron had a bad feeling about this. "Why do you think Mackenzie was one of them?"

"I was meeting her for a quick coffee. She didn't turn up. I tried her phone, and Paul's. I went down to where she works. She hasn't turned up for work and they haven't heard from her. I prefer not to think the worst, Aaron, but I believe both her and Paul have vanished."

"Maybe their train was delayed?"

Kathy shook her head. "No. She would have phoned, or Paul would have."

"Kathy, I'm sure there's something there . . . maybe recent heavy rain has caused some erosion under the road, you know, a sinkhole."

"Maybe . . . but I was over at the site, there are no obvious holes. I don't mean to be rude Aaron, but it's real . . . she has vanished."

Kathy's name was called. They turned to see her husband, James.

James hugged Kathy and gave Aaron a nod.

"Hi, James."

Aaron looked at Mackenzie's parents, holding each other and staring in the direction of the incident site. It was in some ways good that they were both in the city this morning. A large media contingent now assembled around the site, with a lot of pushing and shoving going on.

"James, I'll have to get Kathy to explain what's going on because I need to get to work. I may be able to find out some info at work. I'll give you a call if I discover anything. I'm sure there's an explanation coming."

"Thanks, Aaron."

Aaron headed towards work. He could use some resources there to investigate further. He looked back at the intersection. It was the same intersection where the girl was hit by the car. A coincidence? Or were some places tagged for bad things?

He had a gut feeling that Lucas was involved and he had reneged on his promise.

Lucas had underestimated Aaron's feelings for Mackenzie.

CHAPTER SIXTEEN

LUCAS WAS CONCERNED.

He was driving back from the execution of the transfer. The Professor wasn't with him today. They decided Lucas knew what he was doing, and someone needed to be at the property to look after the guests when they arrived. Lucas leaned forward and looked up at the sky. It was quite gloomy, with dark clouds. He felt electricity in the sky. He punched the steering wheel. *Sorry, Mackenzie. I didn't mean to zap you.* Who was that idiot who pushed her? But it was his fault, not the guy who pushed her. He had chosen to do the transfer at that time so he could catch a glimpse of his darling. The voices in his head were telling him these things happen for a reason. *It's all planned out.*

He would have to agree with those voices. He knew that he had to stay within the strategy. They only wanted to get the law breakers, and he was scheming about how to get that girl. But he no longer had to do that. He hit the steering wheel in triumph. He had crossed from anger to joy. *She's going to be there.* He smiled; he hadn't felt this good for quite a while.

A sign came up on the right, giving directions to a private hospital. That triggered another mood change in Lucas. What if she'd been deformed or something like that? *She'll be fine.* He lost one of the homeless test dummies the other day. The person did not return after a transfer. He told the Professor about it and the Professor told him not to worry, things had been fixed up. *She'll be fine.* There would be no deformities.

Was she okay? The battle in his head continued as he drove and he wondered where the homeless test dummy he lost was.

As Lucas got closer to the property he had to go into a holding pattern behind a red ute. It looked like a painter's vehicle. Tins of paint bounced around the back of the ute, and a dog was pacing and swaying from one side of the ute to the other, restrained by the chain around its neck.

The turn-off to the property was coming up. Lucas got a surprise when he saw the turning indicator for the ute come on. This was not good timing. He followed the ute into the property. The painter pulled his ute into a gravel parking spot near the steps that led up to the main entrance. Lucas pulled up beside the ute and went over to greet the visitor.

"Hello, can I help you?" Lucas asked.

"Oh, hi . . . sorry to disturb you, but I was sent to pick up a ladder that we left here some weeks back. We did a paint job on that large shed of yours."

"Do you know where it is?"

He pointed. "Just down near the shed. We laid it at the side of the shed. That's why we forgot it, you know, out of sight out of mind."

Lucas was not in the right frame of mind for this happy-go-lucky man. "I'll go and get it for you."

"Not sure if you will manage it—it's a big ladder. Now that was a stupid thing to say. You do look like you can manage it. Do you work out or something?

The sooner he got rid of this man the better. Lucas's phone started ringing. He answered. It was the minister, so he asked him to hold. He turned to the painter, hesitated and said, "Well, you best go get it then. Try and be quiet as we have some people in the shed at the moment—we're using it as an activity centre."

"No worries." The painter headed down to the shed.

While he was on the phone, Lucas watched the painter. The shed only had the one large window and it was on the opposite side to where the ladder was, so the painter couldn't take a peek. He watched as the painter walked past the pile of rubbish. Lucas remembered he'd thrown the damaged mannequin on that pile. He noticed the painter hesitate as he walked past the rubbish.

The painter now had the ladder. He seemed to investigate the pile of rubbish in more details as he walked past. Even to the point of pretending to lose his balance with the ladder so he could get a better look at the mannequin. *What a jerk.*

Lucas met him at his ute. "Wasn't a body?"

"Ah. What do you mean?"

"The mannequin. We use it for our first aid classes."

"Oh. No worries. Well, I best be off."

"I suppose you heard a bit of noise coming from the shed. It's one of those self-development courses and the instructor gets them revved up a bit."

"All sounds fine to me."

"Okay, then. Got everything?"

Lucas tapped the ute's roof to signal the visit was completed and it was time to go. The painter's dog gave Lucas a growl. The ute took off.

* * *

The painter's ute turned on to the bitumen road and started heading to the job where the ladder was needed.

A couple of kilometers into his trip, the painter had to slam on his brakes. A man had came staggering out of the bush and up to the ute. The man placed his hand on the bonnet and then made his way around to the driver's window.

The man pleaded for a lift. He was lost. He didn't know where he was.

The painter helped him out. There was a bus stop near the big barrel that advertised the local winery. He dropped the lost man there.

The painter drove off. It was a strange day. Mannequins and people from outer space.

* * *

Lucas hoped there would be no more distractions. He walked back over to the van and retrieved his security duty belt, the one he'd forgotten to return when he left. He let Starkey know that all was clear. It was the minister who called Lucas when he was with the painter—he wanted an update. Lucas told him it was coming.

It was a large shed, its appearance softened by some big trees. Lucas and Starkey headed down towards it. From the outside it looked like a shed, but inside it had been transformed into a separate office and the larger room they referred to as the holding bay. The Minister's department had funded the transformation using some creative accounting. Soundproof insulation had been fitted between the studs, then covered and secured by plasterboard walls, all professionally painted. Security grilles had been added to the windows, and the doors had been reinforced. Creature comforts of air conditioning and heating were installed along with a PA system and media viewing equipment.

Lucas noticed Starkey looking at his belt.

"You expecting trouble, Lucas . . . I assume that's a Taser gun there?"

"It is. Also some pepper spray and a baton." Lucas patted the other side of his belt. "I'm not expecting trouble, Starkey, but what we're up to seems to generate its fair share of unpredictability." Lucas was always impressed with how he was able to convey confidence when he had to, an aura that covered the battle within well.

The shed door creaked as they opened it. They walked into a small office that still had a smell of newness about it. A couple of iPads rested on a bench next to some Richard Nixon face masks. Lucas noticed some empty rice cracker containers and cheese wrappers in a bin near the bench. Next to the bin sat a large box, flaps open to reveal black bicycle helmets.

"What's with the helmets, Starkey?"

"Protect heads when people fall. It's okay when we transport people here, with the softened floor we got put in, but when we send them back it's a different matter. Some do fall, but it looks like it depends what they're doing when they get transported. If they're lying or standing, then that should be the same at the other end. If they are active—like walking or running—then they could be off balance when transported, and fall. I suppose it's an overreaction. Maybe they'll never be used."

Lucas thought of the jogger, the man in the first test. Sounds like Starkey's theory could be right. "You never know."

Their eyes went to a large monitor on the wall. Lucas saw the girl Mackenzie there and smiled. He counted seven people. One man was banging on the door. Starkey picked up the masks.

Lucas took a mask from Starkey. "Well, let's get this party underway." Starkey gave an advance warning over the PA system that they were about to enter.

Lucas made sure they had the remote control for the door. Starkey opened the door to the holding bay. They walked in. The man who was banging on the door took a step back and had a swing at them with his briefcase, then backed off. Maybe it was the size of Lucas or what Lucas had on around his waist. A sense of panic still hovered. One woman was hysterical, demanding answers.

"Lady, would you please calm down?" Starkey asked.

"No, I won't. I demand to know what's happening. And why are you wearing those stupid masks?"

"Lady, you'll know soon enough what's happening. Now, calm down."

A man standing next to the lady whispered something to her.

"No, I will not shut up." She grabbed her mobile phone out of her bag.

"We have told you, that won't work. We have a cell phone jammer set up so there's no receiving or transmitting of mobile signals. So please calm down, and we will explain what's going on."

Lucas watched Mackenzie walk up and put her arms around the lady and raise her eyebrows to the man who must have told the woman to shut up.

The briefcase swinger spoke. "Mate, you can understand the panic we're feeling. One minute we're crossing a road the next we're in a—"

"Oh, I do understand. Please let us explain," Starkey said.

Lucas looked around the room. They all appeared okay, a bit panicky, but it looked like they were all intact. His eyes always came back to Mackenzie and lingered there.

Starkey continued. "As you can see, through your firsthand experience, we have made certain advances with a particular technology that we wanted to bring to the attention of appropriate authorities, but they would not give us the light of day so we—"

"Sorry . . . we're guinea pigs for a new technology? Who do you think you are? You can't treat people like this." The speaker started towards the door, but Lucas blocked his path and directed the man to a seat at the end of the room. After sizing Lucas up, the man agreed with his request.

The man rubbed a black mark under his right eye.

* * *

Lucas moved to stand next to the door. He enjoyed the brief adrenaline rush. With his hand resting on the Taser, he had a feeling of power. Tag once told Lucas that he gave off a sense of unpredictability, maybe not the volcanic type, but you could sense something was simmering and you didn't necessarily want to engage it. That puffed Lucas up. He felt that now.

They had settled. Starkey stood next to Lucas and cleared his throat.

"There's nothing to fear. The event that you have found yourselves involved in is for the good of society. By good, we mean huge benefits. You're all here because you disobeyed a law that was established to protect you."

Lucas watched the response. Some raised their eyes. Some dropped their jaws. Some rubbed their foreheads; most just had a look of disbelief.

Starkey continued. "Some may respond to this by saying 'get a life', but it's a fundamental problem. The law is not being obeyed and many continue to mock the law. We plan to do something about it."

Briefcase man had taken a seat. "You're right. Get a life. Thousands dying in the world, hunger, terrorists . . ."

"Let me continue," Starkey said, with hint of aggression. "Here's a summary. It's a common story. Young girl killed because she chooses to ignore the 'don't walk' indicator. Her family devastated, family disintegrates, dad walks out, ends up homeless, the driver of the car is a shattered man, and two years later the driver commits suicide. So, you say get a life? No, we say save a life."

A few were nodding their heads; the rest looked unconvinced.

"You are the first lot—there are more to come. Jaywalking is the first law we are focusing on. We plan to use our relocation technology in a few more intersections and then move on to other risk areas.

Briefcase man jumped up on his seat. "You mean you used this 'beam me up Scottie' technology because a few people disobeyed a minor pedestrian law—I mean I agree with what you're saying, but come on man, this is going a bit far—and are our bodies going to be okay after this 'relocation'?"

"Your bodies will be fine," Starkey said. "We agree it is a minor law, but it is still law. We can give many more examples where disobeying the law has resulted in a traumatic event. We can talk about speeding, running red lights, talking on mobile phones, road rage. You yourself can name many others, but look at the ripple effect. This is what we want people to focus on, the consequences of their actions. Think about it. The ripple effect."

"Well, how different is 'relocation' to law enforcement then?" someone asked.

"Good question. We want people to obey laws. They're not, so we want to do something about it. We believe a strategy of inconveniencing people will make them have second thoughts about breaking the law. Do you people feel inconvenienced at the moment?"

A few nodded.

"Why not just zap one person? Why a group?" someone else asked.

"It's about capturing lawbreakers. If one person jaywalked, then only one person would have been relocated. But because we got quite a few of you, it shows most people don't give a hoot about the law."

Lucas looked at Mackenzie. It looked like she was going to say something but decided against it. He knew she didn't break the law.

Someone asked, "Are you planning on replacing the law enforcement agencies or something?"

"Not quite. We anticipate that we will develop a close relationship with such agencies, as we offer them a tool. So please don't be concerned—we will send you back soon. We have some refreshments for you. We ask that you trust us, let all this unfold. We mean no harm. You are just messengers."

Lucas thought Starkey's last comment would have them thinking they were aliens. He looked towards the end of the shed and saw that the refreshments had been set up. Starkey must have done that earlier. He would have known once the shock of the transition settled down, they would need something to eat and drink. Such a thoughtful man.

Starkey continued. "But we do stress that this exercise has been one of highlighting the technology. They have ignored all our requests for showing off the technology. They now know what it is capable of, and we want to discuss the use of the technology with the appropriate authorities. They can also explore different applications it can be used for, and can get their best minds working on it. We are sure the military will have ideas as well."

Lucas noticed Mackenzie standing by herself. He was sure her partner was with her at the crossing. He wondered then if they had all made it. He would have to review the 'relocation'. He nodded to Starkey, and moved his head towards the door.

Mackenzie spoke, confirming what Lucas was thinking.

"Excuse me. I'm really concerned about my friend. I was sure he was with me when whatever it was happened. He was with me when we vanished. Could you tell me where he is please. Is he all right?"

"Lady, he probably wasn't transferred. Maybe he didn't break the law," Starkey said.

Lucas and Starkey left the room.

* * *

Lucas grabbed an iPad, went up to the house, and after brushing some ants of a veranda chair, sat down. He tapped the iPad and opened up the transfer log file. Eight bodies were detected and picked up. Only seven arrived at the destination. It looked like they still had a problem with the technology. Where was the missing entity?

When he wanted to talk to the Professor about the technology he felt he needed to use the title, but he'd slipped into referring to the Professor as Starkey now—it had become a habit. He saw Starkey looking at his watch. "Hey, Starkey, I reckon we lost one."

"What do you mean?"

"Eight entities sent, seven received."

"That's not good, Lucas." Starkey checked his watch again. "I have to go and visit the boss."

"That's crazy. Why doesn't he come here?"

"Because he wants to stay away from the scene of the crime."

"That's a joke isn't it?"

"Yeah, of course, Lucas. Tag will be here soon. He can help you look after the people." Starkey walked to the door then turned, rubbing his chin. "I reckon it's the power. There were a few flickers this morning from the unsettled weather . . . we need to install a surge protector or something along those lines. But then again, the transport channel could be affected by electrical storms. Need to ponder this further." Starkey walked down the stairs.

Lucas walked over, leaned on the veranda rail and watched Starkey drive off. The minister probably thought his phones were bugged and tracked, so made Starkey drive to his place. Lucas went inside the house. He looked around. It was quiet—too quiet. He grabbed a pouch from one of his trouser pockets. Time for some grass. He had given up on his path to righteousness—the grass caused him no harm. And he was going to smoke it in this house while he waited for Tag to arrive. Just the thoughts of having a joint made him feel tougher, less inhibited. He told the house that he didn't fear it, and then he thought of Mackenzie and smiled.

Comfortably seated on the couch, he blew out a smoke ring. He watched the circle go out and gradually lose its form as it drifted up to the ceiling. He thought of bubbles. Once the Professor used that as an example of how the people were transported. He explained it was like putting them all in a bubble and then placing the bubble on a conveyer belt. Everything inside the bubble was protected from the elements. The bubble was popped when it reached the destination.

He blew another smoke ring and watched the circle fly off. He wondered how someone fell out of the bubble.

* * *

The Brisbane Koala Bushlands are located fifteen kilometers southeast of Brisbane city, and are popular with bushwalkers.

Koalas are hard to see. Their coloring blends in with the bark of the big gum trees, making them almost invisible.

People wearing red shirts are not hard to see when spread-eagled between the branches of a tree.

A bushwalker discovered the body.

CHAPTER SEVENTEEN

GRANT WINDSOR SAT IN his South Bank apartment, his home away from home. He stared at the security monitor attached to the intercom system, watching Bruce Starke park his car and make his way to the elevator. The sound of television played out in the background. His ears picked up terms like 'body snatchers', 'Armageddon' and 'Mars attacks'. He watched Starkey walk into the elevator and waited for the intercom to buzz.

Windsor suffered from realistic paranoia. He knew his phone calls were monitored, so the last thing he wanted to do was talk to Starkey on a phone after a major incident like this. He welcomed Starkey into his apartment. They walked over to the wall of glass windows and stared down at the Brisbane River. The river sat still with reflections of the city buildings—the stillness broken by a CityCat gliding through the water, city buildings swaying in the wake.

"It went well then, Bruce?"

"By all accounts . . . causing a bit of a commotion in the city, but that's to be expected. But it does look like it went well, Grant. Lucas and I have communicated with the people who got transported."

Windsor continued to stare out at the river. "A little history for you, Starkey—James Cook guessed this great river existed but it took other explorers to confirm it. The exploring of the lower reaches of the river led to the establishment of a penal colony. These colonies were used as correctional facilities. Back in England, criminals were transported to far-off lands instead of being executed. Mind you, some young children were executed for stealing bread. They used a transport system to address a justice problem. We, my friend, are the modern equivalent of that transport system. They will talk about us in the history writings." He smiled to himself. "Notice I didn't say history books, because who knows if books are going to exist in the years ahead."

Windsor turned and looked at Starkey. "We will give them another dose in a few days' time." He looked at his watch. "In the meantime, I need to get ready for a press conference and a meeting with the Police Commissioner. Let's meet again tomorrow to see how things have progressed and do some planning."

Starkey was still staring out the window.

Windsor walked to his desk. "I appreciate you driving out here straight after the event. I know it's a long trip for a short meeting but I wanted to see you in person. Are you okay about things?"

"It's not an overly long trip, Grant . . . you know, this is the first time I've been in your office." Starkey walked over to a portrait on the wall. "Is this your son?"

"Yes."

"It will be worth it in the end, Grant. In answer to your question, considering it was the first time we did a 'group' deployment, we have learned a few things."

Windsor pondered Starkey's last point. "But was it successful?" he asked trying to draw out the doubt that he sensed.

"It was . . . although we had a minor hiccup by losing one of the 'testers' a few days back. I believed the adjustments I made had fixed this problem, but—"

"By testers, I assume you mean one of the street people?"

"Yes, but we also lost one of the people we transported today."

"What do you mean by 'lost'?" Windsor started rubbing the back of his neck.

"They just don't turn up at the transition point."

"Where do they go?"

"Don't know."

"They must drop into the ether somewhere," Windsor said, trying to convince himself. "As long as they come to no harm and turn up somewhere, it shouldn't present a problem."

He watched Starkey. Windsor would prefer not to think of the negative consequences of the transporting. He had convinced himself that no deaths could be attributed to what they are doing. He changed the subject.

"Do you still believe we can automate the process by placing transition devices at all intersections?"

"Yes. I also believe we can develop drones that can monitor and execute the impounding. I also see law enforcement officers having a device to 'impound' people, a bit like the Taser gun they currently carry.

Windsor smiled. "You're a smart person, Starkey. I can just see the smile on a police officer's face when he impounds a person who breaks the law but refuses to show the respect required." Windsor stood up and made his right hand in the shape of a gun, pointed at imaginary person and said, "Zap, you're impounded!"

He walked over to the window from which he could see the reflections of the lights of the emergency vehicles bouncing off the buildings surrounding the incident area. The emergency services were still trying to work it all out.

"Thanks, Starkey, you've done a good job. I've organized money to be transferred over to one of your accounts. You can use that for the next phase."

* * *

It had been a few hours since they had any contact with the masked men. Mackenzie was thinking of the masks that they wore: the grinning smile was quite unsettling. Why would they wear masks? Maybe it was reassuring, as concealing their identities meant that the prisoners would be freed some time. Better than the alternative. If they were able to identify their kidnappers, who knows what the end results would be. She shuddered at the thought.

She knew they were being monitored. The quiet movement of the closed-circuit camera gave that away. *Things will work out. Pray. Just keep calm.* She needed to remain calm to help her think clearly. She wondered where Paul was—they were together, but . . . like a flash, one minute they were walking, talking, and then . . .

She was also annoyed because she didn't break the law. She didn't jaywalk. Her law-abiding ways drove her crazy sometimes. Always has to do the right thing. No speeding tickets, no fines for anything. She strongly believed laws were to be obeyed. It was not drilled into her by her parents, just some inner code inside her. She was obeying the 'Don't Walk' indicator. Somebody pushed her onto the road.

Mackenzie realized she was staring at the man who pushed her, and he was staring right back at her. She turned away. She wondered about the dark smudge under one of his eyes.

She heard the door open and turned to see the hosts return. They had the silly masks on again but that was okay if it meant she would be released. Mackenzie could not get over the size of the nose. But she knew politicians, especially American presidents, were popular targets for caricature artists.

The bulkier man spoke. "If you could all take your seats please, we have a small presentation for you and then you'll be taken to your accommodation".

Mackenzie remained standing. She watched his lips moving behind Nixon's big lips. She noticed hair above his top lip: he had a moustache. Then it hit home what he'd actually said. "Excuse me . . . accommodation. How long are you planning on keeping us here?" she asked.

"Not long. We're quite a distance from the city and we plan to transport you all back there tomorrow, using conventional transport. A bus will be here in the morning."

"Excuse me . . . I look forward to the bus trip . . . but could you tell me if my friend is safe?" asked Mackenzie, she had a nagging feeling about Paul.

"You'll see him tomorrow," the bulkier man said.

The nagging feeling did not go away. She watched as the big man pushed a button on a remote. A soft motor sound came from the end of the room. A screen came sliding down out of its casing. The lights dimmed, a shutter came down on the window. Mackenzie picked up a sniff of something, a musky, earthy smell. She was sure it came in with that big man.

Mackenzie watched the presentation, but her thoughts were on Paul. Maybe he was still back there at the crossing, scratching his head, trying to work out where she had gone. But that was hours ago. Maybe he was with the search party. Where would they look? She had no idea where they were.

The lights were all back on now. Mackenzie watched the shutter going up on the window, the light invading the darkness. She got up and walked towards the window. It must be near or past lunchtime. Her stomach was rumbling. She looked at the table at the back of the room—there was a bowl of fruit there, so she walked over and grabbed an apple.

She turned and looked at the bulky guy. "Sir, I am quite angry with what you have done to us. How you expected us to sit through a presentation is beyond me. But we sat and watched, maybe because we're numb. So we sort of have a picture of what you are up to, but surely there must have been another way of doing this. You talk about the ripple effect. Well, what about the effect this is having on our families and maybe our bodies?"

She sensed some nervousness with the big man and hoped the smaller man would get more into the conversation. She took a small bite of the apple. Her body thanked her.

"We understand but you see this is what we wanted to happen. You have been inconvenienced." The smaller man was now contributing.

But she stared at the big man. There was something familiar about him. She felt like grabbing his mask and ripping it off. She looked again at the smaller man. "Inconvenienced. Yep, you've certainly got that part right." She looked at her apple and took another bite. She watched as a few of the others walked over to the table and took some fruit.

"You will be back in touch with your families tomorrow and they will be much relieved." The small man was nodding his head like it was bobbing on a spring, almost as though he was trying to convince himself.

"Yep, they will be relieved." Mackenzie thought of her parents, then thought of Aaron and how he would sort these men out.

"But think of those that don't come back. This is what we want to prevent. We were saying before we want people to obey laws. They are not, so we want to do something about it." The small man was speaking again.

"But haven't you broken the law by kidnapping us?" asked briefcase man.

The smaller Nixon paused and thought about the question. "I suppose we have, but we don't believe they will pursue us because their energy and time will be taken up investigating the technology we have shown and the suggestions we will make. We believe our message will be strong enough to bring about changes to the law."

"What do you mean by 'suggestions'?"

"Well what you just saw . . . there really is no penalty for the so-called trivial laws. There are fines, there is something called probation for minor offences and then there is prison. We will be offering an alternative penalty.

"And what may that be?" asked briefcase man.

"Let's focus on prison for a moment, while a criminal is in prison they can't commit crimes, can't rob people, break into houses or mug someone. On that level, prison does work. But from the other side, some have said that being in prison made them hard, functioning more like an animal than human. There's a loss of sensitivity, lack of care and not being scared of returning to prison—a revolving door mentality. So we want to avoid prison."

"But people who commit minor offences don't end up in prison."

"Repeat offenders do. And they keep offending because they are not sufficiently inconvenienced by the current punishments."

"Why are you telling us this? Shouldn't you be talking to the authorities?" One of the women spoke up.

"Not at this point. You are our messengers. As you can appreciate, if we were to appear in public we would be arrested, so we will wait for the appropriate time."

Mackenzie looked around. She was tired. Most of the others had returned to their seats. They all looked weary, resigned to the fact that really there was not much they could do but wait it out. She pulled up a seat, and joined them. A bus trip back tomorrow. She couldn't wait. It should be an interesting bus trip. How were they going to conceal their hideout? With blindfolds or blackened windows, maybe. Giddy up, horsey. Yes, she was tired.

Waiting was easier said than done. Mackenzie thought it would be a good idea maybe to get to know each other; it would also help kill some time.

Briefcase man was Graham, an entrepreneur, who owned a

specialty coffee company now expanding into the Asian market. Everybody wanted an espresso after his introduction. Angela was a personal trainer and worked in a city gym. Mark was a backpacker on his way to buy some groceries. He was excited—backpackers want stories to tell, and he reckoned he was on to a good one here. Not everyone shared his enthusiasm. Barbara and Peter were tourists and weren't overly excited about the deviation in their holiday plans. And Mackenzie was Mackenzie. She broke down when she told them about Paul. Barbara and Angela comforted her.

And there was the man with what looked like a tear tattooed on his face. He didn't participate in their team building exercise. People didn't want to push his involvement.

The introductions killed some time. Dimness came over the room. Hot food was wheeled in—pizzas. At least they knew they were near civilization.

CHAPTER EIGHTEEN

AARON RETURNED TO HIS apartment late in the afternoon. He was none the wiser, and it had been a long day. Thoughts of Mackenzie made it hard to concentrate on anything else. His boss was sympathetic.

He had stopped near the site on the way back home and watched as emergency services personnel tried to control people, crazy people. Once news of a big event or accident got out crazy people came from everywhere to see what had happened. And this was a big event.

A group of people had placards declaring the end was near. Repent and be saved. Aaron wondered what church they belonged to—there was a drunk arguing with them, swaying forward and back. Some placard-holder's friend stood ready to catch the man if his coordination skills completely failed.

Aaron needed some air so put on a sweatshirt and headed out to the balcony. He could see a helicopter hovering over the site. Why were people attracted to tragedies? Does it put people on a pedestal if they were able to tell others they saw where those people vanished? Everyone seemed to be seeking significance. He walked back inside thinking about dinner. He looked at his phone on the coffee table. Do people feel significant when they got text messages? Is someone more significant if they have a famous person's autograph?

Why was this significance thing bothering him so much? Mum and Dad always made him feel significant, important. They were good parents. Maybe some seek significance because no one told them they were important. Maybe some take their own lives because they feel insignificant, unimportant, like the world would be a better place without them. It was a frightening thought. Mackenzie was important to Aaron. Did he ever tell her that?

Aaron walked into his study and found the folder he was looking for—the one with his investigation notes on Dad's death. This incident involved the same technology. It was too much of a coincidence not to, and it looked like it had passed its testing phase. He retrieved the number of the security firm where Lucas worked and called it. As he expected, Lucas no longer worked there and there was no forwarding address. Did Lucas still live in that flat in Morningside? He doubted it.

He thought of Mackenzie and he remembered her faith. Aaron whispered to Mackenzie that he was coming but he needed to work out few things. He asked God to look after her.

Aaron went into the kitchen and found some Thai takeaway leftovers in the fridge. He put the leftovers in the microwave and set the timer. He walked over to the TV, turned it on and started flicking through the stations. It seemed every station was covering the event. It reminded him of the TV coverage of the floods that rampaged the city some years back. The microwave timer went off.

He grabbed his tucker and cutlery, sat down and continued watching the TV coverage. The actual vanishing was caught on CCTV and had been released to the media outlets. Aaron watched and recorded the replay. Although he sensed it, the video confirmed that Mackenzie was one of those that vanished. Was he in some kind of denial? He put down his cutlery and placed his head in his hands. He was angry. He took some deep breaths, calmed down, and watched the replay again. Mackenzie and Paul were pushed from behind by a man being chased by police. He hoped that person wasn't still with them. The police must have been after him for a reason.

Where had they gone?

Aaron got tired of the coverage of the event and wanted to watch something different. He started flicking stations again and a man caught his attention. It was a familiar face. Where had he seen that face before? The man was giving his view of the event.

"I'm sure there's a reasonable answer coming. I have met with the

Police Commissioner who will join us soon. Our best people are on the job, so I'm expecting some answers soon".

"As a churchgoer, Mr. Windsor, do you believe this could be something similar to the rapture?" a reporter asked.

"No, I don't."

"Could you elaborate?"

"Well, I'm still here."

"What does that mean?" another reporter asked.

"As churchgoers, we believe that the Lord will return one day to take us to be with him. They say in the twinkle of an eye the Christians will be taken up to be with the Lord. Do we know if any of those that have gone missing are churchgoers? And, as I said, I'm still here."

Aaron shook his head. That's where he had seen this guy before, at church with Mackenzie, and the events after church that night. Aaron had briefly seen this man a few times before and had all but forgotten about him. Then he remembered he was hanging around his mum there for a while. He was thankful nothing happened there.

Now he thought about it, he remembered Lucas was connected to this minister guy. He watched further to see if there were any more questions. More rapture-type questions cropped up. Why were they asking questions about the rapture? Mackenzie once explained the rapture to Aaron. He understood that all the Christians would disappear, but today's vanishing was only eight people.

An aide whispered something in the minister's ear and handed him a mobile. He turned to the reporters and asked to be excused. He stepped away from the podium.

He came back and spoke to the camera. "We have received some correspondence regarding the vanishings. We have been advised to be careful with jaywalking in the city. Do what the red man says or else you may be inconvenienced and have to make your way back to work from a place far, far away. Yes, it will happen again, maybe the same place, maybe not." He continued, emphasizing the need to pay attention to the red man and not break the law, and don't be inconvenienced.

Forget about the rapture. This was starting to sound like a Batman movie. Aaron couldn't make up his mind if the devious Riddler had returned or the Joker has been let loose. But far, far, away? That sounded like Shrek's kingdom. The humor just eased his stress level.

It was all getting a bit surreal. Inconvenienced if you broke the law? Some believe laws are an inconvenience anyway. He imagined a red man running around with horns in his head and a pitchfork. Where did that memory come from? The day had been too long; he needed sleep. His mind was all over the place.

He lay on his bed in boxer shorts and t-shirt, the reverse-cycle air conditioner keeping him warm. The bedroom curtains remained open, the darkness of the room softened by the glow and sparkle of the city lights. He thought of Mackenzie. He thought of his father. Dad would have pursued the perpetrators and Aaron would do the same. That minister guy had strong links to Lucas. They were all together at the café that night—the night that Lucas and his mate paid Aaron a visit.

They were all connected. They must be. Aaron just needed to work out what to do next. He again asked God to keep Mackenzie safe.

* * *

Aaron was tossing and turning as thoughts darted through his mind. He lay there and turned his head towards the window, the city lights reflecting, beckoning him. He got up, walked over to the window, and stared past his ghostly reflection towards the incident site. It beckoned him. He wasn't tired. What time was it? His phone sitting in its bedside cradle told him it was 21:05. When was the last time he'd gone to bed so early? He decided to respond to the beckoning and take a walk.

He left his apartment dressed in a pair of jeans, t-shirt, a grey zip-up styled hoodie, and canvas sneakers. Out in the street things were quiet. He turned and looked down towards the river. A vapory mist was floating up from the river bringing a chill to the air. He zipped up his hoodie and started walking towards the incident site.

St Stephen's Cathedral came into view. Aaron stopped and looked up at the cathedral. A sign described it as the 'spiritual heart of the city'. An angel sculpture guarded the cathedral's entrance and stared back at Aaron. It all felt strange, like something was communicating with him or trying to communicate with him. What was going on? Something was being revealed to him but he could not interpret it. He turned from the angel and continued his walk, puzzled.

The incident site stood out, ablaze with huge spotlights, making it more like daytime than night-time. A slight breeze rocked the blue and white tape sealing off the site.

Some people stood watching investigators pottering around doing their thing with some interesting-looking equipment. Aaron looked over to where he'd helped that poor man a few months back. An eerie feeling came over him. He tried to shake it off. Maybe this area had become some kind of Bermuda Triangle.

He stood, watching, wondering where Mackenzie was and hoping she was safe. He wanted so much to talk to Lucas and get the answers. A trip to Lucas's flat wouldn't achieve much as Aaron felt that Lucas wouldn't be there, but he still needed to check. He'd do that later.

Aaron thought of God and knew He would be helping Mackenzie. It gave him a strange feeling of peace. Was this faith? Since Afghanistan, he'd thought of God a lot more. It was probably fear—reaching out to God was merely a crutch for the feebleminded, a weakness for those that want someone to tell them how to live. Yet here he was, asking God to look after Mackenzie. Did that make him weak and feebleminded?

The spotlights had attracted a large moth and a score of smaller moths—he could see the shadow of the large moth cast onto a nearby wall. Aaron stared at the shadow, a body with wings. Do angels have wings? He looked around the environment he was in and saw a man standing in the shadows, near the stairs leading up to the station. He wore a large coat, and his head was bowed down. The man raised his head slowly and stretched his arms back. It was a street person awakening from a slumber, but looked like an angelic being lifting his head and spreading his wings.

This sudden preoccupation with angels confused Aaron.

* * *

It was time to leave the Bermuda Triangle.

There was nothing to do except to watch investigating officers at work and police officers logging the comings and goings of people entering the investigation site. So Aaron headed home. Maybe a strategy would take shape in his head on the way and the crazy thinking will go away.

He decided to go a different way home. The thought of getting attacked by the angel outside the cathedral helped with the decision. He headed down Ann Street. Passing a smaller church he noticed a man sitting on steps that led up to the old church building. Aaron glanced at him as he walked past and thought he heard him say something.

Aaron paused.

"Mel saw him. Hey . . . are you deaf or something, mate?" The man repeated "Mel saw him."

Aaron hesitated, then turned back to the man. The earflap beanie hid most of his face but there was still something familiar about him. "Sorry. You talking to me?" He pointed at himself.

"Well, there ain't anybody else around is there? What I said was, Mel saw something here today but nobody's listening to him. But listen, mate, Mel can be trusted and he saw something. You should go talk to him. A few of us have vanished before but no one is listening to us. And, mate, did you know you have a pretty big angel standing next to you?"

Maybe coming this way had been a bad move. Or maybe it was just going to be a different sort of night. Aaron looked around to see if there was anyone close to him. He shook his head. These people were out of their heads.

"Listen mate, you probably think I'm crazy, but I'm not. Mel did see something and you need to go talk to him. Your angel agrees with me. And let me tell you, there was something evil going on here today."

Aaron nodded and started to walk away, but a voice in his head made him pause and turn back. He thought about Mackenzie, thought about God, thought about strategy. "If I did decide to see Mel, where would I find him?"

"Pub at the end of the street. It's open for a few more hours. He's easy to find, he wears a red and blue cap with 'The Demons' on it. I keep telling him to throw that cap away, but he won't; it's his footy team and someone in the family gave it as a gift. Go find him. He'll be sitting near the bar. Listen, mate. He's a storyteller, but he tells the truth."

"Do you have a name?" Aaron asked.

"Chris, but everyone calls me Churchie."

Yes, there was something familiar about him. Maybe it was at the sausage sizzle. Pushing that thought aside, Aaron focused on the situation he was in. So, there is a big angel standing next to him and he was to look for a man wearing a cap with the word 'demons' on it. Maybe he was really still in bed and this is all a dream. How do you know? He thought about the book *Angels and Demons* and wondered if it had any relevance.

He decided to go see the man with the cap just so he had a good story to tell Mackenzie when he found her.

* * *

Aaron walked into the bar. The place looked and felt crummy. It had its own atmosphere. His feet seemed to be sticking to the floor—a few too many spilt drinks. Not a hotel that Aaron would want to frequent.

Aaron looked over at the barman who was cleaning a glass. A man with a red and blue cap was leaning on the bar, his head towards the barman so Aaron couldn't confirm if the cap had a logo. Aaron strolled over.

"G'day, how are you going?" Aaron asked.

The man turned and stared at Aaron. "You look like an army fellow."

"You're right . . . your name wouldn't happen to be Mel?"

"It is. Do I know you?"

"No . . . but when I think about it, I did help out at a sausage sizzle a few months back and think I may have seen you before. A friend of yours told me you saw something today."

"We have lots of sausage sizzles." He made an adjustment to his sitting position. "And the friend must've been my mate Churchie. Call him that because he always hangs around that church. He sees things, you know. He reckons I have some nasty characters hanging around me but I can't see 'em. That's why he hangs around the church; he reckons those nasty things can't get past something there."

Aaron raised his eyebrows and smiled. "Could I buy you a drink?"

"Just lemonade will be fine, mate. I'm not a drinker. Used to be. I just sit here most nights for the company. Monday's a quiet night—the rest of the week gets more entertaining."

Aaron ordered the drinks.

"As I said, I used to be a drinker. Got me life in a pretty bad state with the evil drink . . . me name's not really Mel. I had to get out of Melbourne, and when I first got here for some reason the name Mel Bourne stuck with me. The mob I hung around with when I first got here were a strange lot. They got their wires mixed up somewhere."

"So what's your real name?"

"Whatever you want it to be mate, because it doesn't matter. Could I tell you about my fall from grace?"

Aaron wanted to be courteous, so nodded. "I was warned you like to tell stories."

"And my mate Churchie must have told you that, too. You know Gracie, the portable toilet people?"

Aaron knew of portable toilets but wasn't sure of any particular company but then he remembered the truck he saw earlier today with 'Gracie Rentals' on it. He nodded in confirmation.

"In my drinking days I'd leave this pub in a pretty bad way. Started heading up towards the place close to where those people vanished. Was walking past a building site, noticed a portable toilet and realized I was hanging out badly for a pee. After thanking the Lord, I opened the door, did what I needed to do. I thought at the time that it was the strangest sensation I ever had, like I was flying."

Strange topic Aaron thought. But it must be heading somewhere.

"You know why I felt that way. Because I was going up." He started laughing. It was a funny laugh, and made Aaron feel self-conscious.

"You see, the portable toilet was attached to a crane and was being lifted up to a high-rise building. The crane driver didn't realize there was someone in it. Well, I opened the door and stepped out."

"And . . .?"

"Well, the Lord was with me. A canvas sail broke my fall, followed by some branches and then some cardboard boxes. I worked this all out because a loud rubbish truck woke me up hours later. I was in a large recycle container with scratches on my face and some broken branches around me. I looked up and saw the sail I must have broken. It's true, mate. That was my fall from grace."

Aaron now had doubts about what he was doing here. He finished the last of his drink and told Mel he was about to go.

"Hold on, mate, let me tell you what I saw today. It's all true. I was sitting on the park bench that looks down on where those roads cross. People bug me. Bike riders bug me, pedestrians bug me, cars bug me, but I love just sitting watching these things from on high. Maybe it's because I can whine about it because a lot of those folks break the law. I saw a girl get killed down there not too long ago. Talking on a phone and just walked straight into the line of a car— ignored the red man and everything."

Aaron wondered if it was the same incident he was involved in.

Mel continued. "Well, I was watching this morning and people just vanished—which, of course, is quite unusual."

Aaron nodded in agreement.

"I sort of got a bit panicky and stood up and looked around to tell someone and that's when I saw it . . . a big white van, like one of those live news coverage vans. I've seen it before. The van drove off straight away. As it drove past, the driver stared at me and I took off."

So what does one make of this? The white van could have been anything. Aaron took a punt. "Did the driver have a goatee and moustache?"

Mel straightened up. "Come to think of it, he did. How did you know that?"

"Lucky guess." Aaron wasn't being smart. It would've been hard to explain how he guessed it.

"You know, the way he looked at me when he drove past, it was as if I'd seen something that I shouldn't have seen."

A man with a goatee and moustache and a white van? Aaron wondered if jigsaw pieces were starting to fall into place.

"Would you be able to show me where you saw the white van?" Aaron was not sure what would come of it but believed that he needed to be active to make things happen.

"Yeah. That's fine. Can we pick up Churchie on the way. He's good protection. Keeps the nasties away."

* * *

A bus went past. Jason Bourne stared at them. They all looked at his face and his gun—just an advertisement for the latest Jason Bourne movie. It was the largest advertisement Aaron had ever seen, covering the whole bus.

"He's my brother, you know," Mel said.

Aaron turned to look at Mel. Oh no . . . here we go again. No. Be positive.

"Mel Bourne? Geddit?" Mel continued. "You know he has another movie coming, it's called *Bourne Again* . . . just another joke, more for Churchie, that one. But I can see that I may be wearing thin with you, young man, so I'll try and curb my humor."

Aaron grinned and agreed. Mel's comments were spot on and doubts came again about what he was doing. Did this man ever say anything serious? He had come across people like this before; it was all related to a nervous disposition.

But then Mel got serious. "I reckon this vanishing stuff is going to go on. People are already starting to say it's some publicity stunt. I suppose they're expecting one of the television stations to say it's a 'surprise' or what's that other show that used to be on . . .? Candid Camera. But I tell you, we'll see the same thing happen soon. There's something unfolding and I'm not sure what."

Aaron wasn't sure what to say. He looked at Churchie, who nodded.

"As Mel knows, I can see things, and I've never seen so much evil, so many demons. Something's definitely happening."

Aaron wasn't sure how to take this. It was like he'd stepped into another world.

They approached the well-lit park. Mel wanted to be cautious about it. He showed Aaron the bench he sat on. You could hear the comings and goings of the trains in Central Station. Aaron looked around—it definitely gave a good view of the station and the main intersection. The intersection was still closed off. He could just make out the blue and white tape enclosing the area. The bench gave a perfect view of the crossing, and Aaron imagined Mel sitting here talking to himself.

"Do you think it will happen again? You know, I don't even know your name."

"It's Aaron, and it may happen again but not down there. Maybe at another intersection. The people behind this want to prove something."

Aaron heard Churchie yell out. "There's Wally".

And Mel responded. "Where's Wally?"

Aaron wasn't sure whether to laugh or cry. He turned, expecting to see someone in a red-and-white striped shirt, bobble hat and big round glasses, but instead he saw a rough, bearded dirty-looking man heading towards them from the station below. He remembered back at base with some North Americans when a 'Where's Wally?' joke was told. None of the North Americans laughed. Aaron found out it was 'Where's Waldo?' over there.

Was it time for Aaron to make his exit?

* * *

They must have all been good mates, because there were hugs all round. Aaron was glad to be excluded.

Mel asked, "Where have ya been, mate?"

Wally didn't respond, but looked at Aaron.

"Don't worry about him. He is playing private detective looking for vanishing people," Mel said.

"Well, he'll want to hear what happened to me, and he'd better believe it. I ended up in the bush, middle of nowhere and I don't know how I got there. It was pretty scary stuff—lots of strange noises in the bush at night-time. Found an old hut which I stayed in but I got hungry. Eventually found my way out. I think I was going around in circles for a few days. A man gave me a lift. He was a painter."

"Another one to add to our vanishing list," Churchie said.

"Did you know where you were?" Aaron asked.

"No idea, mate."

They walked back down to Central Station. Aaron needed some time away from these men. He needed to take in the days' events. He thanked them for their time and told them he would chase them up if he came across anything. They were all concerned about the vanishings.

Aaron hoped it would be the last time he had to deal with this motley crew.

CHAPTER NINETEEN

THEY ALL WENT THEIR separate ways except for Churchie and Wally.

"You don't mind if I hang around with you for a little while?" asked Wally. "It's just that I'm feeling a bit anxious."

Churchie stared at Wally and raised his right hand towards him. He bowed his head and whispered some words. He then looked up. "Sure, Wal, come and hang around the church with me."

They grabbed a coffee each from one of the volunteer vans. Churchie waited for Wally to put some sugar in his coffee, and they headed over to the church. They got settled on the steps that led up to the main doors.

"You can't see it, Wal, but there's an angry demon down near the gate there. He can't get past the gate because the Lord has made this a 'demon free zone'. Do you feel any lighter? Because he is a big one."

Churchie saw Wally's confusion. "Tell me about yourself Wal. It might be good for you to talk about things." He nodded towards the gate, "That demon can't be good for you."

"You freak me out sometimes, Churchie." Wally stared at Churchie, then turned and looked up at the large wooden entrance doors. "You know, I'm not sure if I've ever been inside a church . . . is that where you find God?"

"That's a big mistake people make. Church is where people go to worship God, but God is everywhere, Wal."

Wally nodded. Scratched his streaked rusty-white beard, "Yeah, maybe one day I'll find him. I've made lots of mistakes too, a real

Wally. I always seem to make mistakes. The biggest one was being born, and since then the mistakes have just kept rolling in."

"That's rather negative stuff, Wal."

"Nah, it's just the truth, Churchie. There's one mistake which hangs around in my head a lot."

"And you can be sure, Wal, that thing down near the gate keeps reminding you of it."

"How does he do that, Churchie?"

"He puts those thoughts in your head. What does he say?"

"I should have been nicer to my mum's boyfriend."

"How weren't you nice to him?" Churchie asked.

"I told him I hated him quite a few times and I kicked him once."

"Why did you kick him?"

Wally started to fidget a bit, fiddling with the chest hair that stuck out of the top of his shirt. "He was hitting Mum."

"Well, I would have kicked him too."

Wally continued. "I yelled at him, told him to stop and then kicked him in the leg. He turned around and slapped me so hard I ended up sliding across the room."

"What did your mum do?"

"Nothing."

"Nothing?"

"Nothing . . . I think she was scared of him. She lived with him for a long time after Dad died. I tried to like him but I hated him. There came a day where Mum had to choose between me and the man—she chose the man, and I believed it was all because of me kicking him."

"Don't think so, Wal. She would have loved you, but was probably confused about life."

"But how could she do that to her own son? I was thirteen when I was shown the door. I remember standing outside the house, looking back at the house, the door closed. I ran back up the stairs and banged on the door. I yelled out saying how sorry I was, but there was no answer. And then the plan came."

This got Churchie's attention. He felt Wally was getting to the crux of the matter. "What plan, Wal?"

"I slept the night in the park. I had done that a few times before. I knew they would be gone to work by eight-thirty so I went back to the house. The shed's never locked, so I got in there and found some petrol. I went round the back of the house, poured petrol on the balcony and back door. I smoked, so I had matches. So I lit a match, threw it on the petrol and ran. At one stage, I stopped and looked back and I could see the smoke and could hear the sirens. I kept running.

"Did the whole house burn down?"

"No . . . I went back to the house later in the day. A few people were standing looking at the house. Only the back half was badly burnt, so I don't know what they were looking at. I heard my mum behind me, asking me if I was happy now and that I was a brat and belonged in hell. She slapped me in the face. After that I just walked away and kept walking. That was the last time I saw my Mum."

"How long ago was that, Wal?"

"Not sure." Wally thought about it. "Must be close to twenty years."

Churchie sighed. What had happened here? Why would a mother desert a child, put him out on the streets?

Wally was still speaking. "They found me a few days later, in the city."

"You know, Wally, you were screaming out for attention. No one was listening. The fire was your last call for help."

"I know, Churchie . . . I blended in to the streets after that."

Churchie put his hand on Wally's shoulder. "Can I say a short prayer for you, Wal?"

"Mel and I spoke about this a while ago. We've noticed that you're really getting into this prayer stuff. We aren't sure if it works but, I'm happy for you to pray for me."

"Lord, what a mess we have made of things. I bring Wally into your presence and ask that you may start a work in his heart so that the truth will be revealed to him. I also ask, Father, that you bring healing to his heart. Healing and forgiveness. I ask these things in the name of Jesus."

"Thanks, Churchie. That was nice. I suppose you believe in hell, too?"

"Yes, I do, Wally. Do you?"

"No, because if it's real, that's where I'm going. Then again, I sometimes think maybe I'm already there."

Churchie reached into his shirt pocket and brought out a small notebook. He held it up to Wally. "My favorite sayings. I write them down because my memory isn't that great." He flipped through a few pages. "Ah, here it is . . . a description of hell for you."

"Our Lady showed us a great sea of fire which seemed to be under the earth. Plunged in this fire were demons and souls in human form, like transparent burning embers, all blackened or burnished bronze, floating about in the fire, now raised into the air by the flames with great clouds of smoke, now falling back on every side like sparks in a huge fire, and amid shrieks and groans of pain and despair, which horrified us and made us tremble with fear."

Churchie closed his notebook and, putting it back in his shirt pocket, he looked at Wally. "Pretty gruesome, hey? That's a vision of hell given to three young Portuguese shepherds by an apparition of the Blessed Virgin Mary in the early 1900s. The Virgin Mary was the mother of Jesus."

"What's an appa . . . apparition?"

"A big word that I learned, Wal. It means a vision, supernatural ghost type of thing." Churchie felt that he was starting to make things hard to understand and wanted to back off.

"And people believe these things?"

"Well, there were three of them, children that is, and the visions are believed by the Catholic Church. Other visions are also recorded. But let's keep it simple, let me tell you what I believe . . . yep, I believe in hell. I think a vision of a sea of fire under the earth with demons and souls shrieking through groans of pain and despair is a good and frightening description. Although I'm still a bit confused about the difference between souls and spirit, I do believe there's an afterlife. We will live on forever either in hell or heaven."

They heard some footsteps coming from the gravel path on the side of the Church. It was one of the ministers from the Church. "Oh, hi Churchie, how are ya?"

"Fine Rev . . . is it okay for us to sit here? We are having a good chat about heaven and hell."

"Okay . . . no problems. There may be a few people coming out soon. We've just finished a Bible study. Pretty late finish tonight. Lots of questions, particularly about today's events, so you may need to let them squeeze past you." He reached out his hand to Wally. "I'm Peter, known as the Rev, and you are?"

"Wally."

"Nice to meet you, Wally. Listen to Churchie. He has a bit of knowledge there. I'm thinking of getting him up to preach one Sunday. Maybe you can come along and listen to him." The Rev winked at Wally. "Well, best be off, a few things I need to do."

Churchie looked at the Rev as he walked off. Since the time the Rev found him huddled up under the bush out at the back of the church, he and the Rev had spent many hours together, the Rev walking him through the Bible, always offering encouragement and telling Churchie how quickly he was picking things up. The Rev said God was doing a bit of work on Churchie.

He stood up. "Must get going now, let's continue our discussion later. It's good news that's coming next."

Wally stood up and stretched. His knees cracked. "Yeah, I got to shoot down to the shelter on Hope Street and confirm my sleeping arrangements. Maybe catch up with you later."

Churchie smiled about the name Hope Street. "Okay, see ya." He watched Wally walk off. The demon seemed to be hanging back a bit now.

* * *

Aaron collapsed on his couch in the living room. Wow, what a day and still not finished. He looked for the remote but couldn't see it. He pushed his hands down the side of the cushions and located the remote. He turned on the TV and was confronted by a news flash.

The body was spotted in a large tree by a bushwalker. Another witness said he heard someone yell and saw something fall out of the sky. It is has been confirmed that the body was one of those that vanished from the city earlier today. A search has commenced for other bodies.

Aaron's heart rate picked up, his muscles tensed, he sat forward. He hoped that wasn't Mackenzie or Paul and that there were no other bodies. No other bodies meant there was still hope.

And then it hit him. The body fell out of the sky. Dad must have fallen and hit his head. Why him? Was he in the wrong place at the wrong time?

* * *

A police officer man sat on a plastic chair staring at his takeaway coffee cup and the logbook that sat on the card table in front of him. His radio crackled about some severe storms out in the suburbs, some dropping huge hailstones. He looked around and found that hard to believe. He was bored: there hadn't been an entry in the logbook for some three hours. Everything was quiet and still.

The police officer sensed something and sat up straight. The pages on the logbook started flipping over and the coffee cup blew off the table. There came a humming noise followed by a popping sound. Figures appeared. The police officer was a Star Trek fan. What he saw reminded him of crew members returning to the transporter platform aboard the U.S.S. Enterprise.

They stood there covering their eyes, the strong lights blinding them. They searched out each other.

The police officer, on his feet now, stared at them. One of the people mumbled something about no sleepover, no bus trip, just lies. He spoke into his radio, then bent over and wrote in the log: *Entities returned 2300.* The sirens and alarms came soon after.

He saw lightening in the distance. Dark storm clouds were coming in from the southeast.

* * *

Churchie had Mel and Wally keeping him company. The city streets could be boring at times, but the incident site was out of the norm, so they headed in that direction. They heard sirens and noticed a commotion at the site. Before they knew it, there was a camera and microphone in their face.

"Are you some of the people that vanished?" asked one reporter.

Churchie wondered if reporters had common sense as the three of them were standing behind the blue tape with other observers. "Well, yes and no," Churchie said.

"What do you mean by that?"

"Well yes, we have vanished before, but no, we are not 'those people'."

The reporter took another look at the trio and shook his head to the cameraman and they walked off.

* * *

Although it was getting late, Aaron wasn't tired. He had just checked his text messages, subconsciously hoping to see one from Mackenzie. Apparently, they were unable to find the location of the missing people using their mobile phones, as their phones weren't emitting signals. The authorities believed some jamming device was being used.

Aaron got up from the couch, walked over to the fridge and started searching for something to snack on. The introductory theme for a news flash caught his attention, and he turned his attention to the television.

The screen showed a reporter interviewing some people. But it was the words travelling along the bottom of the screen that caught Aaron's attention. MISSING PEOPLE FOUND BACK AT ORIGINAL INCIDENT SITE. He looked up at the main part of the screen again and saw the reporter talking to the motley crew that he briefly hung around with earlier. Aaron smiled, as they looked like who they were—street people whom no one would believe. But he was excited because the missing people had returned. He grabbed his keys and sprinted out the door to see Mackenzie.

He passed the church on the way and saw Churchie sitting there. Aaron stopped and looked at him. "Are you okay?"

He turned and looked at Aaron. "Yeah, I'm fine, just came back from the hustle and bustle down there. I assume that's where you're going?"

"Yes. I want to see if my friend is okay."

"They're saying not everyone made it back."

Aaron swallowed. "What do you mean?"

"They did a sort of a roll call. I noticed a person crossing off names on a piece of paper. I heard one of the names called out but there was no response. It was noisy down there but I thought the name sounded like Macca."

"Mackenzie?"

"That could be it."

A wave of wrong thoughts started to attack Aaron. "Churchie, I hope you're wrong."

"I could be, Aaron."

Aaron just nodded. He left Churchie and started running towards the site. The crazy people, the gawkers were back. Aaron worked his way through the crowd. People were whispering, talking. Aaron saw the policeman from earlier in the day. He walked over to him."

"Hi, remember me?"

He looked at Aaron.

"I was here earlier today. I was the army guy that assisted you with moving a lady away."

The officer nodded his head. "Yep, I remember now."

"Could I ask a quick question? Have they all returned?"

"Not 100 per cent sure. It looks like two may still be missing . . . a girl and one other".

Aaron hoped otherwise, but he knew the girl was Mackenzie. He wondered who the one other was.

CHAPTER TWENTY

AARON WALKED AWAY FROM the site. He wasn't sure what to do. Dad's body lying in a car park, bodies in trees, Mackenzie missing . . . he wanted to slam up a barrier to stop the negative thoughts assailing him. Where could Mackenzie be? Was she safe?

As he walked near Churchie's usual abode, Aaron felt the ground moving. He turned to see a group of teens in a car, their heads moving in rhythm to the booming and thumping of some music. He wanted to tell them to turn their music down—it was distracting his thinking. What bugged him even more was that the pace of the car was in rhythm with his walking.

He saw Churchie, still sitting on the steps of the church, so went and sat with him to watch the exhibition pass. Aaron felt the thumping bass from the music vibrating through the cold concrete. Churchie shook his head in unison with Aaron as the car passed.

The vibrations were gone. The distraction passed.

"You were right, Churchie, some people are still missing, and one of them is Mackenzie." Aaron paused and rubbed his head. "I hope she's okay wherever she may be . . . I'm a bit concerned about the character she could be with."

"God commands his angels to guard his children, Aaron. Mackenzie's angel will be watching over her."

He still wasn't sure of this angel thing. He looked at Churchie. Hair trimmed, skin clean, clothes neat and tidy. Not Aaron's image of a homeless person. It was Churchie's eyes that moved Aaron—clear, radiating something. You wanted to look into them, dive into them, like a river.

Aaron pondered what Churchie said. He felt peace for a brief second, then his heart skipped a beat. "I hope you're not saying she is in heaven."

"Don't you think that's where she'd want to be, Aaron? She's a believer, isn't she?"

"Yes ... but—"

"Aaron. I don't know where she is. My angel doesn't either."

"But I assumed they would know everything."

"They don't, Aaron. Only God knows everything. But you need to know that she is being guarded."

Aaron's head was throbbing, his mind racing. Heaven, angels—this God stuff was confusing. He shook his head. He just couldn't get his mind around this stuff. Then something strange happened. It was like he heard a voice from down, way down . . . he wasn't sure where. Like way down in the depths of a stream . . . something flowing.

Stop trying to work things out. It wasn't a thought, it was a voice: a still small voice. He looked at Churchie.

"Are you all right, Aaron?"

Churchie's voice interrupted Aaron's inward focus. "I'm sure I just heard a voice within me . . . within my . . . soul."

Churchie smiled. "What did the voice say?"

"Stop trying to work things out."

Churchie nodded. "God is telling you to be still, Aaron. Distractions are the work of the enemy. Look around us. Our minds are constantly being bombarded. It never stops. Technology is working hard to keep our minds active. Not enough people are stopping to hear God's voice, stopping to smell the roses."

Churchie stood up and stretched and continued.

"Think of those people in the car that drove past. Their minds are being bombarded by meaningless lyrics, some that will stay with them all the days of their lives. You can see that yourself, Aaron. Listen for the words of old songs or jokes that drop into your head every now and then."

Aaron, now also standing and stretching, nodded in understanding.

"Your mind can't work out the things of God—the created can't advise the Creator. Let him tell you or show you his ways, but you need to be still."

"Okay . . . is she okay?"

"Yes, God is in charge. Let me pray for you."

Aaron felt Churchie's hand on his shoulder. Aaron tried to be still, but he didn't realize how difficult it was.

"Lord of heaven and earth, we come before you and stand in awe of your power and majesty. Give this man a spirit of wisdom and revelation, so that he may know you better. I ask, Father, that you protect his friend Mackenzie, a believer, that she would sense your presence and protection. I ask these things in the name of Jesus."

Aaron nodded his agreement. They both raised their heads. Aaron looked into Churchie's eyes. The river flowed, smoothly, quietly, with no booming or thumping.

It was time to go home. He sensed less urgency, as though realizing that he was a tiny thing in this vast universe—an ant. Was that God giving him wisdom, revealing he was but an ant? He understood. *We're out of kilter. Man thinks too highly of himself.*

He turned back and looked at Churchie. "How do you see those things?"

Churchie, now seated, indicated for Aaron to sit down again. "A good question . . . people think I'm crazy, but I do see angels and demons. You'd think it's something easy to prove but it's not. If I told you of a past event in your life that no one else knew, would you believe me? You'd be surprised—people need more than that. You know Jesus' disciples didn't really believe who he was even after the many miracles he performed. They were just as confused as you are, Aaron. "

Aaron nodded. "Good to know."

"His followers saw Jesus restore sight to the blind, raise the dead, and many other amazing things, yet it wasn't until after his resurrection that they saw Jesus for who he really was. Some followers had inklings along the way. Do you know what the first miracle was that Jesus performed?"

"No, I don't, Churchie, wouldn't have the foggiest."

"He turned water into wine."

"Good person to have at a party." Aaron regretted saying that.

"Sorry, Churchie, that was a stupid thing to say."

"It was, Aaron. I think God gave us wine as a pleasure but not something to be abused. Many forget that God's watching over them. I'm sure drunkenness and its consequences grieve the Lord greatly. Aaron, my dad was a drunk and he abused me terribly. I became a drinker and had a terrible accident. It's why I'm here. I have scars that are yet to be healed."

Aaron thought of his own father and the good man he was. A spasm of guilt hit him. He was fortunate to have such a dad.

Churchie continued. "I vanished one night, like the stories you have been hearing. When I returned something must have happened to the wiring in my head. Whatever technology they used did something to me. You know, we're a fragile species. Even the loud music those kids listen to can do damage at the cellular level, besides making them deaf."

This was concerning. Mackenzie, Paul, his own dad: the technology had impacted all of them. No, more than concerning. Things were getting dangerous, very dangerous.

"I started seeing someone or something hanging around me. I was petrified, but eventually learned that he was my guardian angel and he's been guarding me for years. That was over six months ago. The reverend of this church and my guardian angel have been teaching me all about Jesus, our great King. And with this, a feeling of peace that I can't explain has descended upon me."

Churchie dug around in his pockets, retrieved a packet of mints and offered one to Aaron. "Seeing these beings freaked me out, especially the demons. I can tell you what a frightening world it would be if God took away the controls that he has in place, because that's what hell is, Aaron—a place without God's presence or control. I still don't understand why I can see such things, but I trust the Lord and He is increasing my understanding day by day."

Aaron's sucked on his mint and looked around—invisible things flying around? Crazy stuff. His dad came to believe in all this and yes, he was a changed man. Aaron just never gave it much credence. You only believe the things you want to believe. *Be still, Aaron.* He couldn't. He wanted to know where Mackenzie was.

Churchie was looking at his mints but must have decided against another one. "Aaron, angels and demons have a greater influence on this world than most people are aware of. Something is happening in this city. More and more angels and demons are appearing. It is a war, Aaron, not one of flesh and blood, but a spiritual war against principalities, against powers, against the rulers of the darkness of this age, against spiritual hosts of wickedness in the heavenly places. That's from the Bible, Aaron and the battle is for our souls."

Some of this was hard to grasp. Aaron looked at Churchie—those eyes held a peace, like he was looking at somebody else, someone far greater than Aaron could ever comprehend. Churchie's eyes moved and looked at something above his shoulders. Churchie nodded.

"Aaron, the angel that has been with you has returned."

Aaron turned and was trying to work out where the angel was positioned. He moved his hand behind him. Felt nothing."

"Your hand went through him."

"What's his name?"

"Ethan."

"Does he know where Mackenzie is?"

"Yes, but he is the bearer of bad news."

* * *

Churchie struggled to keep up with Aaron, who was sprinting down the road. They reached the taped-off intersection, looked down the road, and saw the crowd gathering around another area. Aaron sprinted towards them.

Police were already pushing the crowd away. Aaron tried to squeeze through but was only able to catch a glimpse of what people were looking at. Two bodies lay on the ground.

Aaron gasped, covered his mouth and walked back. Churchie asked what he saw.

"Two bodies, Churchie. I'm sure one is Mackenzie . . . but they're not moving."

The emergency service vehicles arrived.

Aaron turned to Churchie. "You told me she was okay!"

"Calm down, Aaron. Remember, you were told by the Creator to be still. He's at work here but we don't know at this stage what that work is."

"That girl means so much to me and it looks like she's dead. So what could possibly be at work here?" Aaron stepped back and sat on a concrete bench. "I'm not sure about this religious stuff, Churchie. I'm sorry . . . this proves nothing to me." He placed his head in his hands.

Churchie heard the sobs. He placed his hand on Aaron's shoulder and said a silent prayer. Churchie's angel appeared beside him and they both looked towards the scene. Ethan was hovering over the bodies. He turned and came towards them."

Ethan settled next to Aaron. He stared at Aaron then turned towards Churchie and his angel. He spoke.

"Their spirits have departed, but to where, I do not know."

Churchie was glad Aaron couldn't hear that.

The police now had the crowd under control and the site taped off. Churchie watched as Aaron put on a brave front. White sheets covered the bodies. Mackenzie's parents had arrived and Aaron told Churchie who they were. Aaron was doing his best to console them.

"Churchie."

He turned to see the Rev coming towards him. Churchie stood up and walked towards the Rev.

"What's up?" he asked the Rev.

"Strange things are going on, Churchie. I have had a revelation from the Lord about these people. The Lord will raise them to life and restore their souls. It is for His glory, and also His timing. But for now, I need to go and pray for these people."

* * *

The Rev had an urgency about him. Churchie walked with him as he made his way to the taped off area. A police officer watched as they approached.

"Can I help you, gentlemen?"

"I'm a Pastor and I would like to pray for these people." The Rev had his wallet out, showing his identification.

"But they're deceased."

"That's okay. I'd still like to pray for them."

The Rev noticed a man standing close by, listening in on their conversation. The man tapped the Rev on the shoulder. The Rev turned.

"Hi, I'm James Gordon, the father of one of the victims. Could I have a word with you before you pray?"

"Certainly." They stepped back.

"Pastor, my wife and I are Christians. I'm a bit confused about your request for praying for my daughter as it appears she is deceased and it would now be too late to change anything. Besides, although we are hurting, we are at peace knowing she's with the Lord."

The Rev was nodding his head. "I agree with you. And it's not something I would normally do. But the Lord has put something on my heart and I don't find this easy to say, but I believe the Lord wants to bring these people back to life."

The Rev was overwhelmed with what God had put on his heart and could only imagine this man felt the same, but most probably at a much deeper level.

Mackenzie's dad rubbed his head. "Bring people back to life?" He looked at the bodies and then returned his gaze to the Rev. "I don't know what to say. Yes, I'm a man of faith, but stand here confused. Do such things happen?"

"Yes, believers in Asia, Africa, and South America do this, and there are recorded miracles of people being raised from the dead. But we in western society don't pursue this as actively as those in other countries. Why? I'm sure there are many reasons and one could be that we don't do it because we don't believe."

The Rev paused. They all needed to take in what was happening. Some people—window cleaners, perhaps—abseiling on the next building caught the Rev's attention. See how much confidence they had in those ropes. How much confidence do we have in God? This poor man was really being put on the spot, just like the Rev.

The Rev continued. "I don't want to give you false hope, but I felt strongly that the Lord has spoken to me. It's not something that happens frequently. I rarely hear the Lord's voice. But I have with this situation and when the Lord speaks, you know it."

James Gordon looked at the bodies again. "I don't want to displease the Lord by doing something that is not right."

"I agree and I don't treat this lightly. The Lord has put this on my heart and in a powerful way. I would displease him if I was not to do what he has requested. Please, the last thing I want to do is add to your grieving. I don't know what the Lord has planned. Maybe it will be plain for us to see, maybe not."

The abseilers were now on the ground, feet on solid rock. Their ropes proved themselves and they survived their task. They looked over at the Rev and the crowd, and started tidying up their ropes. There was so little proof of what the Rev was asking.

James Gordon turned to walk off. "Let me talk to my wife."

The Rev watched as he walked over to his wife. After a brief discussion they both came back. Aaron followed behind them.

James introduced his wife to the Rev. "We have decided that praying for the deceased would serve no purpose. We know where Mackenzie has gone and trust the Lord. Although we would dearly love to have Mackenzie back, we understand it is up to the Lord and we believe he does not want us to communicate with the dead."

"But . . . what about the other person?"

"They also have chosen their destination," James said.

The Rev was disappointed. "I understand and will abide by your wishes."

"Thank you." James comforted his wife as the tears began to flow. "We will miss her very much but know that she is with the Father. We do thank you for what you were willing to do."

The Rev watched them walk off.

The Rev hadn't expected this. He was convinced God had wanted him to pray for the people to be raised up. He sensed a presence next to him. Churchie. He gave him a brief smile, then turned back to watch Mackenzie's parents as they headed off.

The Rev felt distraught. He was tapped on the shoulder, "Rev." He faced Churchie.

"There's something strange going on. There are angels and demons around the bodies. They look like they're in a confused state."

"And so am I! What does your angel advise?"

"He says they've lost the souls of those people."

"What does he mean by that?" He thought of what the Lord said to him about restoring their souls.

"When people die, the angels come to take the believer's spirit to be with the Lord and the demons come to escort the unbeliever spirit to a place of torment. But those people? Their souls aren't here."

The Rev took this in. He was aware of such activity in the Bible. There was truth in what Churchie was saying. He looked over at the bodies, imagined the unseen angels and demons hovering over them. What did the angels and demons look like? He said a quiet prayer to the Lord and asked what he was meant to do now, for he didn't want to go against the commitment he just made to the parents and he didn't want to go against the Lord.

No immediate response came. He would wait upon the Lord.

The Rev saw Mackenzie's dad walking back towards them. The Rev's heart lifted. But James Gordon walked over to the police officer. The Rev was in hearing distance.

"What is going to happen next?" James Gordon asked the police officer.

"What will normally happen is that the bodies are moved to mortuary where they'll be formally identified. I say 'normally', because events surrounding these deaths have been strange."

The Rev knew an autopsy would need to be performed and sensed the officer's goodwill in not mentioning that.

"Do I need to go the mortuary?" asked James.

"Yes, if you're going to formally identify one of the victims."

* * *

Midnight was close. Litter from the work day bounced and tumbled down the street, helped along by a slight breeze. Aaron heard the faint sound of machinery coming from another street. Probably street cleaners. He sat in a landscaped area just outside the foyer of a large commercial building. The seat was out of the wind and gave him a good view of the goings-on. He felt like he was watching a movie as the scene unfolded before him.

His soul mate lay there, dead. It felt like part of him had been removed. He had attempted to comfort Mackenzie's parents, but it was really the other way around. What is it with faith? He was sure they were as devastated as he was, yet they managed to display some kind of strength.

He watched as James walked away from the police officer. What had they spoken about? James came back to his wife and they headed towards Aaron. He could see Mackenzie's features in Kathy's face. She walked up and hugged Aaron.

"Be strong, Aaron." She stepped back and looked at Aaron. "We love you, Aaron, just like Mackenzie loved you . . . we'll be in touch. Are you okay?"

Aaron swallowed hard. "What happens now, Kathy?"

James spoke. "There's a formal process that needs to be followed. Then they will release the body." James placed his arms around Kathy. "We're both tired, so we're going to make our way home. We'll be in touch, Aaron. You look after yourself."

"I will." He shook James's hand and gave Kathy a hug.

What would happen now? A process would be followed. Life was a process—birth, death. It's all about process. They would perform an autopsy, work out how she died and then put the body in a box. But he knew how she died and people were going to pay for it. The technology will be found and handed over to the appropriate people—the technology and those involved with it had killed Dad, Mackenzie and Paul. They are accountable and will pay for it. Nothing was going to detour Aaron from this objective.

* * *

Windsor had a miniature camera installed in the lift. Government ministers could do that sort of thing. He only viewed the camera footage when he had visitors, so as far as Windsor was concerned he was not breaking any privacy laws. Besides, it was a security matter anyway.

Starkey was in the lift. Windsor watched as Starkey pressed the elevator button for the sixth floor. Starkey was bent over trying to read some scribbling above the elevator buttons. Windsor knew it was a phone number with some crude suggestions after it. It was meant to have been removed but the cleaners had taken their time getting rid of it. It did not look good for the image of the apartment block.

Starkey looked annoyed and Windsor understood. It was past

midnight and well past Starkey's bedtime. He would not keep him here for long.

Windsor welcomed him. Yes, Starkey was jumpy and tense.

"Couldn't this have waited until tomorrow, Grant? I don't believe being at your beck and call was part of the arrangement."

"Take a seat and calm down." Windsor paced the room. He was also jumpy and tense. "We are now responsible for the deaths of a number of people. This is not good. Why are these things happening? It seems the technology is a bit flaky."

Starkey shook his head. "Losing people is not good. I know that. I'm looking into it and will fix it." That didn't sound confident. He continued. "We've lost so much expertise with the fire and the deaths of those fine young men. But it might be something simple, like weather conditions. There have been electrical storms floating around recently."

"That's nice of you to bring up the subject of more deaths. I'd tried to forget about that fire."

"Sorry, Grant. But they would have helped. As I said, I will fix it."

"I know you'll fix it, Bruce. But people are dead, and we'll be in big trouble if they trace the technology to us."

"We may be, Grant. But there are only a few of us who know about the technology. And we should be thankful about the fire— that's removed any references to the technology."

Windsor ignored Starkey. "They won't listen to us now. Yet we can offer many something that they long for. We can get people to obey laws, not disregard them, and through that we'll save many lives. We can get people back to doing the right thing through fear, for we know fear is the beginning of wisdom."

"That's the fear of God, I believe. I remember reading that somewhere and it struck a chord with me."

"My, you are a wise man. I think fear pushes you in a direction, whether it be God or snakes or sharks. So fear is the beginning of a decision process. I think people fear snakes and sharks more than God."

Starkey's grumpiness seemed to have departed. "I just read about a wise man. He'd been bitten by a venomous snake but instead of getting to a hospital, he stayed home to watch a show on TV that he didn't want to miss. It was only when the headache and cramps set in that he got himself to hospital."

"You go off in tangents sometimes, don't you, Bruce? That man's wisdom is debatable, and it also shows you another controlling mechanism: television. People are weak and easily-led, and that's why we have to do what we have to do. We'll convince the people that they need to obey us, and excuse the arrogance, they will. Our way will lead them to a better and fulfilling life and love thy neighbor will rule again. How can they resist?"

Starkey went quiet. He sat there and just stared at Windsor.

"Everything okay, Bruce?" A twinge of doubt entered Windsor's head but he shut the thought down before it penetrated too far. Now other thoughts attacked him. Was he starting to go off the rails. Was he losing the plot? Maybe there never really was a plot, just a vague idea that two people used to advance their own causes. And maybe those causes weren't clear either. Maybe. He shook his head and told the negative stuff to get out of his head.

"But how are we going to get people on our side?" Starkey asked.

"That's the question, Bruce. Let's find the answer." Windsor felt tired.

CHAPTER TWENTY ONE

AARON WAS NOT TIRED. They were into the early hours of a new day. Stragglers wandered past the church, some barely able to walk. The occasional car drove past. Aaron and Churchie had headed to their homes, with Aaron deciding he would sit with Churchie for a while, as he doubted he would sleep much.

"I'm angry, Churchie."

"Why, Aaron?"

"Because someone is playing around with lives."

"I'm angry too," said a voice above them. Aaron looked up to see the Rev staring down at them.

"Mind if I join you both?"

Churchie smiled. "No worries, Rev." The Rev made himself comfortable on the step below them.

"I haven't actually met you," the Rev said to Aaron.

Aaron put out his hand. "Aaron. And I know you are the Rev. Your friend here has told me all about you."

They shook hands.

"Whatcha angry about, Rev? Churchie asked.

"Maybe angry is not the right word." The Rev paused. "I believe God has spoken to me in a powerful way, and I'm struggling with how to deal with it."

Aaron's mind was on Mackenzie. He felt empty, as though he wanted to shut down, disconnect from the thoughts invading his head. Aaron thought about the still, small voice he heard earlier. "Do you actually hear God's voice?"

The Rev turned to watch some people walk past on the footpath below. He turned back and looked at Aaron.

"Aaron, God communicates with believers in a number of ways. Maybe you read something in the Bible that gives you a kick. Or maybe people, or circumstances, trigger something. And sometimes it's a still small voice that you sense but don't hear—maybe a clear thought."

Churchie jumped in to remind Aaron. "There ya go, Aaron. That's what you experienced before, when you got told not to try and work things out."

Aaron nodded and gave Churchie a half smile. "I already thought about that, Churchie." He turned to the Rev, "I think I can relate to the still small voice."

"Yes, Aaron. Some call that the voice of peace. Peace normally flows with it. But then there's the actual voice of God. I had never heard it before, but I did today. It's like an actual audible voice. It not only comes with peace but also power and the conviction that you need to act upon what was said."

Aaron had reached the point where he didn't know what to think anymore. In his mind, an image of Mackenzie stood before him. He closed his eyes and felt an arm on his shoulder.

"May God's peace be with you, Aaron."

He looked at Churchie. Aaron felt zapped. Where had his energy gone? Even to think was an effort. He would welcome God's peace.

"Thank you, Churchie."

"Rev, what did God say to you?" Aaron was glad that Churchie asked the question because he had run out of steam.

"He told me, 'You are to pray for two bodies that appear today. They are not dead but soulless. You are to bring them back to life and restore their souls. It is for my glory. It is for revival.' That's it."

Aaron felt a quickening in his heart. "Are you for real, Rev?"

"I am."

"Do such things happen?"

"Yes. We talk about the powers of a supernatural God, but do we actually believe it? There are examples of people being brought back to life. But I believe God does it for His glory and for a particular reason. Because, if you think about it, we're sojourners on our way home—when you get there, heaven that is, why would you want to come back? Unless God had something that he wanted you to do."

A surge of energy filled Aaron's emptiness. He noticed Churchie looking at him. Did he expect some kind of response? Sojourners? He sometimes got totally lost when these spiritual people got into their discussions—it sounded like another language. The thought of Mackenzie being brought back to life freaked him out, but also planted a glimmer of hope.

"Did you pray for them, Rev?" asked Churchie.

"No. I need to get close to the bodies so I can lay hands on them. But there's a larger problem. The parents wouldn't allow me to pray as they believed it would serve no purpose."

"Mackenzie's parents?" asked Aaron.

"Yes."

"Why wouldn't they?"

"Because they believe that God wants us to pray for the living, not the dead."

* * *

James could hear the sound of a dog barking.

A newspaper lay on a small table on the back porch. James Gordon picked up his orange juice. A droplet from the condensation build up at the bottom of the glass fell on to the newspaper. It landed on a paragraph in the main news story. James Gordon watched as the paper absorbed the moisture, highlighting a sentence. It was a quote from the Reverend Peter Thomas that a reporter must have heard, about bringing Mackenzie Gordon back to life.

Kathy Gordon stood there with a cloth, looking at the highlighted words.

A mobile phone lay on the table. It started to vibrate.

* * *

Aaron had to do what he was doing. He'd taken the day off work—the boss was okay with him taking off any time he needed. He waited for his phone to be answered.

"Hi, Kathy. It's Aaron here."

"Hello, Aaron."

"Sorry to disturb, but I was wondering if I would be able to drop by and see you both."

"One moment, Aaron."

Aaron knew that Kathy would be checking with James.

"That's fine, Aaron. We'll see you when you come by. We have no plans except for later this morning. When were you thinking of coming?"

"On my way now."

About an hour later Aaron pressed the doorbell. Aaron could see a shadow approaching through the door's frosted pane—James. He hoped that James could not see through the door as there were a number of shadows outside. James might not open the door.

The door opened.

"Hello, James. Sorry to bring uninvited guests with me, but I believe it's really important that you listen to what we have to say."

Was James going to let them in? Kathy walked up to his side.

James spoke. "Aaron, you know this has been a traumatic time. And later this morning it's not going to get much better as we need to go to the mortuary. So I hope your visit is not going to add to our grief."

Yes, it was a negative response, but Aaron expected it. "Please, hear us out."

Aaron watched as Kathy touched James's arm and nodded to him. Kathy's touch seemed to release some of James's tension. He relented. "Okay then, come in."

They were led down the passageway and into the living room, where two comfortable couches greeted them. Kathy gestured towards a three-seater couch while she joined James on the smaller couch. Aaron sat between his uninvited guests. He tried to ignore the pictures of Mackenzie that hung on the wall and sat on the buffet.

"I believe you may have already met the Reverend Peter Thomas." They nodded. "And this is Churchie."

Aaron sat forward. "You know that I'm not of the same cloth of you both, I mean in terms of my religious beliefs. But can I tell you my beliefs have been challenged of late. There's been strange goings-on in the city for the past six months or so. Somebody's been experimenting with technology. The same thing, the vanishing, that happened to Mackenzie has happened to this man here." Aaron pointed to Churchie. "I also believe the technology was involved in my dad's death."

They all looked a bit puzzled by that last statement. Churchie let out a little cough. Aaron guessed he was feeling uncomfortable.

Aaron continued. "And it's happened to others. Churchie is a street person and a few of them have been used as guinea pigs. The technology appears to be unpredictable, but the operators are still playing with it and with devastating results. We need to stop them."

Kathy placed her hand on James's lap.

Aaron looked toward Churchie, then back to James and Kathy. "What I'm about to tell you, you will find hard to believe. But, please, try," Aaron said as he let out a dry cough. He turned and looked at the Rev, who gave Aaron a nod.

"Churchie isn't the same now. It's a result of the technology doing something to him. It's flicked some kind of switch and he now sees things."

Kathy looked at Churchie. "Sees things?" she asked.

"Yep. I can see angels and demons."

Aaron watched James's response to this. James closed his eyes and started rubbing his forehead. "Aaron—"

"Your dad's name is George," Churchie said.

They would believe Aaron told him that. "Churchie, you're going to have to find something better than that."

James was now standing. "I think—"

"Okay, here's something Aaron wouldn't know. Angels communicate. You spilt something on your morning newspaper and it landed on some words about bringing Mackenzie back to life."

Kathy had placed her hands over her mouth and turned to James. James took her hands and rubbed them. "I think it's true, James. He can see things unseen. Do you have news of Mackenzie? Has she gone to be with the Father? Is she in heaven? Is that why you have come around, Aaron? Bless you, thank you."

"No, it's only part of it, Kathy. Please hear the Rev out."

They all looked in the direction of the Reverend Peter Thomas.

"It's to do with bringing Mackenzie back," the Rev said.

James stood upright. "I don't know if we want to discuss this again. We told you before. We don't believe it would serve any purpose."

"But God does and that's why he wants to do it. Not us, but Him. He wants to do it. And He has told me that. Please, if you believe Churchie can see things unseen, please believe me. I heard the voice of God, and He told me that He wants to restore life to those two bodies."

"But is that biblical?"

"Jesus told us to heal the sick, cleanse the lepers, raise the dead, cast out demons."

"But didn't he also tell us not to communicate with the dead?"

"That's not what we're doing. We're laying hands on the deceased and seeking God's direction. We are letting God do what He wants to do. And He has told me He wants to raise these people. It is not for us, it is for Him. He has plans."

Silence pervaded the room.

The Rev stood up. "Could I suggest that we pray for God's guidance here? I only want to please Him and to do what is right for you people. I need your permission to pray over Mackenzie."

The Rev walked over to Kathy and James and placed his hands on them. The Rev bowed his head. Aaron did the same.

"Heavenly Father, creator of life, I have heard your voice and want only to please you, but I also want to do the right thing for my brother and sister here. I ask that you put peace into their hearts so that they may also believe in what you have planned. I ask these things in the mighty name of Jesus."

Aaron thought it would be okay to raise his head but the other heads were still bowed. He watched as Kathy slowly raised her head. There were tears on her face, and she held her husband's hand. He had also raised his head and was looking towards the Rev.

Churchie was standing, swaying, like he was dancing with his angel.

James and Kathy exchanged quiet words, then James spoke to the Rev. "It is done. You can come with us to the mortuary this morning. And my, the world will be a different place today if these bodies are raised back to life."

Part Four – To the Realm and Back

CHAPTER TWENTY TWO

SILENCE. MACKENZIE HAD FALLEN from somewhere.

Where am I?

She needed to sit up. *Lord, be with me.* She could hear faint sounds, screams, shouts. She turned in the direction of the sounds and saw what looked like a solid wall, its color the darkest black she has ever seen. The wall was pulling her, like a black hole sucking things in. Yes, the blackness beckoned her, but she knew that wasn't where she belonged.

"Help me, Jesus," she whispered.

Ignoring the darkness behind her, she stood up and tried to take in her surroundings. Outside, it was night-time, a grayness with no colors. The moon and stars provided ambient light. Her eyes adjusted. She wondered if this was what Aaron saw when he wore army night vision goggles. Out there looked like the normal physical world, a paddock, trees with branches swaying, fences, mist. But there were no sounds.

I wish it wasn't night-time. Brightness came; she saw color and movement, God's creatures coming out of their slumber. *Is it morning?* She thought she heard some kind of positive response to her mental question. She turned to her left—an endless white passageway. Turning to the right, the same, except she saw movement, a figure approached, just a blur. Mackenzie felt no fear. The figure quickened; it must have seen her.

"Hello . . . hello," the figure shouted.

She waited as the figure approached, and watched as a form took shape. She saw that it was one of the men from the 'transit' group, the one who wasn't nice to them, who was a bit different.

"Hello . . . do you know where we are?" Mackenzie asked.

"No idea. Are you okay, not hurt anywhere?"

Mackenzie was surprised by his question; there had been no sign of a caring nature with the group. "No, I seem okay."

They both stared ahead of them, not down the passageway, but out into the world that was presented to them. They could see things—it was like watching the world on a big screen—a fenced paddock, trees, cows. Just past the fence line, the grey bitumen of a road stood out against the greenery. A few cars passed. A cow came towards them, stopped, bent down to chew some grass, then it looked up and continued its stroll. It walked straight through them. They turned to see where it went but the darkness obscured their view.

"It's like we're in some kind of tunnel." The man turned. "I'm not sure about the darkness there. I got close to it when I tried to avoid an oncoming car. It felt like something was trying to lure me in there."

Mackenzie nodded. "I agree. I'm sure I heard screams coming from there. They were faint, as though they were coming from a distance away." She looked down the passageway. "Where do you think it goes?"

She sensed movement and saw a flock of galahs flying straight at them. She ducked and bumped up against the man. The birds flew through them. Mackenzie felt nothing, and realized that she didn't feel any physical contact when she bumped the man either. She stood back and touched his arm. Again, she felt nothing.

The man looked down at her hand. "I think we're out of the physical world."

Mackenzie stood there staring at the man. "Maybe we've ended up in some kind of spiritual dimension."

Mackenzie was excited; she had no fear. Was that possible? There was a clarity in her thinking—no clutter here, no worldly preoccupations. Her thoughts were crystal clear, solid and direct. She looked at the man. She hadn't wanted to be anywhere near him at the other place but this felt different. "I think our senses are different in this world or whatever you call it. Maybe we should explore the passageway."

The man nodded. "Maybe . . . there wasn't going to be a bus trip. They did a transfer on us . . . I think something went wrong with the transfer technology, so we've ended up here. Maybe this passageway is what we got transferred along but normally wouldn't be aware of. Maybe we got off the train too soon, got off at the wrong station. If so, they'll be trying to fix it and locate us."

Mackenzie thought about Paul. She hoped that maybe he'd got off at the wrong station too, and that they would soon meet up.

"Lots of 'maybes'. I hope you're right about them trying to locate us."

"So am I." He raised his hand and pointed to the front. "I noticed the passageway moves with you. If you walk to the front, the passageway advances. Look at that large tree there, and see that it has a sign on it, too far away to read. Watch."

Mackenzie watched as the man walked toward the tree. She was being left behind, so followed him. The passageway moved with them. The tree got larger and the words got larger. 'Private Property. Stay Out.' She wondered about the opposite direction.

"How do we go the other direction? How do we get back to where we started, where we couldn't read the sign? The idea of walking into the darkness doesn't appeal to me."

"A good question. A remote control with a rewind button would come in handy," he said smiling. "I think this passageway has its own navigation system and we just need to work it out. Maybe the passageway detects your presence and anticipates things."

"It's funny—we can't see what lies behind us here. It's the opposite in our world, where we can't see what lies ahead of us. Does that make sense?"

"It does. It would be nice not to see, not to remember what lies behind us."

"Sorry, I didn't mean that to be a negative."

"That's okay. I'm getting over it. But to be honest, I feel a lot lighter here. No negative thoughts have attacked me. But back to your question, how do we go back?"

"Another thought, I believe that we're in some kind of spiritual dimension. I always relate thoughts to the spiritual world. Maybe we just need to think what we want to do or maybe say what we want to do—words translate to thoughts." She remembered something strange happening when she wanted night-time to go away.

"Besides, we have voice commands on our smartphones in the real world, so I'm sure we're in a much more advanced place here. But in reality, I really do believe that what we think will happen, because I believe in a God who is in charge of all these things and I trust him and I think he gave me a demo before. So our words or thoughts may be the key. Let's try it."

The man seemed to be analyzing what Mackenzie just said. "A demo?"

"Night-time to daytime." Mackenzie gave him the go-ahead. She moved her hand indicating he should do something.

The man shrugged his shoulders. "Back," he said, and the passageway did exactly that, but Mackenzie stayed behind.

"Stop," he said and the passageway stopped.

Mackenzie walked up to him. "It works, but I think we need to include the word "together" so we move as a unit."

The man nodded. "You're right. It really is simple, isn't it? Really, we're just telling some powerful, higher intelligence what we want to do and it happens." The man smiled and shook his head. "Wow!"

Mackenzie stared at the man. He seemed to be in his element, in an environment that offered different rules and laws, maybe new beginnings, all things that her Lord provided. She asked the Lord for strength and understanding and praised His mighty name.

"Maybe others have also ended up in here—let's go and look for them. We might find a way out."

The world of nature ambled on outside in silence. Inside, silence also surrounded them, no ambient sounds except for the occasional sucking sound accompanied by faint screams.

"By the way, my name is Joshua."

"Mine's Mackenzie." She thought about keeping her guard up with this man, but the thought dissolved before it had any time to linger. Such thoughts didn't belong in the environment they had found themselves in. It was like wrong thoughts had nothing to attach themselves to.

"All tunnels go somewhere. Wonder where this one goes?"

"I'm sure we'll find out," Mackenzie replied.

They passed what looked like a winery. Wallabies fed on the lush grass that lined the grapevines. A few meters on, they saw flashing lights. It looked like a car accident. Joshua walked right up against the invisible wall, Mackenzie beside him. The wall moved forward with them, so they stepped forward again, closer to the accident.

They watched an emergency worker leaning over a man, pressing his chest down and up.

"Show us what happened here, please." Mackenzie asked.

Joshua turned to Mackenzie as if to respond.

Mackenzie pointed toward the scene; Joshua turned.

They saw a car driving up the hill and a four-wheel drive coming down the hill. The four-wheel drive moved over to the wrong side of the road, the driver distracted by something, his eyes off the road. They heard the impact.

Mackenzie felt a wave of bad vibrations. The emotions of those involved, perhaps. "Back, please. This is unsettling and too hard to comprehend."

The present returned. Mackenzie and Joshua saw others coming to the aid of the emergency worker. They watched as the emergency worker stood up, shaking his head. It was like watching a television show. Could she do anything? It looked like the person had died.

They heard voices singing, indescribable singing, like worship. They saw blurred figures coming. Mackenzie sensed a peace that she had never experienced before. Three angelic beings came into focus, circling the person lying on the ground, and then something departed from the person. The angels encircled their arms around the entity, and then they were gone.

Joshua looked at Mackenzie, "What was that?"

"I think we just witnessed what happens at death. I would also say that person was a Christian, and is now in good hands." It was a privilege to witness.

Mackenzie and Joshua left the scene and progressed further along the passageway. They passed a number of houses and entered some kind of business park. A large number of buildings occupied one area, and Mackenzie worked out that it was a hospital.

A splash-like noise caught their attention. They turned in the direction of the noise as bony green arms and legs penetrated the invisible wall and appeared in the passageway. There were three of them, and they carried something, a person. The beings sensed the presence of others and slowly turned and looked at Mackenzie and Joshua with their glowing red eyes. They returned their gaze to the dark side and floated in that direction, their torn and dirty robes flowing behind them. One set of red eyes had a last look at Mackenzie and Joshua before they pushed the person with them into the darkness and were gone. Screams came from the darkness, and then faded.

Mackenzie called on the blood of the Lamb. She felt no fear. "I think we now know for certain that hell exists, and it sounds like a place of torment."

Joshua seemed transfixed.

Not long after, they came across what appeared to be a retirement village where they encountered another death. Sadly, this person was also escorted to the dark place by the same strange-looking creatures.

"I haven't really thought about death," Joshua said.

"I'm a Christian, Joshua. I have thought about death, but not the way we're seeing things here. If anything, my faith is being consolidated."

"I think I'm a Christian too, Mackenzie."

Mackenzie was about to ask Joshua to expand on what he just said when they came across more flashing lights. This time it was police cars and they were blocking access into a park area. A small pocket of bushland looked to be marked off. They stopped and looked at the scene.

Mackenzie looked at Joshua. "Want to see what happened here?"

"May as well."

"Show us what happened here, please."

They saw a person staring up at a tree. Mackenzie looked up and saw the red shirt. She gasped.

Mackenzie found it hard but she wanted to see. They took it back further and saw Paul tumbling out of the sky, into the trees. Mackenzie bowed her head.

Voices and singing prompted Mackenzie to raise her head. Three angelic beings came into view, floating up the tree, circling the body that lay tangled in the branch, arms covering, enfolding. They were passing and one angel looked towards Mackenzie and spoke to his companions. Two angels floated up with Paul and were gone. The remaining angel came towards Mackenzie.

"Do not be afraid. I am one of the ministering angels sent by God to protect one of his chosen ones in life and death. The chosen one has gone to sleep, and the other angels have taken his spirit into God's presence. But your presence here is not right. This passage separates the natural from the spiritual world. It is used to take the departed to be with the Father. You are here without your angels. How did you get here?"

"Sir, we aren't sure," Joshua said. "We were taken hostage by some crazy people with some new technology and they have been zapping us here and there. I, for one, have no idea what's going on and I'm not even sure if you're real."

"Oh, he's real," Mackenzie said. Why were there no tears? Instead, there were feelings of love, of peace.

The angel looked and smiled at Mackenzie. "The Father has revealed to me that you are one of His. He tells me that He loves you, Mackenzie, and you are not to fear, for this will all come to an end soon."

The angel turned towards the man. "But you young man, the Lord knows you and loves you and wants all to be saved. You are still under the condemnation of God because your sins have not been covered by the atoning blood of Christ. You can still be saved. Listen to Mackenzie: she will explain things to you."

The angel turned towards the dark side. "But, be warned. The dark side is where the souls of the lost go when they die. They do pass through a bright light, but it is on the way to a place of torment—there they stay until Judgment Day. You have been warned. Repent and be saved."

Mackenzie watched Joshua's reaction to this. She knew that he had been given a reprieve that many didn't get.

The angel turned to Mackenzie. "I must go now, Mackenzie Gordon. Your ministering angels are on their way. Mackenzie, it is not sad news, for Paul is with the Father now. It was his spirit we have just retrieved. You know for certain where he is and you know it is a better place. Be in peace about it. He is home."

Still no tears, but love and peace flooded her mind. There are no tears in heaven. She watched the angel float above their heads, and then depart. A thin veil separated them. She continued to watch as more mighty angels appeared.

"Hello, loved one. We are your ministering angels. We have been with your body, wondering where your spirit had departed to. You are away from your physical body at the moment. But the Father does not want that to remain. You will see us for but a short time. But know this: we will be with you forever."

An angel stood next to Joshua who had his head bowed and was shaking. Mackenzie walked over to Joshua. She prayed silently, thanking the Lord for starting a work in Joshua's heart. "Joshua, you have a lovely name. Did you know that the Greek translation of your name is Jesus? Let me tell you about him."

CHAPTER TWENTY THREE

AARON WATCHED A SMALL group of runners as they talked and ran along a path parallel to the Brisbane River. He watched as a colony of gulls broke up and flew to the sky when the runners came too close. Their squawk he had to imagine, as the car windows blocked out sounds from the outside world. He returned his gaze to Kathy, who now had her hand on James's lap as he drove the five of them to the mortuary.

Kathy had decided to give the passengers an update. "We were informed earlier that the coroner has requested that an autopsy be performed on our Mackenzie. So I'm glad we're going to get this thing done before that. I've told them that we would like to come in and pray for our daughter and the other person who were brought in last night. They were unsure about the other person, but said they'd check out if that was okay."

Aaron noticed that Kathy's enthusiasm was dropping off. Aaron understood. He was impressed by Churchie's abilities. He even believed they were supernatural, but like a drug, the effects wear off. Normality soon comes back. He knew Kathy and James would still be finding it hard and wondering if they were doing the right thing. They would all be glad when it was over.

"They're hesitant about who could come in and see the bodies, and would only allow relatives and the Reverend. I tried to get you in, Aaron, but they're quite strict on who could come in. Sorry, Churchie, the same goes for you."

Aaron shook his head in agreement. "I understand, Kathy. When you think about it, what has taken place over the past few days is quite extraordinary, and the investigation process is going to be complex and thorough. They won't want anyone tampering with the evidence."

"You sound so military, Aaron," Kathy said.

"Yeah, soldier boy, get a life," Churchie gave him a nudge. "It's okay by me, too, Kathy."

Aaron saw Kathy looking at Churchie in the rear-view mirror.

Kathy spoke. "You know Churchie, there's something about your eyes. You look excited. You really believe something is going to happen don't you? I have mixed feelings. I really didn't know what to think."

"It will be good, Kathy," Churchie said.

Kathy nodded her head slowly.

The high from Churchie's supernatural dose had all but gone now.

* * *

The Rev sat in the back seat, gazing at the river craft as they started their daily routines. He sensed Kathy was still not convinced about bringing Mackenzie back to life. He could understand that, because he had struggled with it. But the one thought that stayed strong in his mind was the Bible verse about God's power being made perfect in weakness. He asked God to help him to be weak in the flesh but strong in the Spirit.

Churchie, squeezed in between the Rev and Aaron, was full of enthusiasm. "And imagine what's going to take place when these bodies rise."

Good on ya Churchie. You're a man of faith.

They travelled in silence for the rest of the trip, each in their own world.

"Think it's coming up on the left," Kathy said.

The Rev looked at a pinkish two-story building, bordered by native shrubbery and high-security features. The indicator came on, they turned in and James parked the car. Kathy, James and the Rev got out of the car and headed towards the reception area. Just like a cemetery or crematorium, the reception area allowed visitors to be received in sensitively-planned surroundings. They walked up to the reception desk, completed the appropriate paperwork, and were guided into a meeting room. A mortuary attendant soon took them to the viewing room.

The room was cold.

Two stainless steel tables sat in the centre of the room each with a body fully covered in a white sheet.

The Rev stared at the bodies, pleased that both bodies were there. He'd left that for God to sort out.

* * *

Aaron and Churchie leaned on the bonnet of the car, their eyes focused on the main entrance. Aaron didn't know what to expect. A lot had been happening, and there was a lot to take in, but bodies being raised from the dead?

"What ya thinking about, Aaron?"

"Things unseen, Churchie." He smiled. "How do you feel about the dead being raised? What happens if it doesn't happen? How are Kathy and James going to feel?"

"Many questions, Aaron . . . if everyone could see what I see, they'd believe. The angels are messengers of God, Aaron, so I know there's a God and he's mighty. So I have no doubt he can raise the dead as he has created all things."

A line of ants caught Aaron's attention. "Has it happened before, Churchie?" Aaron watched one of the ants carrying something much larger that its size. How did it do that?

"I read something in the Bible about when Jesus was raised from the dead, the tombs broke open and the bodies of many holy people who had died were raised to life. The Rev also told me other examples of individuals being brought back to life—I'm sure you have heard of Lazarus."

"Yep . . . back from the dead like Lazarus."

"Aaron, there's something that you need to remember about these people that were brought back to life. They all died again, eventually. Jesus lives on forever, and so do believers in their next life—that's the thing called eternal life."

"Eternal life?"

"It's the body, Aaron. It's only a tent, a shell that carries something. The something lives on in heaven or hell while the tent returns to dust. This is what people don't believe, and that's why I say if you could see what I see, you would believe. There are angels and there are demons. There is good and evil. And there seems to be some kind of battle going on. I don't fully understand it but—"

"But, Churchie, I do believe there's more to life than what we see. It's just that I never got into the church scene. As my mum would say, it's just not my cup of tea."

"So do you believe you will spend eternity with God?"

"If you mean go to heaven, I would say yes, but I don't say that with confidence."

"But you can know for certain, Aaron."

Aaron sensed movement. He looked up to see someone coming out of the main entrance, but it was only someone coming out for a smoke.

"Don't know about that, Churchie."

"What's that, Aaron?"

"That you can know for certain."

"Oh, you can, Aaron."

Aaron watched the ants again. They just went about their job. They all had a role to play, just doing their part in cleaning up the mess of the world. There was no uncertainty there—they knew their purpose and went about it. Humans were different: most had no idea of their purpose in life. Knowing for certain where you end up when you die must tie in with knowing for certain why you were here in the first place.

* * *

The Rev stood there looking at the two bodies.

Kathy and James had formally identified Mackenzie. The other person was yet to be identified and the authorities were unsure if his body should remain in the room. But there wasn't much credence being paid to what was about to happen so they left the body there.

They all looked to the Rev as if to say it was his show now.

The Rev watched as Kathy and James sat down. The mortuary attendant stood in the background, her white coat blending in with the white walls. The Rev nodded to himself and walked over to the bodies. He stood between the two tables and placed a hand on each body.

"Lord, Father, I'm not sure how to go about this, but I know you are the giver and taker of life. You have put on my heart that you want to restore these people to life." He bowed his head and waited on the Spirit. He prayed softly.

"Holy Spirit, you are invited into this place. Holy Spirit, you are welcomed into this place." The Rev repeated these words a number of times. He then paused and waited in the stillness of the Lord.

And the Spirit came.

"Father, God, I cry out for the souls of these people, restore them, bring them back to life now in Jesus name." Peace came over him, and he felt in his heart that God had done something. He stared at the bodies for a few moments and then went and sat down. He looked over to Kathy and James, who were both staring at the bodies. He bowed his head and spoke to God.

"What happens now?" Kathy asked.

The Rev was silent. He whispered to Kathy. "I don't know."

They sat in silence. The bodies were still. The room seemed colder. They stared at the bodies, nothing. James let out a small dry cough that reverberated around the room, and then stood up to stretch his legs.

The Rev had his head bowed, still in silent prayer. He sensed movement and looked up to see James stretching. He bowed his head again. Doubt was trying to force its way in to the Rev's head but he believed God had done something. The Rev was not going to entertain any thoughts of doubt. His God was a God of miracles. He looked up at James again.

James raised his eyebrows to the Rev and turned to look at his wife. "I think maybe we should go now. It's getting a bit too cold in here."

"Yes, I'm getting cold," Kathy said. "Would it have happened by now?"

The Rev shrugged his shoulders. Were miracles instant? The Rev didn't know. Faith could be short-lived. "You two go for now. I'll stay a little longer."

Kathy walked over to Mackenzie's body. She turned and looked to the attendant, "Could I see her face one more time?"

The attendant came over and moved the sheet down to show Mackenzie's face.

Kathy stared hard and gave her a kiss. She started sobbing. "Open your eyes, Mackenzie, open your eyes. Please."

James came over to comfort her. "I think it's time we left." He helped Kathy to the door.

The Rev got up after they left. He walked over to the bodies and laid his hand on them again. "Father, open their eyes. Open their eyes to see Jesus." He stood there for another ten minutes, then felt the presence of the attendant.

"Sir, I think you need to go now."

The Rev nodded.

They walked towards the exit, and the attendant opened the door for the Rev. They both heard the sneeze at the same time, and looked back. Both bodies were moving, pushing the sheets away. The attendant screamed.

* * *

Aaron was looking at the cloud formation above the building. The clouds looked like cartoon thought bubbles. He lowered his gaze to see Kathy and James walking out of the building. He judged by their body language that nothing had happened. He sighed and turned to Churchie.

"What are you meant to believe, Churchie? Why would our hopes be built up like this?"

The entrance doors were full-length glass. Aaron thought he saw a figure inside, rushing towards the door. The doors burst open. Aaron's chest started thumping as the Rev came flying through the doors. Kathy and James were just near the car, when he yelled out. They turned back and ran.

Aaron looked at Churchie.

"Hallelujah," Churchie yelled.

Kathy and James were now near the entrance door. The Rev was pointing excitedly back inside the building. Churchie and Aaron moved quickly towards the door and managed to get inside before emergency procedures kicked in.

Aaron followed Kathy and James into the viewing room. He saw Mackenzie and another person wandering around, confused, bumping into tables. Attendants were wrapping them in sheets and trying to calm them down. Mackenzie looked in Aaron's direction but she was in a glazed state. The attendant didn't know what to do, but other workers came to her rescue. Aaron felt somebody's hand, and he was ushered out by a security guard along with everybody else.

They stood just outside the main entrance. Kathy and James were hugging each other, both crying.

Amazing. Aaron looked over at Churchie who was with the Rev. They had their heads bowed. Aaron walked over and stood beside them.

The Rev looked up and put his arm around Aaron. "God is at work, Aaron."

* * *

Absolute mayhem followed.

The Department of Defense, although at the periphery of the recent events, now became actively involved. They transported Mackenzie and Joshua to an undisclosed hospital.

Rumors started circulating. Towards the end of the working week the media started ramping up their stories. They tracked down the Rev and set up camp outside the church. Churchie avoided his favorite steps at the church and was bunking at Aaron's.

Many started to believe it didn't happen. They wanted proof. They didn't want to believe.

People were scared.

* * *

It was a cloudless Saturday morning. Windsor was at the property. He was spending more time with Starkey than with his wife. She didn't seem to care if he was home or not.

Old habits die hard. Windsor read the newspaper on Saturdays. Most of the week, when he had time, it was a quick glimpse of online news or reports from his staff. His Saturday paper filled in the holes of the week. He was keen to find out more about the two bodies that were supposedly raised from the dead. Bodies raised from the dead? It must be some kind of stunt. This time the media had gone too far. He read on. Someone they referred to as the Rev was quoted as saying:

"The Lord has spoken. This has been brought about due to the unnatural deaths of these people, and so many can see that God can raise the dead. It is not to be a common occurrence unless God seeks that. But there are many living now who are dead—God wants those to be raised to life."

He must be one of those radical Christians. God wouldn't raise the dead—maybe 2000 years ago, but not now. He got up and walked to the window and looked out. Some kangaroos were feeding on the grass, one with a little joey sticking out of its pouch. They all stopped eating, raised their heads and looked towards the front of the house. It was only a car, now stationary, no danger, heads back down. He heard the front door open and close.

Starkey walked in and glanced at the paper on the coffee table. "I know what you are probably thinking, Grant, but it's true. They have brought those people back to life."

"But how?"

"They believe God did it. But I think it must be tied in with the technology. And I'm sure that's where the media will eventually take this story. Somehow their bodies went into a hibernation state, you know, like they do in space travel."

Windsor just stared at Starkey. It was like God versus Star Wars.

"Whose side are you on, Bruce?"

"What do you mean?"

"God or Star Wars?"

"Star Wars. And isn't that the side you're on, Grant? Considering what you've done with your son?"

"Maybe you're right, Starkey. Maybe I'm on both sides, God and Star Wars. But this is one big distraction from our transportation technology."

"What's that?"

"Well, these people being raised from the dead."

"I'm not sure about that, Windsor. They may start thinking that the technology can be used to put bodies in a hibernation state. But I have no idea how that happened and how the bodies came out of it. Maybe the prayers of that man did bring them back. So the technology is irrelevant. But how do you prove all this?"

"It's a distraction," Windsor said.

"Well, we'll do another transfer. That will get the focus back."

But Windsor wasn't listening. A plan had started taking shape in his mind.

CHAPTER TWENTY FOUR

IT WAS A CRISP Sunday morning. King George Square was known as the ceremonial and civic heart of Brisbane City, but activity in the square was busier than usual this Sunday morning. There was an air of expectation.

It was still some time before the service start time. The Rev and the senior pastor of City Community Church were unlocking the arched doors, and pushing them open. Daylight invaded the inside of the church. What they saw next shocked them.

The Rev stood next to the senior pastor. What he saw reminded him of the days when he slept out for football final tickets. He walked down the steps to the footpath. He heard someone whisper, "That's him."

The people in the queue were smiling at him, so he smiled back. He walked down the queue to get an idea of how many people were here. Hundreds, all shapes and sizes. He greeted or nodded to those he passed.

He turned and walked back up the stairs. "We're full! At least 350 people lined up, and our regulars aren't even here yet."

"What shall we do?"

"I think we need to move the overflow to the deck in King George Square and hook up some audio and maybe video equipment. I'll get in contact with someone. In the meantime, I think we need to reserve seats for our regulars. I'll arrange it with one of the elders."

"Thanks, Peter. We'd be lost without you. Maybe it's a good thing you're preaching this morning—they may have booed me off."

The Rev smiled. He had grown used to his boss's sense of humor.

"Remember, we also had a call about a government minister coming along, so I suppose we better rope off some seats for his party."

"Will do." His thoughts went to his sermon, prepared as guided by the Spirit. The Spirit led him to a sermon by Charles Spurgeon about raising the dead. Very relevant, he thought and may surprise a few. He was going to touch on natural death, but his focus was on revealing the state in which all human beings are naturally found, that they are dead in trespasses and sins.

He went and sat in a pew. He looked up towards the high pulpit and prayed quietly to the Lord. *May the people in this congregation today have a clear sense of their utter ruin and spiritual death. Bring them out of their slumber, Lord. Restore them to life.*

* * *

Churchie told Aaron to meet him at a food van at the end of Wharf Street, near the river. He told Aaron that the food van was a soup kitchen where the homeless went for free food and drink. It was Churchie's favorite. A bakery provided tasty unsold baked goods to the van. Churchie was going to thank the owner of that bakery one day, and he told the volunteer workers this on a number of occasions

Aaron found his way to the food van and located Churchie. After all that had happened, Aaron decided to join Churchie and attend church with him. Mel and Wally were going to join them as well.

Although he struggled with hanging around with the motley crew, it wasn't hard hanging around Churchie: he at least made himself presentable and gave off a hint of intelligence. It was harder with the others—they caused Aaron feelings of discomfort, with Mel dressed and acting like a court jester and Wally getting in shape for a stint as Santa Claus. Aaron knew his attitude wasn't right but he didn't know how to change it. Was it to do with loss of honor or dignity or something like that? He hadn't quite worked it out yet. Mackenzie loved them all and didn't care what others thought. Why were people's attitudes so different? Was it in the genes? Where did the standard of who you should hang around with come from? He'd had a lot of these questions popping into his head recently. It was a worry.

He and Churchie perched on a bench not far from the food van. Aaron sat staring at the queue, both hands wrapped around his disposable coffee cup. He turned to look at Churchie who had just devoured a blueberry Danish lattice, with crumbs from his treat caught by his shirt. Aaron pointed this out, and Churchie brushed the crumbs away.

Aaron was becoming more aware of the mess in the world, of the battle going on. Good versus evil maybe. He was starting to see all the different charity organizations that fed and clothed the widows and orphans as being at the front lines of a war. He was also starting to see that humans were born into this war without even being aware of it. Were the commanders silent, or did people just ignore them?

Churchie waved to someone. Aaron looked to see that it was Mel and Wally standing in the coffee queue. Mel still had his red and blue cap on but looked neat, and Wally looked more respectable than the last time he saw him—less like Santa Claus.

After getting their coffees, they headed over to join Aaron and Churchie. They greeted each other and then made their way over to the church. On entering King George Square they saw a huge line on the footpath, starting from the church and heading well down the street.

"Wow," Churchie said. "Betcha they're all lined up for church. With all that has happened lately, people have become fearful and have come running back to church. Sad thing is, when things settle down and the fear dies off, they'll stop coming. The Rev told me they had their biggest attendances after the Brisbane floods some years back."

"Did he say why?" Aaron asked.

"He did . . . he said people seek comfort in faith when big dramatic things happen, where they have no control over things or don't know what's going to happen. But when things get back to normal, faith gets pushed to the background and it's business as usual."

Aaron understood this. He'd started seeking out faith when he went to Afghanistan and then forgot all about it when he returned home—except these recent events were prompting him to seek again.

"Hey, Aaron, we've gone from one food stall to another." Churchie pointed at the church building. "This is where I found the bread of life."

Aaron smiled and shook his head. This man would be standing in a pulpit one day.

* * *

The motley crew were used to queues; Aaron was not. He tried to take in the happenings around him. Young and old, lots of chitchat, kids running around and parents trying to keep them off the road. A chauffeur-driven car slowed down, as if it didn't want to run over any kids.

Aaron looked down the line and saw the Rev walking towards them and greeting those in the queue. The Rev paused and gave Aaron and the motley crew a brief greeting—no favorites. He told Churchie there were seats reserved for regulars, and he could squeeze his mates in. No favorites?

Aaron looked at Mel. He got the impression that Mel didn't like standing still, his eyes were darting around, obviously looking for some activity to keep him amused and it came.

"Hey, Churchie, did the Rev tell you about what happened when he painted this church?" Mel asked.

Aaron smiled. A 'Mel story' was coming.

"No, Mel, what happened?" Churchie seemed oblivious of what he was getting himself into.

"Well the Rev bought some white paint that was on sale. After he had painted one side, he realized he was going to run out of paint so he got some paint thinner and poured it in the paint. That made the paint last and he was able to paint the whole Church."

"That was good thinking," Wally said.

Mel continued. "Well it rained overnight, really poured. The next morning the Rev went to admire his work and the paint had been washed away. He stood there, and looking up to the sky, yelled out to the Lord in desperation, 'What shall I do?'"

"The Lord spoke back and said, "Repaint, and thin no more.'"

Aaron smiled and nodded. He heard someone in the queue laugh, obviously eavesdropping. Churchie thought it was hilarious and Aaron heard a few other eavesdroppers contribute to the giggling.

Churchie looked at Wally. Churchie had put his pastoral hat on. "Hey Wally, haven't you heard the saying 'repent and sin no more'?"

"No, not really. What does it mean?"

Churchie then put his arm around Wal. "I'm going to explain that all to you one day." He turned to look at Mel. "And to Mel, too."

"Repaint and thin no more." Mel repeated and that brought another round of laughter.

Aaron looked at Mel and chuckled. What a character. Aaron looked at his watch and noticed it was getting close to service time. They had been taking tiny steps and weren't far from the entrance now. He noticed a chauffeur-driven car pull up and watched as the occupants got out. As they walked up the steps to the entrance, Aaron saw that it was the big man, the minister, and his two thugs. Lucas had shaved off his goatee and moustache. He looked different. But Aaron remembered Lucas.

* * *

Aaron's fists were closed tight, his nails digging into his hand. He was trying to embrace the peace that he sensed in the chapel.

They were seated in the church thanks to their regular member, Churchie. Aaron looked around. It was a lot different to Mackenzie's church, smaller and more intimate, but the nice thoughts didn't last long. He was having a major battle with anger. He had an image of himself with a F88 Austeyr assault rifle, standing and scanning the congregation looking for the enemy. Not a good image for the church.

He had extended periods of calmness thanks to the Reverend catching his attention with his preaching. Aaron had decided that inside the church the Rev should be known as the Reverend. Although he only heard snippets of the Reverend's preaching, those snippets were good. Aaron's concentration floated between the Reverend, Mackenzie, and Lucas. The Reverend gave examples of physical restoration of life, but his focus was on the spiritual dead and Aaron sensed that he was one of those. He was confused and made a commitment to himself to talk to the Reverend about this one day.

The Reverend concluded with an update. "Our friends that God miraculous brought back to life are under watch in hospital and should be released within the next few days. In time, sadly, we will be told it wasn't a miracle God had performed but something that science could prove."

The Reverend picked up his Bible and notes from the podium. "But that won't be true. God wants us all to focus on the spiritual not the physical, for when death does come, your body returns to dust and your spirit lives on. God wants us to make sure we live on in the right place. He is giving us a reminder and maybe also a warning."

A few amens came from the congregation.

There was a big queue to see the Reverend after the service. Aaron noticed the big man had joined the line. Maybe he was seeking prayer for forgiveness. His thugs had gone outside.

Aaron was about to go outside when Churchie put his arm in front of him.

"Ethan advises that you stay here for now."

Aaron was not used to having his life directed by an angel but thought it best to take heed. Aaron watched the big man's face getting redder and redder. Did he have a blood pressure problem? Some people were taking a long time to talk to the Reverend. It now looked like the Reverend's assistant was advising others in the line that the minister had another appointment. Aaron watched as the Reverend excused himself and slipped out through a side door.

Aaron looked at the big man. He turned abruptly and muttered under his breath. He bumped into a few people as he stormed out of the church.

* * *

Aaron noticed that Mel had stayed seated. Aaron walked over to him.

"You okay?" Aaron asked.

"There something about this place, a feeling of peace," Mel said.

Mel got up and stood next to Aaron. They watched people as they made their way out. Churchie and Mel stood at the door and waved them over.

They moved outside to sit in Speakers' Corner in King George Square. The area was messy from activities of the previous night. A slight breeze drew out some sour wine fumes from a discarded wine flask and disseminated the smell.

Aaron watched Mel as he shook his head. "What are you up to?"

"The smell. I can't stand it." He grabbed a hanky out of his pocket and covered his nose, then moved it down so he could speak. "Aaron, you remember when I first met you and I told you about the white van and the look the driver gave me?"

Aaron nodded. "Yep, you said it was like one of those news vans."

"That's right . . . well, I'm sure I saw the driver today. His face was a little different, but I'm sure it was him."

"Where?"

"When we were lined up for church . . . he walked past with a couple of other men . . . they were big, bulky men. He was in church, too."

"I think I know the ones you're talking about."

"Should we do anything?"

Aaron turned to Churchie, "Maybe we should take advantage of your hidden talent Churchie. Are you in 'angel see' mode?"

Churchie smiled. "Yep. Tend to be in that mode when there aren't lots of people around. You should have seen the riff-raff hanging around that queue of people at the Church. I switched to 'no see' mode as we got closer to the church because there was a massive build-up of demons outside the church and a mini war was taking place . . . they couldn't enter with the humans they were connected to. And those fellows you were talking about, well . . . they're being influenced by some pretty nasty characters."

"Any advice for us?"

"Things are going to run their course. We are going to need more proof of what Mel is telling us. Wally must have been close to where they do their transporting thing."

Aaron looked at Wally. "Are you always this quiet?"

"I enjoy listening to you blokes. I know what you're going to ask, but I don't know where I was or where I was found."

They spoke about it. Wally told them about the painter who had picked him up. But all Wally could remember was that the painter had a red ute and wore white overalls with specks of paint all over them. Wally stood up. He was looking frustrated and kicked an empty wine cask. He stopped and looked up. "I caught a bus near a big winery not far from where I was picked up."

"That's good, Wally," Aaron said.

"Don't ask me the name, it was a funny name."

"That's even better, Wally, a funny name will be easy to find on Google."

Aaron looked at Mel. He guessed a winery was the last place Mel wanted to go to—he looked like he was still trying to get the smell of stale wine out of his nostrils.

* * *

They drove past the Sirromet Winery. Lucas looked up to see the car park was quite full. Many people travelled from Brisbane to enjoy the spoils of this winery.

Lucas was driving with his tag team partner sitting next to him and the minister in the back seat. The minister wanted to catch up with Starkey after lunch. Lucas looked in the rear-view mirror and noticed the redness in his boss's face was all but gone. Boy, was he spitting nails when he came out of church this morning. Lucas thought people were meant to come out of church feeling peaceful.

Lucas was agitated. It seemed to be getting worse these days. He'd tried to avoid smoking the dope but the voices in his head got worse when he did that. And that army bloke was at church. He must be happy his girl had returned from the land of the dead. Well, Lucas was glad too, he just wasn't sure about what happened. He didn't want to transfer her back but he had no choice. The Prof caught him off-guard when he sent them back, and he couldn't come up with a valid reason to keep the girl. Lucas really hoped there were no deformities. Death was the last thing he expected. But now she was alive. He needed a smoke badly.

Lucas didn't like the idea of the army guy and the girl getting together. He didn't like these men with stunning girlfriends. The other guy she was with was out of the way, unless they were going to bring him back from the dead too. Why did Lucas have to miss out? They should have kept her at the property.

A voice agreed with him. She deserved someone better, someone like him.

His boss was starting to annoy him too. The voices told him that he was being used and his boss thought he was stupid. The voices also told Lucas that the minister was going to get rid of him as soon as he had served his purpose.

He needed a smoke.

* * *

Windsor watched the grapevines pass. He thought about the name of the winery but only briefly—his real focus was on the technology. How easy was it to use? Could he use it?

Windsor looked up to see Lucas looking at him in the mirror. He smiled. "Sirromet is T.E. Morris spelt backwards."

"Huh?"

"The name of the winery is a name spelt backwards."

Lucas nodded and kept driving.

"Lucas, is it easy to transport people? You don't need to use the van all the time, do you?"

"The transmitting device is basically the size of a laptop computer, fits in a briefcase. The van is still a good idea because it gives you privacy and you can hook up some larger monitors. The idea is to bring up an image of the target on the monitor or enter a GPS location. You also need to be in close proximity to the target when you want to transmit. My preference is to use the van but the other way is fine."

"How close do you need to be?"

"Within about seventy meters."

Ten minutes later they turned into the property. Starkey was raking up dead leaves and twigs from under a large Moreton Bay Fig. He leaned the rake on the tree trunk and walked over to greet them.

"Greetings. Windsor, you can't stay away from this place. What brings you out here? I'm sure it's not just for a Sunday drive."

"You may be right, Starkey. Grab some beers, and let's sit out here and have a chat."

Windsor sat down. He looked around to see if he could locate the mob of kangaroos he saw the other day. It was more peaceful out here than in the city. He'd never noticed that before. No kangaroos, but he saw a horse in the next paddock with a white bird standing next to it.

Starkey placed the can on the table.

Windsor turned and looked up at Starkey. "I'm just not used to nature, Starkey. Why's that bird hanging around the horse?"

Starkey looked over to see what Windsor was talking about. He smiled. "It's called a Cattle Egret. While the horse grazes, it disturbs insects and things that the birds feed on . . . saves the birds a bit of work, makes the insects easier to catch."

"Smart birds."

"They even come when we cut the grass—there's bugs flying everywhere when you do that."

"Definitely smart birds."

"Well designed."

"Of course. God is clever." Windsor pondered something. "Do you believe that animals have souls?"

"That's a deep question, Windsor." Starkey paused and had a sip of his beer. "They're programmed to do things, they have a set of instructions they follow. But do they have a moral awareness? I don't believe they have a spiritual aspect. So I suppose if you keep soul and spirit separate you could say they have a soul which holds the design package together."

"Interesting how you talk about a design but don't seem to seek out the designer. As humans, we have a moral awareness that some say it is written on our hearts. But who wrote it? And about seeking out the designer—animals don't do that. They seem satisfied with their lot but we humans are uniquely curious about our origin, purpose and meaning."

"Good point, Windsor. Morals. Gets complex doesn't it? What we're doing with the transporter—we believe it's morally correct, but others don't."

Windsor pondered Starkey's point. He turned and looked out towards the paddock again. The horse and bird were doing what they were designed to do, grazing and eating. They weren't seeking out purpose and meaning; they weren't trying to fix up a mess. But man, what a mess he had made of things.

"Now, Windsor, you didn't drive out here to discuss morals. What did you want to chat about?"

"Yes, you're right . . . I know we've touched on this before, but how do we change the receiving location of the transfers?

"I'm sure there's a good reason for that question. At the moment, the only way we can do it is by placing some switching equipment at the location where you want to receive the bodies. We have three devices. They can all be used as senders or receivers, but for a transfer to take place, at least one device needs to be set to receive. They're easy to configure. That's it in a nutshell."

"Bodies sound too negative, Starkey. Entities sound better."

"Does it?"

"I think so . . . could you show me the equipment?"

CHAPTER TWENTY FIVE

MONDAY. A NEW WEEK.

There was some urgency to Windsor's plan.

Windsor's wife used to volunteer as a church receptionist. She told Windsor that Monday mornings were always the busiest, with people wanting to speak to a pastor—seeking forgiveness for the sins exposed at Sunday services. Then the rug would be slowly pulled over to cover the sin as the week progressed and the cycle would start again. He had laughed at her theory and hoped it wasn't true today.

"Hello. City Community Church," came the greeting.

"Hello, I was wondering if I would be able to speak to Reverend Peter Thomas?" Windsor asked.

"I'm sorry, but Monday is his day off. Could anyone else help you?"

Monday was the busiest day, yet the Reverend had the day off. What was the world coming to? Windsor took some deep breaths. "Would I be able to make an appointment to see him?"

"He's a busy man at the moment. Could I ask the nature of your meeting?"

The lady was irritating Windsor. "It's a private matter."

"Well, sir, as you can appreciate, Reverend Peter is somewhat popular at the moment. I need to assess his appointments for him."

Windsor translated this to mean filter his appointments. "I understand. Look, my name is Grant Windsor. You may know my name; I'm the Minister for Urban Movement. I wanted to have a chat with the Reverend about traffic control around the Church on Sundays."

She was silent for a moment. "The best I could do would be Thursday at ten o'clock."

"That would be fine. Thank you."

Well, maybe Thursday was better as he needed to relocate some equipment that he had borrowed. Yes, Thursday would be better. It would give him some time.

On Tuesday evening, he would go for a drive and visit his son. He would leave the equipment there then.

* * *

Aaron stared at the pile of magazines on the table next to his seat. He bent over and looked at the spines—they covered every topic known to man: fishing, gardening, golf, house ideas, cars, boats, gossip . . . the list went on. None grabbed Aaron's attention, not today anyway. He looked over at Mackenzie's parents. He was happy to accompany them to the hospital. Hopefully Mackenzie would be coming home today.

Aaron got up and walked over to a drink machine. He had two choices: Coke or water. He pondered. His mind was elsewhere. He looked down the corridor. The security guard at the entrance to Mackenzie's room reminded him of Lucas—not his physical appearance, but his uniform. The guard nodded to Aaron. Another guard stood further down the corridor, next to the door at the adjacent room. Aaron saw the door to the second room open. An officer from Department of Defense walked out. He looked familiar.

He was just about to pass Aaron when he stopped. "Fitzpatrick?" he asked.

"Yes." Aaron remembered him from the tour of Afghanistan, but couldn't remember his name.

"Johnson . . . Ted Johnson." He shook Aaron's hand. "What are you doing here?"

"I know the girl. She's a close friend."

The officer nodded. "Apparently she's fit and well. I've just been in with the man. He's also fit and well. Not sure what they've been through. Can't say too much, but it's pretty weird. We've been here a couple of days and now have to go write a detailed report. Good to see ya . . . take care, see you around."

Aaron watched Johnson walk over to the nurses' bay and start taking notes. Aaron sensed movement, turned, and saw the other officer come out of Mackenzie's room. He didn't know him. Still at the drink machine, Aaron pushed the button, retrieved a bottled water and walked back over to Mackenzie's parents—they didn't want a drink.

The other officer walked over to the nurses' bay and joined Johnson. They had a brief chat with a nurse, who must have been in charge. The officers then walked over to one of the security guards. Nodding of heads and handshakes took place, and the defense officers left. Johnson gave Aaron a nod before he departed.

The head nurse came over to Aaron and Mackenzie's parents. "Looks like your daughter will be able to leave today. We just have to finalize some paperwork, but you can go in and see her now."

Aaron's heart jumped a few beats. They headed towards the room. He looked over to the other room and saw some police officers enter the room. That must be the man the police were chasing at the time of the disappearance. What had he done?

* * *

Mackenzie was sitting up in the bed, no wires attached. She smiled at them as they entered. She gave her mum and dad big hugs. She looked at Aaron and told him to give her a hug. He did.

She started crying. Her mum comforted her.

"It's okay, Mum. I'm fine. I really don't know where to start. I know about Paul."

"You do?" asked her mum.

Aaron wondered how she found out.

"This will be hard for you to understand. And I'm still coming to grips with it, but we were separated from our bodies through whatever those crazy people were doing. We ended up in another dimension or something like that. We saw angels and we saw nasty things transporting bodies to—"

Mackenzie's mum held her hand, she gave a squeeze. "Mackenzie, before you get too much into it, we've also been through some things that are hard to understand. You need to know that we'll believe whatever you're going to tell us."

Mackenzie smiled.

"In fact, Aaron has some new friends I'm sure he would be keen to tell you about."

It was a good hour before the paperwork was finalized. A police officer came into the room and asked a number of questions. He told them that it was a joint investigation with the Department of Defense. They wanted to track down who was behind all this, particularly now deaths had occurred. He stumbled when talking about deaths, as originally Mackenzie was one of those. Mackenzie agreed to drop in to the Police Station tomorrow to see if she could identify those involved or the location of where they ended up. She did say they wore President Nixon masks, which would make identification tricky.

Aaron wondered if he should contribute but decided to say nothing. What proof did he have?

A nurse came in at one stage to check if all was okay. The Rev walked past the open door, but Aaron was too infatuated with Mackenzie to go and say hello.

They wheeled Mackenzie out in a wheelchair and got her comfortable in the car. Aaron sat in the back with her. She placed her hand on his lap and gave him a lovely smile.

"You better be a believer now, Aaron, because I have seen where the lost go, and you don't want to end up there."

"It's close, Mackenzie."

"Best we not have a car accident then."

* * *

The Rev felt God put it on his heart to be here. He had made himself comfortable on a chair in the background and sat in the hospital ward as Joshua answered questions asked by the police. Joshua was wanted regarding some unpaid fines that accumulated while he lived in Melbourne. He must have thought that by leaving the state the fines wouldn't follow him.

The police officer left.

Joshua stared over at the Rev. "Who are you?"

The Rev got up and walked over to the bedside. "I'm Peter

Thomas, a pastor at a church in the city." The Rev preferred to use the 'Pastor' title as it was less formal than his normal title. He put out his hand.

Joshua shook the Rev's hand. "I'm Joshua. Nice to meet you."

"Sounds like you've been through a bit."

"Do you mean the fines or my recent adventures?"

"Both, I suppose. Do you have family in Brisbane?"

"I think so. I came here to track down my brother, and boy, have I got myself into something."

"Have you tracked down your brother?"

"No . . . we sort of drifted apart, a bit like our family . . . it drifted apart too."

"I'm sorry to hear that. But you know he's in Brisbane?"

"That's the last I heard from him. He said he was going north to sunny Brisbane. It's taken me a few years, but I got here."

"You have, with bells and whistles. Sorry, that was my attempt at humor." The Rev noted that brought a smile to his face.

"Maybe you can help me find him?"

"I will, Joshua, but first we need to make sure you're okay with the events that you have been caught up in. How are you feeling?"

Joshua swallowed. "Do you believe in angels, demons, heaven and hell, and all those things?"

"Certainly do."

"Well, I do now. The girl with me told me about Jesus and I need to get myself right there. Can you help me, because my eyes have been opened . . . in a big way."

The God appointment became clear. "I certainly can."

* * *

It was a private affair held on Wednesday at a funeral chapel. Just close friends and relatives.

Mackenzie came in earlier than the others. She stood beside Paul's coffin. She closed her eyes to hold back her tears. She saw his face in her mind. He told her that all was okay. She sensed God's peace.

Why was she brought back to life? Why not Paul? The Rev reminded Mackenzie that God's plans are God's plans. Paul was now home, and Mackenzie must still have something that needed to be done on the earthly plane.

* * *

The Rev sat at his desk reflecting on his meeting with Joshua. The Lord and events had obviously changed him. He was working on a strategy to help Joshua out with the fines and other issues. A knock on the door startled him. He looked at his mobile phone, checked the time, and realized he had an appointment. His diary said it was the Minister for Urban Movement.

The Rev got up and opened the door. He noticed the minister recording something on a small note pad. "Hi there, Minister." The Rev put out his hand, "The Rev Peter Thomas, lovely to meet you."

"You too, sir. My name is Grant Windsor." Windsor handed the Rev a business card. The Rev had a quick glance at it.

They entered the Rev's office. It was a small office with a lot squeezed in. Besides a visitor's chair facing the desk, there were two small couches separated by a coffee table. The couches provided the more informal feel needed for counseling sessions. The Rev moved some newspapers from one of the couches and invited the minister to sit down.

"Do you have a business card?" Windsor asked.

The Rev walked over to his desk. He placed the business card the minister gave him on the desk and retrieved one of his own business cards. He came back and handed it to the minister and then sat on the other couch facing the minister. "People aren't sure how to address me. Some know me as the Rev, others use my name, Peter. The choice is yours."

"The Rev has a nice ring to it. I can imagine you've been a bit busy of late. I suppose it's not every day that people are brought back from the dead."

"You're right there. And with that have come the crowds and the traffic. Hence your visit."

"Well, yes and no. I have to admit I've been naughty and used my title to get in and see you."

The Rev felt a little uncomfortable. "Go on."

"I would like you to come and pray for someone for me."

201

"I would be happy to do that. Tell me more about your prayer request."

"Well, Rev, it's my son, and he's dead."

* * *

Windsor got in the car.

"Here are the GPS coordinates." He handed Lucas a piece of paper.

Windsor watched as Lucas entered the coordinates. He'd known the Rev wouldn't agree to his request. He took the GPS reading before he entered the office. Now the only risk they had with the transfer was that the Rev still needed to be in his office.

"All set. Did you want me to execute the transfer?"

"Have you changed the receiver GPS coordinates?"

"Yep."

"Okay, do it."

* * *

After the minister left, the Rev closed the door and sat back down on the couch. He was shaken. The man's demands were strong, intimidating. Do it or else. He knew he was going to get lots of prayer requests for healing, but there was something strange about this request.

He rubbed his head and sensed something. He looked around the room. The walls seemed to be moving. He felt a sense of shutting down.

The Rev opened his eyes. He felt the presence of evil and said a quick prayer in the name of Jesus. His legs felt cold so he started rubbing them. Why were they so cold? He started taking in his environment. He was sitting on a cold vinyl floor. The immediate area was lit by soft fluorescent lights. He couldn't see any windows. He could hear a faint humming noise—the large cylinder shape in front of him, maybe. But where was he? Truth dawned on him. He was the victim of a 'transfer'. His body seemed to be functioning normally. He was happy with that after all the things he had seen and heard.

He got up and headed towards the cylinder with his movement setting off more fluorescent lights. There was a line of cylinders, four in all. They each stood over three meters tall and maybe a couple of meters in circumference—he wouldn't be able to wrap his arms around one. The first cylinder had a bluish glow, the others sat in darkness. A vertical strip of glass ran down the side, about the width of a hand.

What was inside the cylinder? Did he really want to know?

He stepped closer. Through the vertical glass strip he could see some kind of liquid bubbling up. He moved right up close to the glass and peered in, shading his eyes with his hands to get a better view. There, he saw something. He quickly jumped back: it was a body floating in there, upside down.

"Lord, be with me."

He wanted out. He walked over to the exit door. It could only be opened with a card or code number. Obviously they wanted to keep the bodies inside. He gave a nervous laugh at that thought. He walked back to the cylinder, and saw a panel on the front, displaying charts and figures. There was also an emergency number. He patted his pockets for his phone, then remembered he'd left it sitting on his desk. Well, he didn't actually leave it there—he'd had no idea he was going out.

"Lord, what should I do?"

Just around from the monitor, he noticed a plaque on the cylinder. He moved around to read what was inscribed.

Timothy Edward Windsor
Date of cryopreservation: 17/03/2017
Cryonics Inc.

It was that man's son, the minister's son. And now he knew why he was here.

* * *

Aaron followed Churchie to the office. The door was closed. Churchie gave a soft tap. No answer, so he gave a harder knock and the door creaked open a little. Churchie gave the door a gentle push.

"Hello, are you there Rev?"

No answer. Churchie opened the door all the way. They walked in. It looked like the Rev had stepped out for a moment. His mobile phone sat on the table. Aaron picked it up. A message. 'Lunch is on us. Be with you in an hour.'

"Looks like he didn't get our message."

"Aaron, my angel tells me things aren't right. The Rev's been a victim of a transfer."

Aaron pondered that. "What purpose would that serve? Do we know where to?"

"No. The Rev's angel is still here."

Aaron wondered where the angel was standing. "The angel still being here must have something to do with the technology. It must transfer things, humans that is, at a particular frequency and angels are outside that frequency. Only a theory. Surely the Lord knows where the people go. Why doesn't he just tell the angels?"

"I'll ask them." Churchie appeared to be listening to his invisible friend, then nodded.

"Aaron, they're messengers from God. They're not omnipresent."

"What does that mean?"

"They can only be at one place at any particular time. But as messengers from God, they may be told things." Churchie was nodding again. "And I've been told that a meeting with a man was just held, and that man is behind all this."

"How would we find out who that was?"

"I'll go and find out. Either the church secretary or the senior pastor should know."

Churchie left, and Aaron looked around the room. Lots of books. He saw a photo frame on the desk, a business card beside it. Aaron picked up the card while he glanced at the picture in the photo frame: a lady and boy, maybe his wife and child. Aaron thought about how little people know of each other. There was also a picture on the business card. His mobile phone vibrated.

It was Mackenzie.

"Hello, Kenz."

"Hello, my lovely friend. What are you up to?"

"Just out and about with Churchie at the moment . . . how are you feeling?"

"Good, Aaron. The funeral yesterday helped with some closure,

God's doing the rest. When are you going to come visit? I'd like you to meet Joshua. I think you two would get on well." Aaron felt a twinge of jealousy.

"How about I come around this evening, say six?."

"That sounds good. Why don't you bring your friend Churchie? I think he'd find what we experienced interesting. Mum's been telling me about him."

"I'll try and do that . . . and look forward to seeing you and meeting Joshua." The call ended, and Aaron placed the phone back in his pocket. Mackenzie needed to be busy at the moment—it would help keep her mind off things.

Aaron looked at the picture on the business card. It was that man again. He should have guessed. There would have been a motive for him to be at church last Sunday. Aaron wondered what it was.

Churchie walked back in.

"The Rev had a meeting with the Minister of Urban Movement," Aaron said.

"Who's that?" Churchie asked.

"Someone who has been cropping up in my life a bit too often. We have his number. The question is, should we ring him?" Aaron didn't want to put the Rev in any danger.

CHAPTER TWENTY SIX

GRANT WINDSOR STARED OUT the window as the vehicle cruised along the Ipswich Motorway. He felt exposed. He was starting to think what he had done was too risky.

He assumed that the Rev was at the location. He knew there would be no visitors—no one else had access to the building. It was all remotely monitored and Windsor had 'visitor rights'. Cryonics Inc. didn't have any other clients at present, although he was told they were getting more enquiries, so that might change. But for now, the facility only stored his son.

Having access allowed him to place the switching device where it needed to be.

What was he to do with the Rev after he did what Windsor hoped he would do. He thought that sounded like something from what the Apostle Paul said in the Bible. What was it he thought, something like, *"I don't understand what I do. For what I want to do I don't do, but what I hate I do."* And then he thought about the sin that was living in him. What a wretched man he was. Windsor smiled, and knew God would forgive him.

Only a few knew about the technology. A few he could control. But now another person would know how it all worked. Gaps were starting to appear. Maybe the question isn't what to do with the Rev, but the appropriate time to make a run for it. Yes, things were starting to get out of hand. He would work out what to do once his son had been brought back to life.

* * *

The Rev paced the room. He preferred not to look in the cylinder.

206

Something was reflected in the ambient light in the corner of the room. The Rev walked over and found an aluminum briefcase on the floor. He bent down for a closer look, expecting to see a combination lock but instead saw a couple of unsecured latches, and what must be ventilation grilles. What was inside? He flicked the latches open and lifted the lid.

It was some kind of electronic device, cushioned in grey spongy material. The device was plugged into a power point. He touched the screen, expecting it to prompt him for a password, but it didn't. He saw a video image of himself on the screen. At the bottom of the screen were two buttons, labeled *Transfer* and *Receive*. The *Receive* button was pressed down. There were two toggle switches under the *Transfer* button. He could probably use this interface if he had to. He may need to explore that further.

There was a CCTV monitor above the exit door, showing an empty car park.

He looked at his watch. He found a cheap black folding chair, and sat there watching the monitor. After a period of nothingness a car pulled up. He stood up and moved closer to the monitor. It was only a few young people—it must be lunchtime, as it looked like they were eating. He sat down again and thought about food; he was hungry. Food wrappings and drink cartons came sailing out of the car windows as the car departed. The Rev shook his head.

The monitor showed an empty car park again. The Rev looked away from the monitor and thought about the environment and what options he had to get out of this place. Movement on the monitor caught his attention. Just some crows jumping around in the car park, happy to investigate the mess.

Maybe it was time to experiment. He walked over to the briefcase, and flicked the first toggle switch under the *Transfer* button. A green light came on next to it and the transfer button lit up—he had an idea what might happen if he pressed that button, but wasn't sure if he wanted to risk it.

What was going to happen next? Was he going to be forced to bring this person back to life? He didn't believe that would happen— God hadn't put that on his heart. So what would be the consequences of that?

This man, Windsor, wasn't in his right mind. Maybe he was still grieving, maybe even depressed. Windsor had exposed himself as the person behind the transfers, technology that had already left at least one person dead. He looked up at the cylinder and thought about post-traumatic stress disorder. Maybe that was driving the man.

He again looked at the *Transfer* button. "Help me here, Lord."

* * *

The crows scattered as the car turned into the parking bay. Lucas pulled up the hand brake and they all sat, motionless, staring towards the building.

"Why are we here, boss?" asked Lucas.

"Just a piece of technology I need to check." Windsor opened his door and then turned to Lucas. "Lucas, could you come in with me. Tag, you stay in the car."

Lucas nodded and got out of the car.

They stood outside the car. "Lucas, I'm expecting the pastor I went to visit to be inside here. He may not be a happy man. So you may need to manage the situation."

Lucas walked with Windsor towards the entrance to the building. "I've been here before. What is this place?"

"It's a storage facility, Lucas. You may have heard about it in the media. Have you heard of cryonics?"

"Doesn't ring any bells." Lucas had been here before. He wasn't sure why he wasn't thinking straight.

"Cryonics is the practice of preserving a dead person for future revival when medicine, science, and technology can provide a cure or solution. My son's in here." Windsor scanned his ID card and the door opened.

Lucas felt uneasy. They walked in. His mind was assailed by voices as he stood staring at the tall cylinders. What were those big things? But the voices in his head disturbed him more. Why were the voices in his head now? He moved closer and saw a body floating upside down. *He will do this to you soon.* "Who said that?"

"Are you okay, Lucas?" Windsor asked. "Who are you talking to? Did you see the Rev?"

Lucas shook his head.

"Hi Rev, are you there?" Windsor asked, his voice just above a whisper.

Silence.

Lucas thought he saw a shadow move behind the cylinder. He pointed. "Behind that cylinder." He walked up slowly and looked behind it. Nothing there. He turned to Windsor and shrugged. "Nothing." Strange. He was sure he saw something, something with a robe flowing behind it.

Lucas stared at the cylinder. The voice spoke again. *He's going to kill you—that's why you're here. He doesn't like you.*

"Well, no place to hide except in the cylinders and they're empty except for my son's one."

Empty at the moment. Lucas heard the voice again and shuddered. "Maybe the transfer didn't work."

"Maybe." Lucas watched Windsor looking around the room. He saw him looking towards something in the corner and walked over to it.

"Hey, Lucas, come over here."

Lucas walked over.

"You're more of an expert on this device than I am. What do the settings tell you?"

Lucas got down on his knees and looked at the settings and indicators. "Clever man, he's transferred himself to the next receiver station."

"Which is?"

"The property."

* * *

A softer floor this time, but just as cold as the last one. The Rev wondered where he was now.

He stood up and tried to take in the new environment. Bare walls, some seats towards the back, one window with security grilles. It reminded him of the prison cells that he had visited as part of his pastoral duties over the years, except there were fewer items in this room.

He grabbed a chair, sat down and asked the Lord what he was meant to do now.

There was nothing the Rev could do.

This was a jail: there was no way out. Was anybody around? He yelled a few times but his voice just bounced off the walls.

* * *

Smoke filtered up through the trees on the property. It was a common sight to see property owners burning off. The council could investigate smoke if it irritated or annoyed others. Starkey had kept this in mind. He burnt things bit by bit; he did not want anyone investigating the property, not yet anyway.

It was time to flee. To burn what evidence was left. Cover his tracks.

The small fire was down the back of the property near a row of pine trees. The hypnotic nature of the fire had caught his attention. He stood there staring, then nodded his head. It was time to go. He started walking to his car. Something caught his attention—a noise coming from the shed or maybe from an adjoining property. It sounded like a voice, but he just shrugged it off.

His phone sat on the passenger seat. Three missed calls from Grant Windsor. He returned the call but there was no answer. He would drive past Grant's place on the way to the airport.

Starkey looked up at the house. He stared for a few moments and then said goodbye and drove off.

The drive to Windsor's place was a careful one. He tried Windsor's apartment but there was no one home. Starkey wrote a note. It was not his preference. He dropped the note and a spare set of car keys in the letterbox.

He called Lucas before driving to the airport.

* * *

Lucas was in the passenger seat. Tag was the driver for the return trip. Lucas's phone rang. He looked at the screen. *Bruce Stark Calling.* He decided to answer it.

"Hello, Starkey."

"Hi, Lucas. Sorry to bother you but I'm trying to locate Windsor. I had a meeting scheduled with him. You haven't seen him, have you?"

"Not lately. Saw him a couple of hours ago. He told us that he'd be in contact if he needed us." Lucas finished the call. Starkey had said goodbye as if he meant it. He turned to Tag. "I'm going to have a smoke. You want one?"

Tag looked at Lucas. "You're acting mighty strange, Lucas. Never seen you smoke in the car before."

"It's fine, mate. Did you want one or not?"

"Nah . . . you know, Lucas, I reckon the minister was a brave man using the technology. Don't think I would."

"Don't think I would either, mate." Lucas lit his smoke, wound the window down and took a long drag. He thought of the minister, pictured his face and blew some smoke in the direction of the imaginary face.

You're cool, Lucas, the voice in his head told him. *Real cool . . . real tough.* After a few more puffs, the cigarette was flicked out of the car with some aggression—sparks bounced along the road behind them.

"How come you didn't tell Starkey about the transfer?" asked Tag.

"Not sure. Must have forgotten. No drama." Lucas didn't want to tell Tag there was no transfer. He just left Windsor in that cold room with his dead son.

* * *

The Rev got up from his chair and did another scan of the room. It was obvious that the room was built to keep people in. How long was he going to be here for? There was a toilet, a table with some packets of crackers, some bottled water. The crackers and water would keep him alive if he was in for an extended stay.

He was racking his brain for facts. He sat down and placed his head in his hands. *Father . . . help me to be at peace with my circumstances.* Things would be okay. Time for some rest, an opportunity to spend time with God without the distractions of the world. He thought of Jentezen Franklin and how his church began each year with twenty-one days of fasting, a time of restoring energy and spiritual sharpness. He smiled, reminding himself to be thankful in all circumstances.

The Rev was thinking of the past and the future, but knew his thoughts needed to be in the now. How hard it was to be in the present moment, as the mind seeks out distractions. Oh, how to steady the mind. He started saying a prayer that he knew monks and nuns used: they called it the Jesus Prayer:

Lord Jesus Christ, son of God, have mercy on me a sinner.

He prayed the simple prayer over and over. It was his favorite prayer because it summed up the whole Gospel: who Jesus is and who we are.

At one point the Rev, with his head bowed, felt a presence in the room. He looked up and knew God was with him. He thought of the Bible verse when God allowed Moses to see God's glory.

And the LORD said, *"Here is a place by Me, and you shall stand on the rock. So it shall be, while My glory passes by, that I will put you in the cleft of the rock, and will cover you with My hand while I pass by. Then I will take away My hand, and you shall see My back; but My face shall not be seen."*

The Rev thought of God's glory, so powerful it could not remain in front of Moses, it had to pass by him. Even with that, Moses was protected by the hand of God and the cleft of the rock when the glory of God passed before him.

"Thank you Father." He would wait for those that the Lord would bring.

* * *

Should Windsor have seen it coming? He believed not. He saw a look on Lucas's face that he hoped never to see again. The door was slammed in his face and he was told to rot with his son.

He'd left his phone in the car. There was no way out except the way that pastor escaped and there was no way Windsor was going to consider that. Who knew where that pastor ended up?

Solitude scared Windsor. He needed to be active in mind, body and soul. Activity stopped him from thinking. But now he sat, staring at his son floating in the tank, and he was a confused man. Solitude had been forced on him and he didn't know what to do.

The equipment in the room gave off a steady, monotonous humming—there were no distracting noises. Windsor's head was clearing but he did not like what was being revealed: fear. All these years, that was what he had been running from. He could focus now. He listened to the voice in his head, and for the first time he thought that maybe he wasn't listening to the right voice.

He started to sense evil in this place. He saw shadows.

He spoke to God, something he hadn't done for a long time. He asked for forgiveness.

A still small voice told him to press the transfer button.

* * *

It was sudden. But he was sure he saw bony skeletal arms reach out for him. He sat dazed. An arm was reaching out to him, helping him up. He looked up. It was the pastor.

"Well, it works then?" Windsor asked.

"It does".

"I'm sorry what I have put you through, sir. I can't explain to you why, except that I was being dragged along by something. I feel released now."

"Come and sit down."

"How come you're still here? Don't tell me there's no way out of here either?" He laughed and put his hands to his head. "Maybe I've jumped from the frying pan into the fire. No, I don't believe that . . . there was a real sense of evil at that other place, and I don't sense that here."

"I'm pleased to hear that. It's good to have company. Now, let me engage in some trivia and get some atmosphere in here. That saying about the frying pan—it's adapted from a fable about fish thrown live into a frying pan of boiling fat. One of the fish urges its fellows to save their lives by jumping out, but when they do so, they jump into the burning coals, a worse situation."

Windsor was patting himself, looking over his body. He was still a bit shaken. "I wonder what the opposite analogy would be."

"Good question. I did a sermon on this once and gave examples of possible analogies like a leap of faith. I think the best example was out of hell into paradise."

"Must get a copy of that sermon." Windsor looked around. "Maybe we can make a lot of noise and attract Starkey—he's the one who lives here."

"I heard someone drive off some hours ago."

"Oh. Then there is no way out, is there?"

"No . . . but I have faith."

* * *

Time alone passed slowly, time with company, a lot quicker. It was getting darker in the room. The Rev noticed some blankets on a shelf towards the rear of the room, and the leftovers and water on the table would keep their appetites abated. They'd be okay for a few days if necessary. But company made all the difference.

They sat at the table, nibbling on the crackers and sipping bottled water.

"It's nice to have company, Grant. Solitude can be good sometimes. Jesus spent a lot of his time in solitude, talking to his Father and recharging the batteries, then he would go about his tasks with the community of people. We all need each other but we need to be balanced. Solitude, time with God, helps give us that balance."

Windsor placed his bottle of water on the table. "My time alone, although it was only brief, brought with it a feeling of loneliness. I felt isolated, no sense of God or anything. To be honest, it frightened me and gave me a real quick wake-up call. In fact, I feel like I've been hit by a lightning bolt."

"Why are you involved in these things, Grant?"

Windsor stood up. "I was getting so frustrated with everyone making up their own laws. No one seemed to show respect anymore. People just didn't care. They cross pedestrian crossings when they felt like it, they run red lights, they drive while talking on mobiles, they throw cigarette butts out of car windows, they tailgate . . . the list goes on."

"A lot of those things annoy me too, Grant."

"And many others too. The idea of the technology was to relocate such offenders to a place of 'inconvenience'. I know it sounds bland and not well thought–out, but the technology was so impressive, and then my son committed suicide after running over a girl who walked straight in front of his car. This just gave the plan a further push. Then I read about Cryonics, Inc. The feelings from then took over."

"I'm sorry to hear about that."

"I loved my son so much and felt guilty about not spending enough time with him. I know now that he was screaming out for attention. And there were other mistakes. I took out my guilt on someone from my church. I believed he treated my son badly when my son was younger, but now see that it may have been a mistake. Now the man's dead. That wasn't meant to happen. I just wanted to spook him. It was all about power. I loved my son. Now he's dead. Could you bring him back to life?"

The Rev had turned his seat and was facing Windsor. The man was still grieving, and was filled with guilt and remorse.

"That's a difficult question, Grant. I believe God brought the other ones back because of the circumstances. It's the first time I've seen such things. It's God who brings them back to life, not me. I'm just the vehicle He used. That's why I needed to get away from that place. I just didn't know what you might have done to get your way."

Windsor put his head down. "I'm so sorry and embarrassed by my actions. I do ask your forgiveness."

"Just get right with God, Grant. We need to think about what death is. I believe those who don't know Jesus are dead—maybe this is what we should be focusing on, bringing those dead in the spirit back to life. I have no idea where your son was at. Maybe he had already been raised from the dead."

"I would like to believe that, and will." Windsor looked around the room again. He put his hand out to the Rev.

They shook hands.

"Let's enjoy each other's company. Besides, this is a nicer place than where we came from. Enrich me, Reverend. It looks like we may be here for the night.

CHAPTER TWENTY SEVEN

AARON CALLED GRANT WINDSOR'S phone a number of times. He wanted to know what Windsor was up to with the Rev.

No response. He thought about calling the police, but wasn't sure how they would react to angels, demons and things like that. They'd probably lock them all up thinking they were mad, even though the proof was out there: bodies vanishing and reappearing, the dead brought back to life. But then, at times, Aaron wasn't even sure if he believed what was happening around him.

Their appointment with Mackenzie had turned out to be a barbeque and she wanted Aaron to bring along the motley crew. She still liked the idea of looking after the homeless. Aaron had forgotten that's what they were. Aaron told the motley crew that he would pick them up outside the church on Ann Street.

He felt nostalgic, so had some old Beatles music playing in the car. He slowed down and saw the motley crew waiting. He pulled up as close as he could and gave them a toot, as they hadn't seen his car before. They waved and came running along like excited schoolchildren. Aaron smiled. And they all had made a big effort to present themselves well.

Mel and Wally climbed in the back seat. Mel still had his red and blue cap on. Churchie jumped in the front with Aaron and asked if there was any news on the Rev.

"No news, Churchie. I've been trying to work out what to do. I believe we need some kind of proof so I can call the police. Maybe we can come up with some strategy today, when we're all together."

"Don't be concerned about the Rev . . . don't worry about him. God will be looking after him."

Aaron looked at Churchie and thought about what he said. Seeing the invisible world must strengthen one's faith. And that invisible world was there with the Rev and around everyone. It was a powerful thought.

"You know this Windsor guy is a churchgoer," Aaron said. "I've come across him before at Mackenzie's church. You know, the church has a bad reputation because of guys like him. The church is seen as hypocritical. What sort of role model is he?"

"The church is full of people. All people are sinners, Aaron. The only difference between believers and non-believers is that we believers have accepted God's forgiveness for our sins, but those that haven't asked for forgiveness stand condemned."

"So you're telling me this Windsor bloke is forgiven for what he's been up to."

"Only God knows a man's heart, Aaron. Only God knows if a person is a genuine believer."

"Hey, will you two cut out the religious talk? We have no idea what you're going on about," Mel said. "But let me add my two bob's worth: 'The Lord said come fourth and receive eternal life, I came fifth and received a box of chocolates.'"

That one caught Aaron off guard but he thought about it and laughed. Mel did have the ability to relax things. Mel needed to expand on the joke before Churchie and Wally responded.

The rest of the journey was taken up by the boys debating the best places to get secondhand clothes from—there were quite a few options.

As they got closer to Mackenzie's place, Aaron told them that the man with Mackenzie on her little adventure would be at the barbeque.

Mel asked his name.

"Joshua." Aaron looked in the mirror as he responded. He saw something in Mel's face—a kind of reaction, but to what, he didn't know.

* * *

Aaron turned the car into a quiet tree-lined street, tidy gardens on one side, and well-kept parklands taking up half of the other side. He pulled up outside the Gordon's house. Aaron told the crew that his parent's house was across the road—he would drop in and see Mum before he left. Mum's lawn needed mowing. He wondered how she was coping without Dad.

Aaron stared at the familiar woven wire gate. It brought back fond memories of the past. He held the gate open and ushered them all through, closed the gate, and then led them up to the front door. Mackenzie had already opened the door and came bounding towards them. She jumped up and gave Aaron a hug, nearly knocking him of his feet. Aaron freed his head from Mackenzie's headlock and looked at the smiling face of Churchie.

What a welcome, she's just so glad to see us all. Aaron was touched by the welcome, but thought of Paul and felt guilty.

Mackenzie led them inside, through the house and into the backyard where they were greeted by a barking Jethro. Aaron took in the floodlit scene: Mackenzie's dad manning the barbeque, her mum down the back of the garden inspecting her favorite shrubs with a man Aaron assumed was Joshua, flashes of Jethro as he sprinted along the fence line.

They all turned when Aaron and the motley crew made their entrance. Kathy and Joshua made their way up from the back of the yard. Aaron walked down the steps, over to Kathy, gave her a hug and turned to the man with her.

"You must be Joshua." Aaron held out his hand. "I'm Aaron." They shook hands. "Thanks for watching over Mackenzie for us."

"No, you've got that wrong. She looked after me."

Aaron's eyes moved to the black botch under Joshua's right eye. Not wanting to stare, he fixed his gaze elsewhere.

"Nope, that's not true either," Mackenzie said as she came up beside Joshua. "It was a team effort, helped along by things unseen."

They headed back up the steps. Aaron smiled. "Let me introduce you to what I refer to as the motley crew." Where was Mel? "I think you all know Churchie. Maybe you don't, Joshua."

Churchie walked over and shook Joshua's hand.

"I hear you have a gift of seeing the unseen world?" said Joshua.

"A gift . . . maybe you're right there, Joshua. It's just taken me a while to realize that."

"And this is Wally. He's a quiet man but is a loyal friend to Churchie and Mel." Wally gave everyone a wave and a smile. Aaron looked around—still no Mel. "Now, I need to find the last member of the motley crew."

Aaron quickly ran up the steps and went inside. Mel stood beside a partially open lace-curtained window, staring into the backyard.

"Whatcha doing, Mel? You haven't gone shy on me, have you?"

"No, Aaron." He turned to Aaron, his eyes watery. "That's my brother down there."

"What do you mean, Mel . . . your brother?"

Mel let go of the lace curtain, which swayed gently with the breeze before settling back in place. "Aaron. My name isn't Mel, it's Scott Jones. Joshua and I got separated years ago and went our separate ways. I saw his picture in one of the articles covering the recent events. I wasn't 100 per cent sure it was him but I thought it could be, and it is."

Aaron walked over and put his hand on Mel's shoulder. "Mel . . . Scott. What should I call you?" He said that with a smile. "Maybe we should get you two reacquainted."

"Call me Mel. That's who you know me as."

Outdoor sounds filtered inside as Mackenzie parted the colored plastic strips hanging on the back door.

"Everything okay?"

Aaron turned and looked at Mackenzie. "I think we're just in for another surprise on this journey. I'm seeing quite clearly now that there's no such thing as a coincidence."

Mackenzie gave Aaron a puzzled look.

"You know Mel."

"Of course I do." She walked up and gave him a big hug.

"Well, his name's really Scott. And . . . your friend Joshua is his brother."

Mackenzie gave Mel another squeeze. "Wow!"

The breeze had picked up and was now dispersing the smell of sizzling sausages.

Aaron and Mel walked out together and found Joshua assisting James on the barbeque. Aaron tapped Joshua on the shoulder. He turned.

"I believe you know this man." Aaron moved Mel forward.

Joshua stood there, speechless. He paused, moved his head slightly. "It's not . . . it can't be . . . Scott?"

They embraced.

Aaron sensed Joshua was overcome by the situation, so grabbed a chair and placed it near him. Joshua sat down and shook his head. He waved Mackenzie over and took her hand. "Mackenzie, this God of yours is amazing."

"He's your God too, Joshua."

Aaron looked around and noticed everyone staring at the unfolding scene. "Sorry, everyone. I was going to introduce Mel to those that didn't know him . . . but as it turns out, his name's not really Mel. It's Scott, and this here is his long-lost brother, Joshua."

Mackenzie's mum placed her hand to her mouth. Wally and Churchie looked at each other. James, with a sausage in a set of tongs, said, "Let's eat and celebrate this great surprise."

On the patio, everyone sat on canvas director chairs. Aaron had already spilt some sauce from his sausage sandwich on his hooded sweater. Mackenzie stared at him with her eyebrows raised, and threw him a paper napkin. Aaron wiped the sauce and looked at the reunited brothers.

"So, Joshua, is Scott the reason you came to Brisbane?' Aaron asked.

"Yep. Our mum is dying and she wanted to see Scott again. And I needed to get away because I'd been a naughty boy, not paying fines and things like that. But it's all turned out good. We'll head back to Melbourne as soon as we can.'

Mackenzie came over with a wet napkin and gave it to Aaron. He needed to do a better job on the sauce spill. Mackenzie looked over at the brothers.

"Joshua and Mel, if there is anything we can do to help, let us know. We can check out some flights for you later. We mean it; we want to help you both," Mackenzie said.

After dessert, Mackenzie located some discounted airfares and had them on a flight back to Melbourne on Saturday morning. She also helped find the winery with a funny name.

* * *

A simple Google search located the winery, at least what they believed to be the one with the funny name. Sirromet Winery was located in the Mount Cotton area about forty minutes from the city, midway between Brisbane and the Gold Coast.

So the next day they hastened together a posse and went looking for the Rev. Aaron believed it might set off some triggers if they took Wally, Joshua and Mackenzie for a drive around the area. Mel and Churchie joined them. James lent them his Prado, as it gave them the required seating.

In twenty minutes they were out of city traffic and the suburban blocks were being replaced by large properties, some well hidden, their existence given away by long driveways. With the large properties came paddocks with horses and bags of horse manure for sale.

Aaron saw a white cross on the side of the road as he took the Prado around a slight bend. He thought of the cross at the business park, of the parents of the boys that lost their lives in the fire. He hadn't forgotten his promise to himself that he would seek justice for the parents if it wasn't an accident.

Aaron noticed Mackenzie turned to look back at the cross. "Aaron, could you pull over here? There's something familiar about this place." Mackenzie turned to Joshua. "Does this ring any bells with you, Joshua?"

Joshua looked around. They both got out of the car to have better look. The others watched.

"Hey, Aaron, once when I was out driving with my window down, a police man pulled up beside me and pointed at me and said, 'Pullover'." I looked at the police officer, tugged the top of my clothing and said, 'No, it's a cardigan'." Mel said.

Mel made Aaron laugh, even though at times it may have been inappropriate. Churchie and Wally were laughing at this one.

"I think I've heard that one before, Mel," said Churchie.

Wally chirped in. "Me too. It was in a movie called *Dumb and Dumber*. I think Mel was in the movie, too." Wally started laughing.

Aaron looked at Wally in the rear-view mirror. Wally was starting to come out of his shell.

Mackenzie came up to the driver's side. "This is the right area,

Aaron. Joshua and I agree we've been here before. We witnessed an accident. But we're unsure which direction we came from.

"I agree, Aaron. I remember driving past here," Wally said.

"Well, where to from here?" Aaron asked.

"Let's get something to eat at the winery. I'm sure they would have a snack bar or something like that," Mackenzie said.

There was all-round agreement.

* * *

Aaron turned the Prada into the Sirromet driveway and headed towards some buildings at the top of a hill, looking for a place to eat.

Grapevines lined both sides of the road. Wallabies stood feeding among the grass patches between the vines, oblivious to the passing of the four-wheel drive. Aaron parked the vehicle, and they made their way over to where they could order some food. While in the queue, Aaron looked up at some posters on the wall. They were posters of past events—music concerts. This place attracted good bands, good singers—a future date with Mackenzie, maybe.

After ordering some snacks and drinks, they found their way over to an area that gave great views of the valley. A number of vacant benches and tables greeted them. As the winery advertising material suggested, the sky was impossibly blue. Aaron looked down to a large grassy area, probably where they had their concerts.

Mackenzie sat down next to Aaron. "Do you think the Rev's okay, Aaron?"

"Should be, Mackenzie. Don't know why he'd come to any harm."

"I feel a bit guilty. You know sitting around eating . . . relaxing . . . when he may be in trouble."

"I know what you mean. But we need to eat and I'm sure he wouldn't want us moping around. We will find him."

Churchie looked at Wally. "Hey, Wally, my angel's telling me that you should go around the side of the building there."

"Why?"

"There's someone there you need to see."

Aaron sensed Wally was unsure about this. "Come on, Wally, I'll go with you."

Aaron looked at the plate of potato wedges. He grabbed a couple before he stood up. They were hot. He juggled them as he walked with Wally around the side of the building. They stopped and stared at an extension ladder with a man three-quarters of the way up it. The man sensed their presence, looked down at them and gave them a smile.

Wally looked at him. "You don't remember me, do you?"

He came down the ladder and walked over and started topping up his paint tray. He looked hard at Wally. "Not sure if I know you."

"You dropped me off at a bus stop not too long ago."

"My . . . you scrub up well."

* * *

The painter was a friendly man. Aaron asked if he could tell them where he had picked Wally up from. The painter took his smartphone out of his pocket and brought up a map of the area.

"It's not far from here. I'd just picked up a ladder from this property here and then started driving down West Mount Cotton Road. It was about here that you jumped out and scared the living daylights out of me."

"Sorry . . . these phones are amazing," Wally remarked, moving his head on an angle to get a better view.

Aaron thought that he would expand on things to see if the painter may have an idea of the property they were looking for. "Have you been hearing the news items . . . sorry, what was your name?"

The painter grabbed the ladder, looked up and moved the ladder a few paces to the right. "I'm known as BT. I'm not a real 'news' person, but catch the news in the van every now and then."

"Nice to meet you BT. I'm Aaron and he's Wally, just in case you didn't exchange names at your last meeting. Have you heard about people going missing, dead bodies being raised . . ."

"Pretty hard not to. Every time I put the radio on there seems to be some discussion about that—pretty weird stuff, hey?"

Aaron nodded and watched as the painter went over to a large paint bucket. "Wondering, would you have any idea of any well-concealed properties out where you found Wally."

BT stopped and looked at Aaron. A look of enthusiasm came

over him. "Of course . . . why didn't I think of this sooner? The place I picked the ladder up from, we did a paint job there . . . and the more I think about it, it must be the place. Let me call my boss and see if I can get an early mark. I'll take you there."

Aaron watched as BT made the call. He was wondering should they go there or should they contact the police. Maybe make sure it was the right property first, and then call the police.

BT was off the phone now. "Boss not keen on me leaving the job. If you can grab some paper and a pen, I'll draw you a map."

CHAPTER TWENTY EIGHT

THEY BOTH HEARD IT the same time. They got up from their seats.

"Was that a car door closing?"

The Rev nodded. "I think so." Another door closed.

"Sounds like a couple of doors closed . . . looks like we're going to be out of here soon." The Rev prayed a quiet thank you. His ears pricked up as a door opened up just outside the room. He could hear muffled voices, then sensed movement above his head. He looked up and saw a video camera scanning the room. He pointed it out to Windsor, who gave a wave.

They heard a crackle and then a voice boomed into the room. "Hello, Minister. Didn't expect to see you here. Didn't think you had the guts to do a transfer. And I'm annoyed that I left that transfer box there. Maybe I should have at least password-protected it. Must return and get it, but then again, how often do they go and check a dead body?"

The Rev saw the look on the minister's face. "Who is this?" he asked Windsor.

"One of my assistants," Windsor said.

"One of his assistants," Lucas repeated. They heard laughter.

"You're a puppet, Windsor. Starkey just used you to get funding for the technology. Now that things have gone off the rails he's probably bolted. And it looks that way, if you could see what's happened in this room. All the filing cabinet's drawers are open and there are no papers to be seen. He's either taken the secrets of his technology with him or burnt them."

"That's not true. He is a friend."

"Wake up, Windsor . . . prestige was what he was seeking."

"And you, Lucas, where do you stand?"

"I bumble along in life, Windsor. Circumstances come and go. I have the technology now and I'm sure it will prove useful. As for what, I don't know yet."

"My, you're showing your true colors now, Lucas. What has brought this about?"

"You, Windsor, and this stupid world we live in."

The Rev had decided to try and find an exit clause. "Hello, Lucas, could you let us out of here? It's starting to get quite stuffy. Couldn't we talk face to face?"

"Would love to, preacher man, but what would happen then? No, it's best you remain there. We need to make a getaway. I'll let someone know where you are. Anyway, I'm sure your God will look after you, maybe drop some manna from the sky."

They heard laughter again, followed by a clicking sound. The microphone had been turned off. A few moments later they heard the door open and close and voices yell out goodbyes.

The Rev looked at Windsor.

"He's snapped, or something like that. I think he's a dope smoker; I was starting to pick up sniffs of something like burnt grass clippings."

"It does happen," the Rev said as he went and sat down. "There have been many reports over the years of people losing the plot and going a bit weird after prolonged use of marijuana. Its most probably caught up with him. Needs some rewiring to be done in his head. Sad, and to think there are people out there who want to legalize the stuff. Crazy world, hey? Got to have our drugs."

"Well, it sounds like it's caught up with Lucas. There were many days, more recently, where I noticed a glazed look in his eyes, not that he took his sunglasses off too regularly. He must be taking other stuff now because the episode I had with him in the cryonics facility was not pleasant. It was like I was dealing with a different person."

"You could have been. Drugs can function much like an ouija board in terms of being a gateway to the demonic world. You could have been dealing with a possessed man."

Windsor shuddered.

"It's all about mind control. I believe drugs, alcohol, and even meditation techniques give demons access to the mind. They control the individual and make them do things. And the longer they've been on the stuff, the more depressed and unpredictable they become."

"That's a worry, Rev. I don't think the technology and unpredictability are going to be a good match."

"Well, let's hope he has a moment of sanity and does let someone know we're here."

* * *

Lucas turned left on to West Mount Cotton road and started heading towards Cornubia. The transporter device was safely tucked away in the boot of the car. He had two devices now. He would have to work out how to retrieve the other one at some point, although he wasn't overly keen on being in that room with the oversized coffee flask.

A plan started to form in Lucas's mind. He didn't understand why, but he just couldn't get that girl out of his head. He thought of that obsessive melody put out by Kylie Minogue and tried to recall the beat.

"Hey, Tag, how did that Kylie Minogue song go? You know the one: Can't get you out of my mind."

"I'm not sure, Lucas. Think it was 'head' not 'mind'. Is it something like: *la, la, la, . . . la, la, la*?"

"That's good, Tag." Lucas hummed the tune.

Lucas was obsessed. Was she close by or something? Maybe he was picking up her vibes. Best if he put his thoughts elsewhere.

"Hey, Tag, you okay about things?"

"Yeah, no worries. All an adventure. Besides, we've been behaving ourselves too much of late. What are your plans with the technology?"

"Nothing yet, mate, but we may need to vanish for a while."

"I hope you don't mean using the technology."

"Nope." Lucas laughed. "The technology is a transporter, point A to point B. It won't turn us into invisible men. We just need to go away for a while until the dust settles, until something else catches the attention of the media. Does your sister still have that place up in the hinterland?"

"Yep."

"We should give her a call."

Lucas sang the song to himself. He just couldn't get her out of his head. Lucas was entering a strange world. And the voices joined in with his singing.

* * *

Aaron saw a car appear from the shrubbery just up ahead of them and turn on to the road in the opposite direction. Dust, lifted by the car, momentarily hid the departing vehicle as it drove off.

Mackenzie sat forward in the car, looking for the entrance. "We may need to slow down here, Aaron. The painter guy said the driveway was easy to miss."

Aaron slowed down. They passed a rusted-out car sitting in a well-grassed paddock. The dust raised by the other car was settling, so he could just make out the driveway the car came from. There was a small break in the greenery, which he pointed out to Mackenzie.

"That could be where that car came out from. Maybe the road leads to a couple of properties," Aaron said.

"Maybe. It's close to the painters map. Okay . . . let's turn up it."

They passed an old sign lying in the bush and turned into a dirt road. After a short drive an old Federation home came into view.

"Isn't that place cute, Aaron? "

Aaron wasn't into cute houses yet. "It has character, Mackenzie."

She laughed.

Churchie moved in his seat. "This is the place, Aaron."

Aaron got out of the car and looked around, telling the others to stay put.

The place looked deserted. He sniffed and saw smoke from something smoldering down near a row of trees. Someone had been here recently. Aaron walked up the steps on to the veranda and headed towards the entrance, to be greeted by a large lion's head holding a brass ring. It seemed out of place for a farmhouse. He lifted the ring and rapped it a few times—the raps returned a booming echo. He didn't expect anyone to answer; the place had that deserted feel.

Aaron walked to the end of the veranda and stared out towards a shed. He turned towards the others. Churchie was out of the Prado and pointing towards the shed. Aaron came back down the stairs and headed in that direction.

He heard footsteps on the gravel as Mackenzie came up behind him. He would have preferred her to stay back, but maybe she wanted to exorcise some past demons. He told her to stand back while he opened the shed door. He looked in: benches, monitors on the wall, filing cabinets with drawers open. He walked in. He looked inside one of the drawers—empty.

Mackenzie came in behind him. "They're in that room there, Aaron."

Aaron looked at the handle. It had a combination and sensor light. "Must be a remote somewhere."

Mackenzie found it.

Aaron opened the door and jumped back as two men stood there, staring at him.

"Are you two okay?"

"We are, and thank you."

* * *

They all sat on the steps. Another police car came down the driveway, sending another plume of dust into the sky. The thump-thump of a helicopter sounded close by. Next the media vehicles would arrive.

Aaron looked around the property. This place was going to be gone over with a fine-tooth comb. The ramifications of the technology meant a number of agencies would be involved in the investigation.

They watched the minister being taken to a police vehicle.

"He's a remorseful man. He'd been initially driven by a lust for power, and finally grief took over. He lost his way with his faith," said the Rev. "One of the last things he said to me before you found us was that he didn't fully understand the things of God like he thought he did. He realized that his heart was deceitful and desperately wicked. He was burdened by this and was a shattered man. I told him to seek out God again; his faith and understanding will be restored. He knows that with God, all things are possible."

Aaron listened to the Rev and decided he was a special man. You could feel his love for others. Aaron watched as the Rev turned his attention to Mackenzie.

"Mackenzie . . . he's burdened by the sins he has committed, by what he has done. He realized that his so-called righteous acts are like filthy rags in God's sight. I know this won't be easy but you will need to forgive this man and uphold him in prayer."

"I understand." It was an uncomplicated reply.

Aaron took it all in. *But me?* He was struggling . . . sin? It seemed so old-fashioned. But one thing remained: Aaron's dad's death had not been addressed. Lucas was still out and about. The police had told Aaron they would find him. He believed they would—but if they didn't?

The Rev walked over to Aaron and handed him something. "Put this in your pocket, look at it later."

Aaron did as he was told.

CHAPTER TWENTY NINE

AN OCCASIONAL BEEP BROKE the silence. Small splashes of green from the monitor's indicators lit up in the darkness. A door opened, the florescent lights sensed movement and switched on. The hooded man looked around the facility, and saw the small silos and the aluminum case on the floor in the corner. He walked over, picked up the case and left the facility.

He blended into the darkness; his car parked in the adjacent block.

A police car pulled into the Cryonics, Inc. facility not long after.

* * *

The Cryonics facility manager parked his car in his reserved spot—not that he needed a reserved spot, as the car park never overflowed. He walked over to the police officers and introduced himself. An officer from the Department of Defense sat with them. They all headed to the facility's main entrance.

The facility manager flashed his card over the security pad. A click resulted. He pushed the door open. They wandered around; they could not locate the case.

The Defense officer looked up and noticed a monitor in the room. "What's the purpose of the monitor?"

"Maintenance and security," the facility manager said.

"Are you able to bring up who has accessed the room recently?"

"Sure, wouldn't expect to see much, maybe the occasional maintenance access visit."

"That's fine. Let's have a look."

The facility manager double-clicked an icon that resembled a large key with a small clock underneath it. He entered his user ID and password, then clicked on the appropriate menu. Entries were listed in date order, the most recent first.

"Looks like Grant Windsor paid a visit twenty minutes ago." The Defense officer turned to the police officers. "He's in custody, isn't he?"

They nodded in agreement.

"Wonder who it was then?"

Part Five – Crazy Man

CHAPTER THIRTY

September 2017

THREE MONTHS. A NEW season sprang into life.

Aaron had put in many hours at work to make up for his time off. Now his boss told him he was working too hard, and to take a day off. So he did.

He rode his bike out to Mackenzie's place and then caught the train into the city with her. He wanted to make sure she was coping okay now she'd returned to full-time work. He knew she would be but was just being over protective. She had changed her appearance a little but still got the occasional *'hey isn't that the girl that came back from the dead'* look from strangers.

"Maybe I should have moved interstate like Joshua," Mackenzie said.

"Why's that?" Aaron asked.

"I spoke to Joshua recently. He's doing well and he keeps a low profile as not much Brisbane news filters down to Melbourne. Which would be nice as I still sense a lot of people look at me because of what happened."

Aaron noticed that Mackenzie had her head tilted down slightly as she spoke to him.

Mackenzie continued. "His mum passed away recently and he and Mel have been busy sorting out things. They hoped to come visit around Christmas time. Mel was building up his collection of jokes."

Aaron missed Mel in a funny sort of way.

She continued. "Their mum got things right before she died. He said that if Churchie was there he would have seen the angels come and take his mum's spirit away to be with the Lord. Joshua said there was a nurse in attendance that told them that she had a happy feeling when Joshua's mum passed away. She puts it down to the presence of angels and has experienced it before but not often. Joshua had coffee with the nurse and he told her about his experience. She cried and thanked Joshua for such a beautiful insight."

Aaron wondered how often Mackenzie spoke to Joshua on the phone. "That all sounds good Kenz."

Aaron stared out the window as the train pulled into Central Station. He knew Mackenzie was getting frustrated with him and the faith thing. After all they had been through, she couldn't understand why he hadn't asked Jesus into his life. Aaron wasn't grasping what that meant.

They stopped at the entrance to Mackenzie's work. Aaron placed his hands on Mackenzie' shoulders so she was facing him. He looked her up and down. "You look beautiful, Kenz. Go get 'em."

Mackenzie gave him a peck on the cheek. "I love you, Aaron."

Aaron smiled and watched her walk off.

The Rev had taken Aaron under his wing, and Aaron had a spring in his step as he headed off to meet with him.

* * *

Aaron walked up the concrete steps. He remembered the first time he saw Churchie here, and his comment, 'You deaf or something.' The memory brought a smile to Aaron's face. Funny thing was, he was a little deaf thanks to his Afghanistan experience.

"Aaron, my mate," Churchie called. He sat on a concrete bench just outside the main entrance to the church. "You've come to set your ways right?"

"You're cheeky, Churchie. Where's the Rev?"

"Follow me."

They walked into an area with a large kitchen bench. The Rev came over and gave Aaron a hug. He pointed to the couch. Aaron made myself comfortable and felt a bit nervous. He wondered why he felt that way. Churchie sat on a chair near the window.

The Rev came and sat. "How are you, Aaron?"

"Good, Rev, recovering, like all of us . . . I've just got to deal with my dad issue and the Mackenzie issue, and I'll be as right as rain."

"What's the dad issue?"

"Justice . . . that Lucas fellow had something to do with my dad's death. And he's still out there somewhere."

"What about Windsor and that Starkey bloke? The one that bolted?"

"Good point. I think their involvement was indirect. With Lucas it was a personal thing, we crossed each other's paths. He made it personal by involving Mackenzie."

"That's right. I'd forgotten that. What's the issue with Mackenzie?"

"Something called 'unequally yoked'." Aaron looked around the room as the Rev flipped through a notebook.

"Well I will try and help you understand what's she's saying, Aaron," the Rev said. "Do you like music, Aaron?"

"I do."

"I'm sure you have heard of that famous song *Highway to Hell*."

"Yep."

"I heard the song recently and it made me think about a highway the Bible talks about. It refers to a highway to holiness and says that the unclean will not walk on it. So when I hear that song, *Highway to Hell*, I feel quite sad because many are on that highway. The unclean cannot enter God's highway—they are on the highway to hell."

Aaron wasn't sure if he was doing the right thing, being here. He still wasn't really into this Bible talk stuff, but he was doing it for Mackenzie. "Unclean, meaning dirty people . . . sorry Rev, but this is where I get a bit lost. It's like the Bible is written for another age. Who would say 'unclean' these days?"

"Good point, Aaron. Unclean refers to sin. But then sin isn't a fashionable word these days, either."

"Sorry. I didn't mean to be rude."

"Not at all . . . let me tell you what we're going to cover with these little chats. I'm going to walk you down what's known as the Roman Road."

"Highways . . . roads . . . I look forward to this."

"Sounds like you don't know much about the Bible, Aaron?"

"No, not really . . . I have heard people quote from it, and I did do a stint at Sunday School and remember some of the stories, but that's about it."

Aaron watched as the Rev picked up a Bible and started flicking through the pages. "Well, here's a quick description for you. The Bible is made up off sixty-six books, two major parts known as the Old Testament, which has thirty-nine books, and the New Testament, which has twenty-seven books. We believe the Bible is the word of God, where God has inspired or instilled his words into the heart or mind of the writers."

"Learned something already, didn't know any of that."

"Good. I could go into a lot more but I won't for now except that the navigation system used for the books of the bible is chapter and verses. The Roman Road, which I mentioned before, is a number of verses from the book of Romans. Romans was written by a man called Paul, who wrote a number of letters to the early churches."

"Okay. Hit me."

The Rev handed Aaron and Churchie a piece of paper. It had written on it:

Romans 3:23 For all have sinned and fall short of the glory of God

"So we're back to that sin word. It is indeed an old-fashioned word—modern society would be more familiar with the word 'crime'."

"Now I have heard of that one."

"Sin is the cause of most crimes. But it even goes further, into all facets of our lives; our relationships, our thoughts. Sin is all about missing a target, a standard that has been set by God. As the verse says, we have fallen short of God's glory, the way he wanted us to live."

"For all have sinned, Aaron . . ." said Churchie, "that's the thing that hit me, it hit me hard. I realized I was a sinner and sensed that I wasn't right with God and needed to do something about it. And with those angels hanging around, I knew this was serious stuff."

Aaron had to agree with Churchie but thought that seeing angels was a big advantage. Aaron started pondering his condition.

"Another thing with sin, Aaron, is that there aren't different categories for sins. There are no little sins and big sins, just one sin and you're stained. And that little sin could have been a little white lie to your mother when you were five years old."

Aaron smiled. He was stained. He thought of Mel's joke. Repaint and thin no more—it made a bit more sense now.

The Rev continued. "I'll tell you this now, it will make sense later. The blood of Jesus covers your sins. We need to be covered by the blood of Jesus."

Some words penetrate deeply. These words did, and for good reason.

CHAPTER THIRTY ONE

THE HINTERLAND PROPERTY HAD a sunroom attached to the rear of the house. Lucas was seated on a wicker sofa, taking a deep drag on the glass pipe. He waited for the effects to kick in, for his mind to relax; it came not long after. But it wasn't all good: his thoughts went everywhere, and for a crazy moment he wondered who he was talking to in his head. He would talk aloud to something but get no response. His mate referred to it as a spirit of madness.

But then, as always, after his mind storm ended, his thoughts would focus on the girl, on Mackenzie. He turned as expecting to see her sitting on the sofa next to him. He stored many memories from the property, he had watched her on the monitor, her every movement. He knew where she worked. That's how he got her the first time—that was an accident but it turned out okay. He knew her path to work. She had always followed the same routine. Did she change it after what happened?

He laughed—he now had the technology. But he couldn't think of anything to do with it.

The drugs were working now. He was tuned into his surroundings, and his heartbeat was so loud, he looked down to his chest expecting to see his chest pushing out with each beat. The magnified sound of plastic door strips rubbing against each other made him turn. Tag entered the sunroom.

He looked up at Tag. Lucas thought he saw someone, something, standing beside Tag, but he shook his head and it was no longer there.

"Why the shake of the head, Lucas . . . you're not stoned, are you?"

"Nah . . . just relaxed. Whatcha up to?"

"Just got off the phone to my sister. She said she'll be back in three to four weeks. Hoped we were looking after the place and that you hadn't pinched all her dope. She also said we're welcome to stay longer after she returned. I think she likes you, Lucas."

"You're making me blush, Tag . . . where does she hide her dope? . . . just joking."

"You've already found it." Tag walked over to the window. "Have you worked out what we're going to do with the technology? Is there a way we can use it to make money?"

"I've hit a brick wall with it, Tag. The boss was going to use it to 'relocate' law breakers, the theory being that they would be so 'inconvenienced' it would deter them from breaking the law again."

"Do you think it would have worked, Lucas?"

"What's that?" Lucas had forgotten what they were talking about.

"Inconveniencing people." Tag walked back towards the door. "Let's continue this discussion later. Could you stay away from the dope? I want to have a proper discussion with you soon. I have to go and get my sister's dog from a neighbor—they can't look after it any more. I think it may have attacked one of their dogs or chooks."

"Make sure you keep a low profile with them. Where are they?"

"Nearest neighbors around here, Lucas, are about half a kilometer away and these are another couple of kilometers further."

"What sort of dog is it?"

"Pit bull."

"Aren't they a bit violent?"

"He's okay. Just feed him and he'll love you."

He watched as Tag pushed his hands into the hanging door strips, separating them and then headed back inside the house. Lucas watched the plastic strips as they jostled with each other, fighting to get back into their positions. He pictured Mackenzie standing behind the strips. *Yes, love, I will come and get you soon.*

* * *

Lucas climbed out of bed, opened the curtains and looked out into the paddock. The grass and fallen trees were all wet from overnight dew. He saw the dog walking around, leaving his paw prints in the dew. His mother was standing in the paddock wearing an apron and collecting daisies, waving to him. He shook his head . . . where did that image come from? He could barely remember his mother.

He went back and sat down on the bed. He didn't want to look at the window just in case his mother was still there. Instead, he stared at the devices sitting on the floor. *What am I going to do with you?*

Here I am, in the middle of nowhere. He got up and walked into the passageway and into the spare room. A single bed. He walked over to the window. No curtains. His mother had gone. This room needed to be made secure. He needed to go buy some things.

He found Tag in the kitchen. "Your sister won't mind if we make the spare room more secure, would she? He walked over and saw Tag was making himself some eggs. "Could you make me some of them?"

"Scrambled okay?"

"Sure . . . I have a bit of a plan coming into my head. We could relocate a rich kid here. Hold them. Get a ransom."

"Go on."

"Use the technology to zap a rich kid, get the money dropped off somewhere, zap the money, return the kid. A bit tricky, but I reckon we could do it. Maybe go for a million, and then get out of the country."

"Is a million enough?"

"Are you getting greedy?"

"No, Lucas, but think about it. That's only half a million each. But it sounds like an idea. Another one could be to sell it to some criminal mob and then get out of the country."

"That's a good idea, Tag. That could be a better one, cleaner. Just pass the technology on to someone else and get out of the country. Maybe we'd be safer if we just stay in the country. The airports may have alerts on us."

There was a renewed enthusiasm at the kitchen table that morning.

* * *

Tag sat in the white car with a briefcase open next to him. He had the image of a biker on the screen.

There was a bit of confusion when the bike fell over. Tag would have been confused too if he saw someone vanish.

They chose this biker because he was well-known for having connections with all the local criminal elements.

* * *

Lucas was glad he had the shotgun. Biker Bill sat on the floor, with his helmet in his hand, staring at Lucas.

Lucas smiled inside the mask because he realized how stupid the old man mask looked. He moved the gun barrel towards the bed. "Please stand up and take a seat on the bed there." He watched the biker stand up and sit on the edge of the bed. "I know you may be somewhat confused with things, but I know you are a person of authority so I wanted you to have first-hand experience with a product that is up for sale."

Biker Bill just stared straight at Lucas.

"Go on," Biker Bill said.

"Although it's been some weeks, maybe months, I'm sure you've come across the media coverage of the vanishing people and associated goings-on."

"I have."

"We are the owners of that technology and would like it to put it up for sale."

"Wouldn't it have been easy to put it on eBay?"

Lucas laughed. "We're looking at two million dollars. There's a piece of paper with a number on it on the bedside table there. I'm sure you would consider the technology a good investment. If you would like to pursue the investment, leave a message at the number on that piece of paper in three days' time."

Lucas waited for him to grab the piece of paper. "Put your helmet on. This technology's really easy to use and I don't want you to hurt your head." Lucas walked backwards with the gun still pointing

towards Biker Bill. A device sat on a table near the door. "Real easy."
He pushed a button. Biker Bill was gone.

Lucas felt that three days gave them enough time to think about
the benefits of the technology. It also gave him time for another
activity he wanted to pursue.

CHAPTER THIRTY TWO

AARON HAD GONE INTO protective mode with Mackenzie. His daily regime involved a bike ride from the city to Mackenzie's place and joining her on a train ride back to the city. He completed the regime with a bike ride back to the city after he got her home safely. She had finally convinced him that he didn't need to do it every day; they settled on just every second day. He tried to use the excuse that he needed the exercise. She had laughed at that.

He was on protective duty today.

Aaron looked around the train carriage. Everyone was stained, covered with spots of sin—some with a few, some with many.

Aaron reckoned he had worked it out—well, most of it. There was no connection to God, no relationship with God, because of his sins. He was stained. But he hadn't quite worked out what he was meant to do about it. The stains needed to be covered and he knew it had something to do with Jesus. The Rev referred to Aaron as a dead man walking. Aaron had laughed and asked how a dead man could walk.

The Rev told him that in the scheme of things man was going to live forever, but sin through Adam brought an end to that. With sin came death, which we were all born into, hence the term dead man walking. We are all born dead, spiritually dead.

"Thinking about something, Aaron?"

Aaron smiled as he turned to Mackenzie. She had her iPad on her lap. He saw behind her that they were passing Roma Street station. "Just pondering things that the Rev has been telling me."

"Can I help?"

"Just thinking about sin, death, and living forever."

She smiled. "Take a look at this."

He leaned over. She tapped an area of her Bible. It said:

For the wages of sin is death, but the free gift of God is eternal life in Christ Jesus our Lord.

"Ponder that, Aaron. Ask God to give you understanding."

* * *

Aaron was still pondering when they pulled into Central Station.

He had an appointment on the other side of the city this morning. He didn't tell Mackenzie. She would have insisted that he not walk her to work. But there was time. He could do both.

Mackenzie was in good spirits, and keen to cross over where the incident occurred. She said it was time they put it all behind them. She was busy at work and had just completed a number of technology proposals for some clients. Aaron knew her busyness was helping the healing process but it was also making her a bit careless. He knew danger still lurked.

They crossed over the road without incident and headed towards Mackenzie's work. Aaron was a bit more vigilant today as there were rumors circulating about another vanishing, a biker fellow. Aaron knew that the police would find it hard to get any information. But Aaron was concerned. If Lucas was behind the latest disappearance, his appetite for using the technology had been activated again. He remembered how stoned Lucas was that night he visited Aaron, and he knew drug users could be unpredictable.

What was Lucas up to? Aaron wanted Lucas to make an appearance as they had unfinished business. He had moved from his Morningside flat, and Aaron had been unable to track him down.

Aaron still had a battlefield sixth sense. He could become overly sensitive to the environment he was in. There was short-term parking available on the road across from Mackenzie's work. A number of parking spaces were available. One space was taken up by a white Ford Taurus. There was a large man sitting in the car. Aaron looked toward the car. The man looked the other way.

"Mackenzie. You know I'm paranoid, but there's a white car over there that concerns me." Aaron looked around and noticed a coffee place just behind them. "How about you drop in there and grab a coffee and I'll go and check out the car."

Mackenzie looked at the coffee shop. "Okay, but I'm sure it's nothing. There are lots of white cars in the city . . . okay . . . be careful."

Aaron walked away from the car, crossed the road and came up behind the vehicle. As he got closer to the vehicle it drove off. He recorded its number plate—if he saw it again in the vicinity he would follow it up with the police. But then again the person may work around here. For some reason Aaron doubted that.

Aaron dropped Mackenzie safely off at work and headed towards his appointment. He jumped on a free City Loop bus to get over the other side of the city. There were a few work messages on his phone. He looked up to ponder a message and watched cars going by. A white Ford Taurus passed and he glanced at its number plate. It was the same car, and it was heading back in the direction of Mackenzie's work.

Aaron fought with himself. Was he being paranoid? But there was a knowing spirit at work in him. He got off at the next stop.

He kept telling himself that all was okay but he still rushed along the footpath, back towards Mackenzie's work. He could see the car in the distance working its way through the traffic.

At an intersection, he had to wait for cars to pass and watched the Taurus go over a crest. When the cars had passed, he crossed the road, ignoring the red man, the Don't Walk symbol. He had to do the same at the next crossing. The roads were busy.

* * *

Mackenzie looked at her phone. The battery was dead. She left it on her desk, recharging, while she hand-delivered a proposal to a client just down the street.

She stepped out into the street. It was quiet. The client's office was in an old renovated building a few blocks away. She crossed the road, heading towards the building, and noticed a white car. Was it the same white car again? Aaron must be getting to her. Now she was feeling paranoid as well.

She knew it was happening. How stupid. It wasn't paranoia: it was the Spirit prompting. She entered the realm again.

CHAPTER THIRTY THREE

"Hello, Mackenzie."

Mackenzie's reaction to this transfer was different. She knew what had happened and she was alert to her surroundings. The man had the same build as the one from the shed. "No mask today?" she asked.

She was ignored. "Are you feeling okay, all intact?"

"I am. Thank you for your concern." This was different. She felt God's strength like never before. "Why are you doing this?"

"Well, I wanted to have a date with you, and I don't think you would have accepted if I just called you up out of the blue."

This man was in another world. Mackenzie looked around the room, a bedroom. It wasn't as secure as the shed that she was in before. She could probably smash the window and run for it. That didn't seem right. Too easy. No masks. This time was different.

"What sort of date?"

"I was thinking of a dinner date. I know we don't know each other very well but I sense that we are meant to be together, you know, like soul mates."

The man was not in his right mind, and was possibly dangerous and unstable. She started weighing up her options.

"Do you like that idea?"

"The dinner sounds nice, but there's going to be a lot of people worried about me at the moment."

"You can call them tomorrow. Do you have your phone?"

Her handbag sat on the floor. She bent down to pick it up. On the way up she caught the way he was looking at her. She shivered. She rummaged through her bag, but remembered her phone was still at work.

"Are you cold?"

"No . . . and no I don't have a phone. I left it at work, recharging." She sat on the bed.

"Your bag, please." He walked over, grabbed it and emptied the contents on the bed. There was a photo of Mackenzie with some people her age. He picked it up and studied it. "These are the men in your life?"

"Close friends of mine . . . sadly, your technology killed one of them." Mackenzie regretted that comment as soon as she said it. Her mum's words jumped into her head. *Consider what great forests are set on fire by a small spark.*

"I didn't kill anybody. It was the mad professor: he invented the technology."

Mackenzie sensed heaviness in the room. She asked the Lord to be with her, to be her strength and refuge. The man's face had hardened. He walked over to her, grabbed her and dragged her to her feet. He closed in on her face.

"I didn't kill anybody," he repeated.

This man was a different person now, and she felt fear. "Are you here by yourself?" Her head was scrabbling for ideas. *What to do?*

"At the moment. My mate who did the transfer will be back soon. Let me show you around the house."

Mackenzie followed him into the passageway. He showed her the bathroom, which had a nautical theme, with a fishing net hanging from the ceiling. Back in the passageway, he stopped at a window and pointed to the view outside.

"Lovely rural setting but we're in the middle of nowhere." The loud distinctive call of a peewee could be heard. Mackenzie spotted the bird and watched as a dog came charging at it. The dog stopped and watched as the peewee flew off.

"And the dog . . . I think he's a very dangerous dog. If you decided to venture out there without me, you could be in a spot of bother."

He seemed to have switched back to the other person. Mackenzie nodded her head in agreement. She had a quick thought of Jethro and wished she was back at her old home. She decided the next time that other person visited, she was going to rebuke the spirit in the name of Jesus.

* * *

The police tracked the Ford Taurus to a 24-hour car park. It was a hire vehicle. The police dusted the vehicle for fingerprints.

A man with what looked like a shiny briefcase stepped into the train carriage on Platform six at Central Station. This was Lucas's idea. He reckoned they would be on the lookout for the car so he told Tag to catch a train back.

Tag sat down and made himself comfortable for the two-hour trip. He would call Lucas near the end of the trip to come and collect him. He assumed the transfer went well. It was a favor for Lucas, because he desperately wanted that girl. The technology would be out of their hands in a few days so Lucas had wanted to do the last transfer on the girl.

Tag hoped Lucas's spaced-out behavior was wearing off.

* * *

The kitchen had a small wooden table painted green, and four heavy wooden chairs sat tucked in under the table. Lucas dragged out one of the chairs and told Mackenzie to take a seat.

"Cup of tea or coffee?" A picture of a cow's face on a tea coaster smiled up at her.

Mackenzie looked around the kitchen. She noticed a knife block near the fridge. Could she do that? No, too dangerous.

"My name's Lucas and yours, I know, is Mackenzie. I would really like you to get to know me Mackenzie. I know these circumstances aren't the best for starting a relationship, but I do believe that we're meant to be together. This may sound crazy to you, but I hear voices in my head. They told me that we're going to be together and I believe them."

Mackenzie listened and spoke silently to her Lord.

"I'm going to go into town and get some stuff for tonight. Now, I trust you, Mackenzie. There's no phone in the house, and don't try and befriend the dog because he will attack and probably kill you, so please don't do anything stupid."

Lucas started walking out of the kitchen and turned back to Mackenzie. "One other thing. You won't be able to transfer yourself back—the device is now password protected." He learned that lesson after the Rev transferred himself. "So we can receive but can't send unless you know the password, and I'm not going to tell you that unless you are nice to me."

He walked off, chuckling.

* * *

She watched the crazy man drive off.

Mackenzie walked to the back door and stood there. She started to open the door and heard the dog barking. She closed the door. The dog stood there, looking up at Mackenzie, eyes shining, teeth glowing and mouth frothing.

Mackenzie searched the house for something to feed the dog with, but couldn't find anything. *Okay, dog, you win. This time I won't come out.* She walked back down to the bedroom and started picking up her handbag items from the floor. The photo of Aaron and Paul had her crying. She got up, sat on the bed and wiped her tears. "Please Lord, help me."

She looked at the transfer device. There were lights flickering. She opened the case and saw the password prompt. Should she turn the device off? Best leave it for now.

Mackenzie walked out of the bedroom and closed the door, headed back to the kitchen, found herself a glass and poured some water. She looked out the window and saw a tractor in the distance, plowing the land, dust rising. Was there any way she could get the driver's attention? Maybe set fire to the house?

She sat down. It was deathly quiet. She got up, opened a window and was greeted by a bark and growl. *How quick is this dog?* She sat down again. *Lord, please help, I'm frightened.* What was that noise? She looked around and saw a bird sitting on the window ledge. It was calling out to someone. She gave a nervous smile. Silence returned.

Thump. What was that? It was loud and came from down the passageway. A dull sound, like something had fallen onto the carpet.

In the silence, she was sure she heard a creak. And then another. A door was being opened.

She got up silently, walked over to the knife rack, found the largest knife, and concealed herself behind the kitchen door. She stood there, shaking. The mirror under the clock reflected the passageway.

Someone was moving in the passageway, coming towards the kitchen. They stopped and pushed open a door, Mackenzie thought maybe that was the bathroom door. They were looking for something. Back in the passageway again, the mirror picked them up.

Mackenzie was shaking uncontrollably now. She screamed. "Who's there?"

A voice came back. "Mackenzie . . . is that you?"

Aaron?

CHAPTER THIRTY FOUR

AARON CAUTIOUSLY ENTERED THE room. Mackenzie burst into his arms.

Aaron looked around. "Are you by yourself?"

"Yes . . . the crazy man has gone to buy some things from the local shops."

"He went shopping and left you here?"

Mackenzie hugged Aaron even tighter. "He's crazy, Aaron . . . I think he's in some kind of psychotic state. He's living in another world." She pushed back and looked up at Aaron. "How did you get here?"

"I have access to the technology, Kenz. I have one of their devices."

"But how?"

"The Rev gave me a security card that gave me access to where one of the devices was stored. I think he got the keycard off the minister when they spent their confinement time back at the property. But we can talk more on this later. I need to get us out of here."

"We can't use the technology. You need a password for the device. There's a mighty mean dog out there. I searched for food to pacify him but the place is bare."

"Pity about the technology. That's what I was planning to do. Mean dog . . . no food?" Aaron walked over to the kitchen window. The dog soon made its presence known. A nice pat wasn't going to work here. "Do you know if the man has a rifle or something in the house?

"I haven't seen anything . . . besides, I wouldn't let you shoot a dog."

Aaron looked at her, still a loving spirit no matter what the circumstances. He thought of something he saw in the bathroom. "Kenz, I have an idea." She followed him back to the bathroom. He pointed to the net hanging from the ceiling. "This caught my attention when I looked in here before. I think we could throw it over the dog. It may not hold him, but should give us enough time to get out."

Aaron pulled the net down. Bits of plaster floated down from the holes left in the ceiling. It was a good-sized net and more than enough to entangle the dog. He placed the net on the kitchen table.

"Let's go to the front door and see how far we're going to have to sprint."

They came back to the kitchen with a clear view of what they had to do. "Okay, Kenz. I'm going to distract the dog around the back and when I yell, you run to that gate. You'll have plenty of time because I'll throw the net over it, then come and join you."

"You sure this will work, Aaron?"

"It will, Kenz. Either way, you'll get free and I'll be okay. I can look after myself." Aaron walked over and gave her a hug.

"Okay, go to the front door. Make sure you can open it. Give me a yell when you're ready."

Aaron watched her walk off. She looked back, giving him a nervous smile. He got the net off the table and gave it a good look over—the rope was thick and heavy, and he was surprised it stayed hanging from the ceiling. There were no tangles. He felt confident that it would do the trick.

"I'm ready, Aaron."

"Okay, wait for my call."

Aaron went to the back of the house and opened a window. It wasn't long before the dog made its presence known. It started jumping up, trying to get Aaron. Aaron put his arms out with the net. The dog stopped jumping, tilted its head and looked up at Aaron.

Aaron threw the net over the dog. It barked and then started squirming around trying to get the net off its back.

Aaron yelled, "Go Kenz."

The front door shut with a loud bang. He saw the dog's ears prick up. It tried to run but was tangled. Aaron sprinted to the front door, opened it and saw Mackenzie safe behind the gate. Aaron opened the flyscreen door, but paused when he heard barking and saw the dog coming around the side of the house, almost free of the net—it was trailing behind. The dog ran to the gate and jumped up at Mackenzie—the net now completely off. Mackenzie stood back. The dog turned and started coming toward Aaron. Aaron closed the flyscreen door. "Get help, Kenz . . . try and contact the police. Don't worry about me I'll be fine."

Aaron watched Mackenzie run off. He thought of getting a towel or something and wrapping that around his arm. It was a mean-looking dog. Aaron looked down the road in the opposite direction to which Mackenzie was heading. A dust cloud was moving along the road. Was that Lucas coming home?

* * *

The dog was at the front gate barking, its tail wagging.

From behind a front bedroom window Aaron watched through lace curtains as Lucas got out of the vehicle. He paused at the gate. Aaron saw him looking at the net on the front lawn. He walked back to the vehicle and came back with what looked like a rifle.

Lucas told the dog to be quiet and threw a bone that he must have purchased on his shopping trip. He walked up to the front door and opened it.

Aaron made his way to the kitchen and heard light footsteps as Lucas came down the passageway.

"Mackenzie . . . are you there?" He asked.

Aaron was not afraid. His soldier spirit had kicked in. He wanted answers. "No, she's not, Lucas. Come down and join me: it's about time we caught up with each other again."

Aaron watched as Lucas walked into the kitchen. "I hope you don't plan to use that weapon."

"Well, it all depends what you have done with my girl, Mackenzie?"

"She's just gone for a walk."

"How did you get here?"

"I got a device courtesy of the Minister."

"How did you do that?"

"It was left at the cryonics place."

"Spooky place, hey?"

"Didn't spend much time there, Lucas. How many of those devices are there?"

"Is it really any of your business?" Lucas positioned himself so he could see down the passageway. "But I will tell you anyway. Three all together. They all act as switching devices, you know. You can jump from one to the other as long as they're turned on. Now your device is still turned on, so I can jump to wherever that is. But you couldn't follow as I would turn it off. And I'm thinking that's what I might do."

Aaron watched as Lucas walked over to a kitchen cabinet, rifle still pointing at him. He opened a drawer, pulled out a plastic bag then threw some black cable ties at Aaron and told him to join a few of those cable ties together and tie up his legs. Aaron weighed up in his mind whether he should try and disarm Lucas or not. Still too much of a risk factor involved, so he decided to follow orders. For now.

"You know, my dad died as a result of your technology."

"I had nothing to with that. I was a pawn used by some crazy ambitious men. The minister suggested your dad. He told me where he would be and what he would be wearing, a Beatles t-shirt. How could I forget that? He had something against your dad. I don't think he expected your dad to die; I think he just wanted to scare him, something like that. I was that stoned when I did it, it took me ages to remember. "

Minister guy? Something against Dad?

Lucas continued. "And about the fire—Starkey gave me a package, told me to leave it in the office those young men worked in. I can't prove it, but I believe it was some kind of explosive."

Lucas was shaking his head every now and then, like he was trying to get something out of his head. He nudged Aaron with the rifle to encourage him to hurry up and complete the task with the cable ties. They both jumped when a large clap of thunder shook the room. Lucas went over and looked out the kitchen window. It was getting noticeably darker. He came back and pointed the gun in Aaron's face.

"Get a move on. Do the same with your hands. Use your mouth to tighten the ties." Lucas tested the ties to make sure they were tight. He looked at Aaron. "What have you done with Mackenzie? You've hurt her, haven't you?"

Lucas was having a severe mood swing. The whole atmosphere changed, like some presence had entered the room, some darkness. Lucas's mood was getting darker. He rubbed his head and moved his hand down over his face. Was he fighting something in his head?

"You know, I hear voices in my head. And they're getting loud and angry. They're telling me I should kill you. But I ask, why? And they say that you're going to stop me from getting to Mackenzie."

Aaron thought of something the Rev told him. "Lucas, do you know that Mackenzie is covered in the blood of Jesus?"

Lucas's face changed briefly, "What does that mean?"

"It means you can't get near her."

Now, that brought a nasty response from Lucas. He hit Aaron across the face and was about to do it again when he heard the dog barking.

* * *

Lucas ran to a front room and peered out the window. A police car.

He rushed to the bedroom and stood in the doorway. The device sat on the floor, lights flickering. He looked to the window and saw the darkness converging on the room. Another loud clap of thunder. It was risky using the device with the stormy conditions outside. He always believed the problems that occurred with the transfers were due to climatic conditions. The weather when that man's dad died was similar to today, but the voices were telling him it would be fine.

He doubted Tag would have his device powered on. He should be on a train now. What about Tag? Did he have time to call him and warn him? Not now. He'd call after the transfer.

The voices told him to do it now. He heard scraping noises coming from the kitchen. That man was probably dragging himself to get something to cut the ties.

Lucas walked over to the device, entered the password, and pushed the transfer button.

* * *

The sound of thunder travels great distances. A severe electrical storm was bearing down on Brisbane. Power outages hit a number of properties.

The receiving device sat in Aaron's study, plugged into a power outlet, its lights blinking. A loud clap of thunder, and lights flickered. The lights fought to stay on but their source of power was severed; the lights dimmed, cycling down, power was gone but the device's backup battery took over.

The device displayed a message.

'Connection to other devices lost. To attempt manual reconnect, press F5.'

* * *

Where was he?

He stood there staring at the police car. Mackenzie was standing beside two police officers. He wondered who the other people were. They looked like beings from a science fiction movie. There was also a group of creepy-looking things, but they were standing back with some hovering around the dog. One police officer sprayed something at the dog.

He sensed a presence behind him, turned, and there was darkness with eyes like live coals staring back at him. Voices beckoned. A shrouded figure came towards him.

Lucas screamed.

* * *

Mackenzie sensed something.

She looked up at the sky for a second, and then returned her gaze to the police officers. She thanked the Lord for the man on the tractor and the quick response of the police officers. Probably not a lot of excitement in a community this size, but they looked like they knew what they were doing.

One police officer had sprayed the dog with capsicum spray, which was enough to get the dog to retreat and for the officers to get inside the house. The dog lay under a tree, its paws rubbing its face. Mackenzie was told to stay near the police car.

* * *

Aaron heard the police officers as they declared their presence.

"This is Aaron. I'm okay and I'm in the kitchen at the end of the passageway. There may be a person in the first room on the right."

Aaron knew they would take their time getting to him. They needed to move with caution, ensuring there was no ambush waiting.

There was silence. Just the occasional floor board squeak. They entered the kitchen.

"Hi there. I'm Aaron. Love you to get rid of these cable ties."

"We will. When we can confirm you are Aaron." He turned to the other police officer. "Go get the girl."

"No one in the house then?"

"Just a body in the first room. No pulse."

The other officer returned with Mackenzie.

"Yes. That's Aaron."

The police officer cut the cable ties and Aaron gave his wrists a hard rub. He stood up.

Mackenzie ran up and hugged Aaron. "Are you okay?"

"I am, Kenz."

She turned to the officers. "Thank you ever so much."

"That's okay. Look, we will need to do a few things like get details and things like that. There's a body in the room down there so we need to contact the appropriate authorities. We have also been advised that there is a Department of Defense involvement in this, and we need to wait until they get here."

Notes were taken while they waited.

The thump, thump, thump of helicopter rotors could be heard above the occasional roar of thunder. One of the police officers commented that he wouldn't want to be up there at the moment.

They saw the helicopter land and armed personnel jump out, followed by an officer of some kind.

The dog stayed away, still under the tree rubbing its eyes.

Mackenzie stood next to Aaron as more people made their way into the kitchen. It was a dark house, lights needed to be turned on. The rifles on the armed personnel glistened from the kitchen lights.

There were issues that needed to be addressed—they knew that it was possible that the dead man could be brought back to life, because the circumstances were the same as Mackenzie's. The Defense personnel wanted to know where the other devices were. They had Lucas's phone, and were tracing a number of recent unanswered calls.

The storm clouds hung over the hinterland. A huge clap of thunder shook the house, and the lights flickered, once, then twice, then the power went out. A soft glow came from one of the bedrooms.

The transfer device displayed a message.

'Connection to other devices lost. To attempt manual reconnect, press F5.'

* * *

Tag sat on a bench at the Nambour railway station.

He had tried to call Lucas several times but got no answer. He watched a gang of boys out of the corner of his eye. They looked bored, as if they were searching for something to do. A man with a shiny briefcase was a good target. He looked down at the briefcase— he knew they were scheming something. He couldn't let them get a hold of it. There were people on the other side of the platform. There must be another train coming soon, going back to the city. He would be safer if he was on that. Lucas not answering worried him.

A few of the boys were coming closer. Tag reckoned he could probably take out three of them, but there were more than that. And he could not expect help from the other platform.

What about a transfer? Would Lucas have the receiver turned on? But that would mean he would have to leave the device here.

He was still watching the gang as they got closer. All of a sudden a wolf-whistle broke the silence of the night. One of the boys standing guard must have seen something. The boys jumped on the tracks and ran. Tag looked back on the platform and saw two police officers coming towards him, guns raised.

He pushed the transfer button.

* * *

Aaron watched as the Defense officer took a call on his phone. He walked out of the kitchen and came back after a few moments.

"We have another deceased person our hands," he said. "Apparently, he pressed something on the briefcase he was holding, and then keeled over."

"Sounds like another transfer gone wrong," said Mackenzie.

"What do you mean," asked the officer.

"It happened to me."

"Are you the girl that . . . came back from the dead?"

Mackenzie nodded.

"But their bodies haven't been transferred anywhere," said the officer.

Aaron said, "That's a good point. I would have expected Lucas, that's the name of the man down there, to end up at my apartment in the city."

Aaron watched as the officer raised his eyebrows but continued. "I have a theory. This is a pretty mean storm we're experiencing at the moment. It must affect the communication channel that the devices use. So one question remains: are they in the same situation that Mackenzie ended up in?"

Aaron looked at Mackenzie.

She nodded. "I know, and we have a decision to make."

* * *

How long Lucas was transfixed for, he didn't know. He saw an ambulance arrive and saw what he thought was his own body being brought out to the vehicle. More of those creepy things were hanging around his body. The voices in his head were telling him it was okay to go into the darkness, but he was resisting.

He walked on. He didn't know what to do except walk, and walk very carefully. He passed a property where a farmer was tying down things. His wife was out the door yelling at him, her apron and hair blowing in the wind. It reminded him of the image he had of his mother. How he wished she was here with him now. She had tried so hard to protect him from his dad. He knew she would protect him here. *Please, Mum.* The voice in his head told him he was a wimp, a wuss.

He saw a figure running towards him.

It was Tag.

Part Six – Endings

CHAPTER THIRTY FIVE

AARON SAT HAVING COFFEE with Mackenzie and the Rev, not far from the Rev's church.

It had been a few days since the episode up in the hinterlands. The Rev had a meeting with the Police Commissioner regarding the bodies of Lucas and Tag, and he would be going to the mortuary later today. They decided that he should try the same thing he did for Mackenzie and Joshua. The Rev felt the same in his heart: God had confirmed his action.

The Rev looked at Aaron. "Our journey along the Roman Road is a slow one, Aaron. I can imagine with everything that's going on, your eyes are being opened wide!"

Aaron nodded and thought of what he said to Lucas. "I really sensed evil when Lucas and I were having our confrontation. I told him that Mackenzie was covered in the blood of Jesus, and he went off the deep end. So I think I need to refine that."

"Demons tremble at the name of Jesus," said the Rev. "You did well, and yes, it is a refinement process. I'll have to go soon but it really is important for you to continue down the Roman Road. The next verse I was going to tell you had to do with sin, in that the wages of sin is death but the gift of God is eternal life. So the payment for your sins is death. But there's a gift waiting for you. Remember, a gift is like a present, something you receive from someone. Talk to Mackenzie about it."

The Rev stood up, shook hands with Aaron and gave Mackenzie a hug. She told him to be careful.

They watched as the Rev headed off towards the church and crossed the road. Mackenzie let out a shriek as a cyclist ran a red light and nearly collided with the Rev. The Rev lost his balance and fell. The rider stopped and looked back.

* * *

A crowd had gathered. They could hear the Rev telling them all he was fine.

The cyclist and his bike stood next to the Rev. Many spectators were heckling him.

"Are you okay, Rev?" Aaron asked as he came over to him.

"I'm fine, Aaron. Just a bit of a shock." The Rev turned to the bike rider. "Why do people like you run red lights?"

The cyclist looked at his watch. "I'm sorry, mister. It looks like you're okay. I'm really sorry but I need to shoot. I have to get to an appointment."

"Could you answer the question, mate? Why do you people run red lights?" Aaron said. He also wanted to know the answer. "Do you think you're above the law or something?"

The cyclist made moves to go. Aaron grabbed his arm. "Listen mate, you nearly collected a friend of mine. You don't seem too concerned about it, and seem more interested in getting to your appointment. Now, we don't want you to be inconvenienced with what's happened and have to stay and face up to your responsibility but could you just answer the question? We all want to know."

The cyclist looked at Aaron's hand on his arm. Aaron released his arm.

"I don't know, I just do it. I'm into ethics not laws. As long as I don't hurt or hit someone it's okay. I see red lights as something telling me to yield, have a quick check, and then if no one is in danger, go for it. Now I'm sorry, I won't do it again. But I do need to go."

Aaron placed his hand on the bike's handlebar. "So you're telling us you're a changed man, that this incident has taught you a lesson. For some reason I don't believe that, but I'll give you the benefit of the doubt."

"Tell me, mate, do you ever jaywalk?"

He was right. Aaron had broken laws before. He had just never focused on such things to the extent he was now.

"See. I'm not Robinson Crusoe. Lots of people break the law." He looked down on Aaron's hand, and then at Aaron."

Aaron stepped back.

The cyclist looked at the Rev. "Look, I'm sorry. But I need to go." The cyclist moved his body on to the bike.

They watched as he rode off.

Mackenzie tucked her arm in Aaron's. He looked down at her. She gave a sigh. "Aaron, it's all a bit close to home, this. I couldn't help thinking of the minister and what he wanted to achieve with his technology. He wanted to stop people breaking laws. You know, he may have been on to something. See how inconvenienced, put out, that person was starting to feel."

They looked at the Rev. He was fine.

"Laws are there to protect us. But most people are a law unto themselves. The Lord knew this would happen. God's law is written on their hearts. They choose not to obey them unless it suits them," the Rev said.

Aaron watched Mackenzie nod in agreement.

* * *

Aaron and Mackenzie walked down to the Botanic Gardens. They sat at the river's edge and stared at some of the moored boats. An expensive-looking yacht sat in the water. Aaron thought of the cost. Maybe it was a gift from someone. He thought of the gift the Rev spoke about.

"How do I get this gift, Kenz . . . the one the Rev spoke about?"

"It's all about Jesus, Aaron. It's about what he did on the cross and you seeking forgiveness and believing in him. This all comes from the heart. God will soften your heart and give you understanding—you just need to ask him. God sees your heart, Aaron. He knows if it is genuine or not."

Aaron watched as she grabbed a piece of paper and pen from her bag and then looked up at him. "Why am I doing this? We have technology. Open up the notes app on your smartphone, Aaron."

Aaron did as Mackenzie suggested.

"Type in Romans 6:23, 5:8, 10:9-10. Remember, the first number is chapter, followed by the verse. Study those verses and we can discuss them next time we meet."

"I have to meet Mum soon. Let's go, we pass your place on the way there, I can drop you off."

They reached the *M on Mary*. Mackenzie gave Aaron a hug and told him that she loved him. "You can also download a Bible app for your phone." She gave him a wink and off she went.

Aaron smiled and watched her walking off. She was safe now. The technology was locked up in some super-secure Defense establishment. What would Defense do with the technology? Aaron was sure that modern warfare would make use of the technology. He was also sure that some world powers were hovering.

He watched Mackenzie crossing the road. Saw some more jaywalkers. What was that minister's goal? To stop people breaking laws? Most people were a law unto themselves. They do things their own way and follow their own ideas about how to live, instead of following laws or customs. What can we do? The minister had a plan—it just wasn't well thought-out. It was clouded by things, emotions, feelings. He wondered about the other person, the Professor. What were his intentions?

CHAPTER THIRTY SIX

ABOUT AN HOUR SOUTH of Brisbane city, a coastline of golden beaches stretches for fifty-seven kilometers. The coastline was given a name by real estate investors: they called it the Gold Coast. Aaron and Mackenzie were heading there for a day trip.

Aaron wanted to stop off at Eight Mile Plains on the way, to share some things with Mackenzie and pay his respects.

He hadn't noticed the sculptured lions at the entrance to the car park before. Last time, he'd had a different mindset. Now he told the lions to lift their game in guarding this car park.

They got out of the car. Aaron put his arm over Mackenzie's shoulder.

Aaron pointed "That's where my dad's body was found."

Mackenzie squeezed his arm.

Aaron looked over towards the bush where the track went. He wasn't going to tell Mackenzie about the animals. There was still some scaffolding up around the building, but most of the fire damage had been repaired. They headed down to the building's main entrance where a cross and some fresh flowers sat. Aaron took an envelope out of his pocket.

"What's that, Aaron?"

Looking at the envelope, Aaron turned to Mackenzie, "Around the time of Dad's death, there was a fire here, Kenz. Two young men lost their lives. I encountered a grieving couple when I first came here. They believed the fire wasn't an accident, and it turned out they were right. I told them that I would do what I could to help. I've written a letter to tell them that new information has come to light— the suggestion of an explosive device and the suspect being hunted down." Aaron placed the envelope under the flowers.

"They may already know, but I wanted to make sure. I also

wanted to thank the man, because he trusted me with information that helped track Lucas down."

They walked back to the car. "I spoke to the Rev yesterday," Mackenzie said. "He told me that after Lucas and Tag were 'brought out of hibernation'—as the secular experts put it—he has been busy but hoped the government media campaign to curb the panic will work. The government wants people to know that the deceased cannot be brought back from the dead. The experts stressed that the hibernation was caused by the technology, and that these people didn't die, so they weren't brought back to life. People can't be brought back from the dead, they say."

They stopped at the car, Aaron looked back. "I suppose the Rev would be happy with that. It takes the pressure off him. People don't want loved ones to die. God has a plan though, doesn't he, Kenz?"

"He does, Aaron, and we just need to make sure we're part of it."

They drove out of the car park and headed towards the motorway.

* * *

Windsor sat on his bunk. It was good of the Reverend to visit him.

He had a lot of time to think in here.

The Prison Ministry had asked Windsor to speak at a Bible study class recently.

"Evil lives in all of us," he told them. "It's waiting to strike. Stress and emotions lift the boom gate, and evil sprints through. It's what happens to those affected by drink and drugs—the boom gate gets lifted, and those pesky things get in there and run amok."

"What are the pesky things?" someone asked.

"Demons." Windsor told him. "Demons . . . those pesky things are demons. They do a lot of damage." And he wondered what the statistics were in relation to crimes being committed while under demonic influence. "I've met a lot of people in here who have told me they were not in their right mind when they committed their crimes, and they believe they were influenced by something."

A few of the men had nodded in agreement.

"Things unseen can do a lot of damage. Let's ask the Lord to open our eyes."

Windsor lay down on his bunk. He told the Lord he was sorry.

CHAPTER THIRTY SEVEN

AARON SAT UP ABRUPTLY. He sensed a presence.

A slight breeze fluttered the curtains. City lights filtered in, providing night shadows. He looked around his bedroom. He was alone. Lifting the bed covers, he got up, walked over to the window and stared across the city lights towards the intersection. It was peaceful and quiet.

He looked up to the illuminated night sky with the artificial lights blocking the light of the stars. *I miss you, Dad, and you too, Jack.* He now believed in the reality of God, heaven—and the other place. *Yes, Mackenzie, I believe everything you have told me.* We are stained because of sin and cannot enter God's presence because of that. *Yes, God, I am stained, but what do I do?*

A heaviness came upon Aaron. He hadn't thought about it before, but his past had displeased God. The heaviness sat in his heart. He felt burdened and dirty. A light caught his attention in the distance. It was a large cross that sat atop one of the old church buildings. He stared at the glowing cross. *He has come to set the captives free.* And then it all became clear: he understood what Jesus had done.

He went and sat on the bed. One of the Bible verses Mackenzie gave him spoke to his heart.

"If you declare with your mouth, 'Jesus is Lord', and believe in your heart that God raised him from the dead, you will be saved."

* * *

The smell of eucalyptus floated through the air. A parrot flew past, its mate calling from behind. As the parrots veered left the sun reflected off their rainbow plumage, their red chests glistened. The pair flew and settled in a large eucalyptus tree. Their call echoed through the Koala Park's woodland.

Aaron had watched the flighted spectacle. He returned his gaze to the cross that sat under another large eucalyptus tree. Mackenzie was leaning down, placing some flowers near it. Aaron watched as she stood up and wiped some tears from her cheek.

She came over to Aaron. He placed his arm on her shoulder.

"I miss him, Aaron."

"I know you do, Kenz."

Light drizzle filtered through the woodlands, enhancing the smell of the eucalyptus trees and melaleuca shrubs and trees. The drizzle had the parrots singing. Aaron and Mackenzie walked over to a sheltered area where they sat on one of the picnic tables.

"I had a fun day yesterday, Kenz. I went to the Bible study that Churchie now runs for the homeless under the guidance of the Rev. Wally was there. They're all doing well and send their love. They'd like you to attend one."

"Did you learn anything, Aaron?"

"I did, Kenz. Last night, I asked Jesus into my heart, to get rid of the heaviness that sat in there."

Aaron looked at Mackenzie. Her eyes were watery.

"Things became clear to me, Kenz. It was like something was lifted from my eyes. I saw that we all follow in Adam's footsteps. He put himself before God, and we all do the same thing. It's us first, not him."

"That's right, Aaron. It's called self-centeredness."

Aaron nodded. "I was told that the gate and the road that leads to life is narrow, and only a few find it. I decided to walk through that gate because I believe there is a God and He made me. I just need to understand why, and I'm sure that will become clearer in time. But Kenz, I do believe now. It all makes perfect sense when one gives it the attention it deserves—if you explore and think, you find the truth. And all this stuff that's been happening, it's all good background to build my faith on. So there ya go, I'm a believer now."

Mackenzie's arms were wrapped around Aaron in a flash. "Yes, it all becomes clearer . . . much clearer."

They heard a flutter. They turned to see a white pigeon had landed in front of them. The pigeon wandered around looking for seeds and then flew off.

Mackenzie smiled and looked at Aaron. "There ya go, Aaron. God likes to entertain us with his nature. He's given you a confirmation."

Aaron watched the pigeon flying off. He thought of God. He thought of the mighty angels, the unseen angels, in their presence.

Mackenzie stood up and put out her hand to Aaron. "Well, my friend, let the journey begin."

ABOUT THE AUTHOR

Phillip Cook was born in South Australia and has been heading north via the east coast ever since, collecting life experiences along the way. He currently lives in Queensland. Dead Man's Journey is his first novel.

Printed in Great Britain
by Amazon